Derrida on the Mend

Derrida on the Mend

by
Robert Magliola

Purdue University Press
West Lafayette, Indiana

Published 1984

Library of Congress Catalog Card Number 82-62779
International Standard Book Number 0-911198-69-5
Printed in the United States of America

Dedication

Iam (etiamnunc) pro dimidio animae meae, notwithstanding . . .

This book,
Flori Carmeli oblatus,
is
dedicated
to

Karl Rahner, S.J., keen votarist of the 'whither';

Paul Ricoeur, generous sage (letting others grow 'between' his ideas); and

Gayatri Chakravorty Spivak, lovely deconstructionist (and Indian "on the '—gress' ").

Contents

Pre/Face   ix

Acknowledgments   xiii

Part 1   Between the Tao: Derridean   3
            Differentialism

Part 2   a/Mid the Tao: Heideggerian   57
            Centrism

Part 3   Across the Tao: Buddhist   87
            Differentialism (Athwart the
            a/Mid and Between, I)

Part 4   Across the Tao: Christian   133
            Differentialism (Athwart the
            a/Mid and Between, II)

Appendix   Deconstructive *Démarches*   165

i.   Everything and Nothing: A   165
            Demonstration of the Third
            Lemma

ii.   Next to Nothing: A   176
            Demonstration Just Short of the
            Fourth Lemma

Notes   189

Post/Face   233

Index   235

This

Pre/Face
bears

a

tear.

The tear is not ineffable, yet
you cannot name it.

This preface can be
read

simply

or

differentially—
the tracks and off/tracks

are

true.

The preface talks about a text, *Derrida on the Mend*. *Derrida on the Mend* came about as follows.
For a considerable number of years I have been plying the fabric (*tantra:* "warp-threads") of phenomenology, hermeneutics, and 'theory of text'. For a long time already I have been also researching Buddhism. And for a long time already I have been using Buddhist meditative forms—adapting them to my prayer life as a Carmelite tertiary. (It is fair to say, indeed, that my practice has been more rigorous than casual.) One be/wildering day several strands crossed: I found that Derridean deconstruction and Nagarjunist Buddhism, the former to dismantle the principle of identity, the latter to dismantle an entitative theory of *dharmas,* resorted to the 'same' logical techniques. But in the Nagarjunist 'text'—as rational and off/rational discourse and as meditative experience—there is an 'excess', a 'surplus', which continues *dissémination* and still 'preserves' organic theories. (If you are unfamiliar with Jacques Derrida's work, I beg your patience—you will come to understand these terms as they are rationally devolved in the book now being prefaced, for this preface as all prefaces is also body and open postface.) Thus I could reinstate organic theories of philosophy, literary theory and criticism, and so on, while introducing a 'differentialism' which liberates and bears bliss. Professional Buddhologists, for the most part overwhelmed by

ix

'centric' interpretations of Buddhism, would come upon a Buddhist differentialism. In the West, theologians would come upon a 'differential theology' in excess of 'deconstructionist theology'. And strangely, the differential theology which is released from the surplus of deconstruction is a disciplined and even 'con/servative' one.

For example, two strategies which we shall come to know in the book ahead as 'Derridean *dédoublement*' and 'Derridean pure negative reference'—while deconstructing Augustinian models—will confirm in unexpected ways conciliar definitions of the Trinity. Across the tangle (vernacular: "an alter/cation") of comparative religion, Karl Rahner's call for a 'theology' of a more-than-personal-God can find in differentialism the means for fruitful dialogue with the impersonal 'going on' of Buddhist *paramārtha*. In the realm of human interpersonal relationships, differentialism's 'pure negative reference' will proffer at least the wherewithal for accounts (and justifications) of experiential claims like those of William Johnston, S.J.: "When people meet at the level of personal love achieved through radical non-attachment, they do not merge, nor are they absorbed in one another; . . . There is at once a total unity and a total alterity" (Johnston, *Silent Music*, Perennial Library, 1976, p. 147). Such an experience, so confounding to organic (entitative) thought, becomes accessible by off/way of differentialism because, in differential terms, pure negative reference is constitutive. In comparative literature, the contrived de/vices of Oriental poetry belonging to the differentialist tradition can teach to the West new enactments of deconstruction and *dissémination*. In literary exegesis, historical criticism and American formalist criticism can be reinstated by the Nagarjunist version of what we shall come to recognize as the Buddhist 'two truths'. *Ita porro* (Lat.: "and thus, further," or "and so on . . .")!

"Derrida on the Mend" has a history as manuscript. Because my text proffers unexpected off-(the)-track a/Betting, it met that reactionary prejudice which is not authentic *Vor-Urteil*, or fore-judgment. The 'mal-alliance' of judges moved me to tears. The verdict of traditional judges was that the text was too avant-garde; the verdict of deconstructionist judges was that it was too traditional. Judges winced at the 'off-weaving' ('intertextuality'!) of 'closed' disciplines such as literary theory, hermeneutics, philosophy, Buddhology, theology. If life be Derridean *écriture*, *Derrida on the Mend* is written in my blood. Dear reader, if you be an 'entitative' sort of thinker, give *Derrida on the Mend* a chance: I think you will find that the body of the text—unlike this strange preface—adheres to a format which is rational, straightforward, even conventional. If you be a 'deconstructive' sort of thinker, give *Derrida on the Mend* a chance: I think you will find that the "body" of the text self-deconstructs, though with a re/lease.

Here are some ex/plications, provisos, and demurrals, and even some intimations. When *Derrida on the Mend* speaks of the "differential 'between','" a very specialized usage is being brought into play. The reference is not to the "conventional 'between',"" that is, an "intermediate" situation of some kind. Terms like 'Taoism' also receive personalized de/finitions, though of course in other contexts — also charted with care — Taoism is treated as a purely historical phenomenon. The title of part 1 (see my general table of contents) suggests that Derridean activity is a differential 'between' which cleaves (or better, eludes/elides) the 'Taoist' unity of opposites, or any other organicism. The title of part 2, and the typographical play with the preposition, suggests that Heideggerian activity is an organic (i.e., 'logocentric') 'between' which centers 'Taoist' and other kinds of unity (even if the centering be a closed contrary of intimacy/withdrawal). Parts 3 and 4, among other concerns, demonstrate and then celebrate the free "moving across" of the differential mystic, — that is, the 'diagonal' movement by which he/she slides at will from logocentrism to differentialism and back. Due to the protracted length of time it took to write *Derrida on the Mend,* the reader will find the bibliographic references and other critical apparatus somewhat "dated." My apologies. Part 2 and the Appendix were originally written for other occasions and are considerably older than the other sections. My treatment of Heidegger, in particular, should be understood as my adaptation of his texts: part 2, in other words, is an adaptation which is analogous, technically, to what exegetes call recension and redaction. My intention was to generate a Heideggerianism which would address the questions vexing Anglo/American critics at the time. The treatment still serves, I think, as a "quintessential Heidegger," that is, Heidegger presented as he "in the long run" alters the philosophical tradition. I think many so-called contemporary "left-wing Heideggerians" confound their Derridean *deconstruction* of Heidegger with a Gadamerian *appropriation* of Heidegger. Their work, which I — by the way — very much affirm, performs the former; in part 2, I perform the latter.

There is 'more' in this preface than "meets the eye." For some, the OED, a scriptural concordance, and some "basic Latin and Greek" may abet differential reading(s), what I call 'off/tracking'. As for imagery which can evoke a Freudian rendering, the deconstructionist reader would do well to re/call that Freudianism and its permutations are very logocentric — so Freudian renderings — like all logocentric renderings — dissolve in turn. Differentialism, I shall argue, deconstructs all logocentrisms but re/appropriates according to a dissemination which I call variously the Buddhist trace, *śūnyatā,* the differential 'going-on'.

. . . nonpresence and nonevidence are admitted
into the blink of the instant. There is a
duration to the blink, and it closes the eye.

— Jacques Derrida, *Speech and Phenomena*

> . . . in an instant we shall all be
> changed, as quickly as the blinking
> of an eye [ἐν ῥιπῇ ὀφθαλμοῦ], . . .
>   —1 Cor. 15:52

O Buddha, going, going,
   going on beyond, and always going on
      beyond, always *becoming* Buddha.
            Hail!
               Hail!
                  Hail!

                     —the *Heart Sutra,*
                        Jiyu-Kennett Roshi, trans.

   Yonder.—What high as that!
      We follow, now we follow.—
                  Yonder, yes yonder, yonder,
      Yonder.

                     —Gerard Manley Hopkins

P . . .

Acknowledgments

I thank the National Humanities Center, Research Triangle Park, North Carolina, for the fellowship which enabled me to write this book. My deep gratitude to William Bennett, director of the center during my residency; to the center's staff, which abetted my research in so many ways; and to the other grantees, who stimulated and provoked my work during pleasurable hours at desk and table. I express my warmest gratitude also to the managing editor of Purdue University Press, Mrs. Verna Emery, who toiled long and cheerfully. Whatever stylistic infelicities ma/linger in this text are a consequence of my decisions and indecisions. My gratitude to Donald Carter, the press's graphic designer, who designed artistically and 'graphically'. My appreciation to Mrs. Cherylynn Knott Horvath of Purdue University, who functioned so efficiently as my copyright permissions editor; and to the typists of the National Humanities Center, elegant *dactylographes* one and all. To my heroic wife—Rosa Tsung-Yu; my heroic children—Lorinda-marie, Jon-carlo, and Clara-marie; my fondly caring mother—Florence Magliola; and my devoted father—Hugo Magliola: I acknowledge my deeply felt debt. As calligrapher of the Chinese and Japanese characters in the text, aforesaid distaff Rosa Tsung-Yu doubled as calligraphic staff: double thanks to her. *Eine Dankesschuld* to Professor Lawrence Radner, a specialist who knows seventeenth-century German verse much better than I and who diligently checked my personal translations from Angelus Silesius. Traces of the past I acknowledge and appreciate as well, such as my graduate formation at Princeton University—Professors Ralph Freedman, Joseph Frank, Robert Fagles, and many others—for they too did me good. And now at the closure of a beginning, I thank those Purdue University colleagues, friends, graduate students who have remained with me to the ending, for all endings that are good dissolve in turn, and we are the move which is per/petual trace.

• • •

I thank the following copyright holders for permission to quote from the works cited:

The Pennsylvania State University Press, University Park, for quotations from Mervyn Sprung, "Being and the Middle Way," in *The Question of Being,* ed. Mervyn Sprung, copyright 1978.

Hyperion Press, Inc., Westport, for translations from *Angelus Silesius: Selections from "The Cherubinic Wanderer,"* trans. J. E. Crawford Flitch, reprinted by Hyperion in 1978 and originally published by G. Allen and Unwin, London, 1932.

Excerpts from *The End of Religion,* copyright 1971 by Aelred Graham, are reprinted by permission of Harcourt, Brace, Jovanovich, Inc.

Mouton Publishers (division of Walter de Gruyter and Co.), Berlin, for quotations from Bimal Krishna Matilal, *Epistemology, Logic, and Grammar in Indian Philosophical Analysis,* copyright 1971.

The Charles E. Tuttle, Co., Inc., for the quotation of a Buddhist story appearing in Zenkei Shibayama, *A Flower Does Not Talk,* trans. Sumiko Kudo, copyright 1970.

The Hokuseido Press, Tokyo, for the translated *mondo* "Bowing and Rising," found in *Games Zen Masters Play* (New American Library) and originally appearing in R. H. Blyth, *Zen and Zen Classics,* Vol. 5, copyright 1966.

The Pennsylvania State University Press, University Park, for the reprint of portions (modified) of my *"Eigentlichkeit* and *Einfall:* The Heideggerian Return 'To Things Themselves'," in *Literary Criticism and Philosophy,* ed. Joseph Strelka, copyright 1983.

The Johns Hopkins University Press, Baltimore, for excerpts from Jacques Derrida, *Of Grammatology,* trans. G. C. Spivak, copyright 1976.

Northwestern University Press, Evanston, for selections from Jacques Derrida, *Speech and Phenomena,* trans. D. B. Allison, copyright 1973.

Jiyu-Kennett, Roshi, for the translation from "The Wisdom of the Patriarchs," published in Jiyu-Kennett, *Zen is Eternal Life* (Dharma Publishing, copyright 1976) and also found under the title *Selling Water by the River.*

E. A. Burtt, for the translation from E. A. Burtt, ed., *The Teachings of the Compassionate Buddha,* published by the New American Library, New York, copyright 1955.

The Hokuseido Press, Tokyo, for quotations from R. H. Blyth, *Zen in English Literature and Oriental Classics,* reprinted by E. P. Dutton and Co., Inc., New York, copyright 1960.

The Hokuseido Press, Tokyo, for quotations from R. H. Blyth, *Zen and Zen Classics,* Vol. 4, copyright 1966.

PART 1

Between the Tao:
Derridean Differentialism

i

All the metaphysical determinations of truth, and even the one beyond metaphysical onto-theology that Heidegger reminds us of, are more or less immediately inseparable from the instance of logos, or of a reason thought within the lineage of the logos, in whatever sense it is understood: in the pre-Socratic or the philosophical sense, in the sense of God's infinite understanding or in the anthropological sense, in the pre-Hegelian or the post-Hegelian sense. Within this logos, the original and essential link to the phone has never been broken.[1]

By "metaphysical determinations of truth," Jacques Derrida means all judgments and measurements of "truth" which are *logocentric*, that is, centered on a concept of truth as logos. And by "logos" he means truth defined as the *expression* (or 'signifier') of an originating *factor*[2] (or 'signified'), no matter what that factor may be (and it is clear Derrida holds that the whole Western tradition,[3] in one way or another, is logocentric). In its most classic form, logocentrism posits a 'transcendental signified' (or absolute Origin) whose 'voice' (or transcendental signifier) is so immediately and essentially 'proximate' to its 'other half' (its 'originating factor', that is, the Origin), that the two 'halves' constitute a supreme Identity.[4] In Patristic and medieval theology, for example, the supreme Identity is God, whose internal working involves an originating factor (*Pater*, or *Genitor*, God the Father) and a voice (*Filius, Genitus*, the only-begotten Logos or "uttered Word," God the Son). This Logos is the *imago Patris*, the perfect expression of God the Father. This Logos is begotten but not created. To put it another way, God the Father, as originating factor, is eternally "begetting" God the Son, but not "making Him from nothing," for to understand the Father's activity as "creation" would be to reduce the Son to creaturehood (a consequence orthodox theologians had to avoid, of course, since it disestablishes the divine status of God the Son).[5]

3

Whether the transcendental signified be a Christian God whose thoughts *ut foris* (i.e., as directed "outside" Himself) create the things (*res*) of the world according to their senses (*sensus, eidoi*), senses which are determined in and through divine Logos; or whether the transcendental signified be an Aristotelian First Cause, the "active reason" in which Forms know themselves and proffer themselves as the potential and actual objects of human knowing; or whether it be Rousseau's divine law[6] breathed into the "sensible cogito"; or Husserl's ideality, operative in the *Logical Investigations* as guarantor of verbal sense and in the *Ideas* as guarantor of noetic-noematic meaning—an inevitable hierarchy of concepts can be seen to unfold. With the internal workings of a transcendent signified as the precedent (and prototype), even when not acknowledged, *meaning* (*vouloir-dire*) as such is taken to be the binary combination of originating factor (the signified) and voice (signifier). That is to say, Western theories of meaning comport a sense (an idea acting as signified) and an utterance (a signifier which usually bifurcates into 'inner voice' and 'vocalization'). The ontological hierarchy in control, as it were, requires (1) that 'sense' and 'inner voice' keep priority as the binary constituents of meaning, (2) that 'vocalization' (the 'phone') function as the privileged mode of expressive communication, and (3) that 'writing' (the 'graph') occupy the last place in the chain of command.

In so far as 'writing' is concerned, however, even the locution 'chain of command' is somewhat misleading, because Derrida's most crucial claim at this juncture is that the tradition considers writing not just the least important "link" but as *modally* distinct from (and inferior to) the other links. The tradition, says Derrida, confers privileged ontological status on the binary combination of sense and utterance and renders writing (*graphie* or *grammè*) accidental and derived. Writing is just the "sign of a sign,"[7] that is, the instrument whereby the primary sign (sense and utterance) is communicated. Writing is the "supplement of the spoken word," as Rousseau puts it.[8] Or writing is just "phonetic" (as opposed to the privileged "phonic"), and, thus, *exterior* to the "word" which is a "thought-sound," as Saussure puts it.[9] So the operative model the tradition provides us is not only hierarchical (with a kind of chasmic "fall" occurring between the penultimate and the bottom link), but also concentric (with a movement from privileged "inside," where "presence" is constituted, to "outside," where only "operations" take place). Though Derrida rehearses (1) the ancient Greek, (2) the Hebraic, and (3) the Christian (including early, medieval, and Renaissance Christian theology) lineage of logocentrism, his purpose of course is to take aim at modern "thought," be it post-Hegelian, anthropological, structuralist, or even "Heideggerian." Indeed, he takes what is clearly a mischievous delight in arguing that even the most defiantly non-metaphysical approaches are founded *directe vel indi-*

recte on a "philosophy of presence," on logos.[10] Moving from the infinite subjectivity of Spinoza and Leibnitz to the individual "con-.sciousness as presence-to-self" which characterizes Descartes and the rationalism which follows him, Derrida continues on to "decon-struct" the logocentrism of Rousseau, Hegel, and Husserl (whose "principle of principles" is "the most radical and most critical resto-ration of the metaphysics of presence").[11] His most telling attacks, in terms of the *sollicitation*[12] or "unsettling" he proposes, are on Marx-ism (a dialectical materialism!), on Saussurean linguistics (a system which parenthesizes the referent!), and on Heidegger (who himself intends to deconstruct metaphysics!), as well as on Lévi-Strauss, Austin, and Foucault.

It seems to me that Derrida's endeavor is best taken as an assault upon the principle of self-identity, at least as that principle has been understood by the preponderance of Western systems of thought, past and present. When giving an account of the conventional prin-ciple of self-identity ("whatever is, is"), Derrida—since he is here recapitulating the movement of thought which characterizes the tradition—quickly reduces all issues of self-identity to the issue of personal self-identity[13] (the identity whereby "I am I"). Derrida ex-plains that conventional ideologies, either overtly or covertly, understand personal self-identity as a binary combination of "originating factor" and "expression." Here I, as explicator of Der-rida as explicator, am going to intervene just long enough to insert an additional maneuver, and my intention is only to clarify Derrida's own explication. Since the personal self-identity constituted by "originating factor" and "expression" has been given so many differ-ent names over the centuries and has been understood at more elaborated levels of personal identity in so many different ways, I shall simply call this 'founding' binary combination of personhood the *nominans-nomen* ("the naming and the name[d]").[14] Thus we can, I think, avoid the confusions which would arise from popular terms such as "soul," "self," "ego," "self-consciousness," and so on. Such terms, in the past and present, have referred sometimes to the founding structure and at other times to various forms of psychic superstructure.

What Derrida is "getting at" is the 'founding' structure of person-hood as all these ideologies understand it, and he is "getting at" this *Urstruktur,* if you will, so he can later dissolve it. As Derrida explains the matter, personal self-identity according to the convention arises when the originating factor (*nominans*) recognizes itself (the *nominans* expresses, no matter how, an "I," the *nomen,* name) in some kind of reflexive reference. Whether the *nominans-nomen* be unconscious or conscious; whether it be conscious but affective, or conscious and rational; whether it be substantive, or "constructed" from awareness of action (internal action or "directedness" towards the "outside" or "others"); whether it be dependent on "memory" or body-awareness—whatever the formulation, says Derrida, the tradition understands personal self-identity to be founded on an originating factor recognizing itself by or through its own expression. Thus, from the beginnings in Socrates and Plato, through Saint Augustine, who tells us "The mind knows itself by itself,—because it is incorporeal" (*De Trin.*, IX, 3), and on to Saint Thomas Aquinas, who says "The intellectual knows itself not by its essence but by its act" (*Summa*, I, Q. LXXXVII, A. 1), the pre-modern period witnesses to the formula, though surely its thinkers disagree on the exact working of the *nominans-nomen*.

And the post-modern period, if anything, speeds the same drumbeat: so Locke can insist a person "can consider itself as itself, or the same thinking thing, in different times and places, which it does only by that consciousness which is inseparable from thinking and essential to it" (*Concerning Human Understanding*, chap. 27); William James can aver "our considering the spiritual self at all is a reflective process . . . to think ourselves as thinkers" (*The Principles of Psychology*, chap. 10); and Husserl can assert "the meaning of 'I' is essentially realized in the immediate idea of one's own personality" (*Formal and Transcendental Logic*, no. 27). The formula recurs overtly, in some thinkers, through the post-World War II period,[15] but becomes especially apparent in theories of identity which do not focus on personal identity (a situation all the more ironical, as Derrida would see it). Linguistic schools of the Saussurean kind and some philosophies of "correspondence theory," though preoccupied with the identity of linguistic elements *in se*, or "factual" elements *in se*, and "relations" between elements and ideas, comport themselves as they do only because their formulae are cryptic displacements of the classic principle of personal self-identity, *nominans-nomen*. Derrida regards these theories of identity as displacements of what is, for him, of course, a false notion of self-consciousness because he operates within the modern European approach to language, which, at least since Gottlob Frege, frames all questions of identity in terms of "meaning." And according to this approach, the "meaning" of things is how things *appear* in language. Thus to study the principle of identity, that is, how things are self-identical ("whatever is, is"), is to study language. When "I" identify a thing as self-identical, the formula is, "'I' identify you as 'such-and-such'" (and the identification is a binary combination of "originating factor" and "expression," of "signified" and "signifier," no matter whether understood in a narrower or broader sense). Derrida's strategy will be, then, to assault the principle of identity, that is, the theory of signified and signifier, as it functions in explanations of language and of how language composes the identity[16] of things. Then he feels he can, step by step, "close in" on the citadel which is personal consciousness itself, and its precious "center," the *nominans-nomen* (the principle of personal identity).

Perhaps the influence of Frege not only on Continental philosophy, but also on early Anglo-American 'Analytic' philosophy, can account for some parallels in the respective projects of Derrida and the 'Analysts'.[17] Some philosophers and historians of philosophy have seen the similarity,[18] but their number has been few. The styles of argument and rhetoric which characterize Continental thinkers on the one hand and the Anglo-Americans on the other are so divergent that for the most part Derrida is unnoticed by professional philosophers in the United States. As for Derrida, it is to be admitted, first, that he too glibly stereotypes the European tradition when subsuming just about all of it under the title of logocentrism; and second, that he ignores Anglo-American thought almost vengefully, thus missing the chance to encounter what are perhaps less logocentric formulations and increasing proportionately the chances of self-deception (that is, he may think his claims more original than they really are). Be all these things as they may, the influence of Derrida on both European and Anglo-American belles lettres, especially literature, literary theory, and literary criticism, has been—as is commonly acknowledged—nothing short of overwhelming. So we pursue our explanation of Derrida's "deconstruction" of metaphysics. As indicated above, his tactic is to attack first the principle of identity and then the principle of personal self-identity.

Among the deliberations that I consider the most crucial for Derrida as he "builds his case," the deliberation which is logically prior to the others[19] is the "argument from Saussure's principle of arbitrariness" (*l'arbitraire*). Let us recall that for Saussure, the linguistic sign is a binary combination of signified (the idea, the sense) and signifier (the phonic form). Writing, the graphic sign, is not properly "linguistic," but an "external system."[20] One of Saussure's constatations, certainly, is that graphic signifiers are arbitrary. (Pictographs and the like belong for Saussure to another category of representations, those which naturally "figure" what they represent and which Saussure calls not graphs but symbols.) What is important here, though, is that for Saussure phonic signifiers too are arbitrary; that is to say, specific sounds are not *naturally* bonded to specific senses. (Onomatopoetic words, insofar as they are onomatopoetic, are excluded from consideration on the same grounds as pictographs, viz., they naturally represent what they mean.) But Saussure wants very adamantly to hold that when speaking of phonic signifiers there is a *natural* bond between the *order* of sense *in general* and the *order* of sound *in general*. By "natural," he means that the need to express sense through sound is "built into" mankind's very mode of being. Sense "in general" or the "order of sense" naturally requires sound "in general," the "order of sound." Why, asks Derrida, is there so often in Saussure's work this insistence on the natural bond between these two "orders"? Derrida's claim is that Saussure, half unknowingly, surmises nonetheless that if he yields on this point—the natural affiliation of the two orders—the consequence "down the road" will be the dissolution of human self-identity. Such would be the consequence because the *nominans-nomen* itself is the binary combination of sense and sound, translated from linguistics into the workings of the psyche, into, indeed, the reflexive act. For in the reflexive act, the factor (signified) whence a reflexive intention issues and the utterance (the signifier, here an inner voice) which is the "I" that mirrors the factor TOGETHER constitute personal identity. If the order of sense and the order of sound are not naturally bonded to each other, this means the *nominans* is not naturally bonded to the *nomen*. My uttered "I" *need not reflect* the intending factor which "places" the "I." Indeed, it is not *natural* for it to do so! What is more, since reflexivity has dissolved, the moment wherein the human mind is "together" and, thus, capable of knowing (naming) *other things* no longer exists. The human mind cannot constitute for itself the identity of other things.[21]

Yet, continues Derrida, the *sum total* of phonic signifiers, that is, *each and every one of them,* is arbitrary. No less arbitrary than the sum total of graphic signifiers.[22] Since such is the case, Derrida concludes that to distinguish the natural bondage between alleged "orders" from the arbitrary bondage between individual signifieds and signifiers (whether the latter be graphic or phonic) is just a "trumped up" maneuver, a semi-conscious hypocrisy, if you will. Derrida finds Saussure, *volens nolens,* in latent self-contradiction. Saussure argues that all graphic signifiers, individually and as a totality, are arbitrary. And Saussure argues that arbitrary signifiers are by this very fact *unnatural* ("external," "institutional"). Thus, he concludes here that graphic signifiers, individually and as a totality, are *unnatural.* Saussure continues, indicating next that all phonic signifiers, individually and as a totality, are arbitrary. But as a totality they are *natural* (which does not logically follow). So Saussure's conclusion contradicts his premises (Saussure's argument leads to "self-contradiction"). And Saussure's attempt to alchemize a "totality" into another ontological mode—into an "order" with different properties if you will—*even though* his premises give no such warrant, is a merely cosmetic move (though probably founded on a deep-seated urgency, as explained earlier.)[23]

"All is writing [*écriture*]," proclaims Derrida. Keeping in mind that he has abrogated what is considered classically the essential distinction between speaking and writing, namely, that the former is more natural and more proximate to sense than the latter, perhaps we can now understand the polemical (and it is polemical!) reason for Derrida's extension of the term "writing" so it covers *all* signs. What is gained by this obviously rhetorical gambit? Simply this. Derrida wishes to shift our attentive focus to where, in his opinion, it properly belongs. By applying to all signs the term "writing," he coerces us into the "recognition" that all signs are artificial. The "only irreducible kernel of the concept of writing," he tells us, is "the durable institution of a sign."[24] Both phonic sign (which is not to be confused, of course, with the phonic stuff which is its "carrier") and graphic sign endure for the duration of a language community (and often beyond that), and both are "instituted" (that is, not naturally begotten, but artificially composed). If "writing," as a concept, is to be understood "over and against" something, then Derrida at this juncture would say it should be "over and against" what is "not a sign" (the "matter," for example, which is phonic or print "stuff"). Precisely because the contemporary sciences of linguistics and semiology are founded, though unknowingly, on the model of hierarchy, and also on the model of inside and outside, these sciences should "convert," as it were, and become *grammatology,* the study of "writing." (It is not inappropriate in this context to recall that the word "linguistics" suggests, even etymologically, a study of sounds—*lingua* means "tongue" in Latin; and "semiology" suggests, etymologically, a privileged "unity"—the root *sem* indicates "oneness" or "togetherness" in Greek and Sanscrit.) And grammatology as a concept performs as the great leveler: at this point, the leveler of signifiers, graphic and phonic both, and shortly, as we shall see, the leveler of signifieds. Derrida next engineers a more frontal assault against the principle of personal self-identity.

ii

Representation mingles with what it represents, to the point where one speaks as one writes, one thinks as if the represented were nothing more than the shadow or reflection of the representer. A dangerous promiscuity and a nefarious complicity between the reflection and the reflected which lets itself be seduced narcissistically. In this play of representation, the point of origin becomes ungraspable. There are things like reflecting pools, and images, an infinite reference from one to the other, but no longer a source, a spring. There is no longer a simple origin. For what is reflected is split *in itself* and not only as an addition to itself of its image. The reflection, the image, the double, splits what it doubles.[25]

I shall call Derrida's second argument, heralded by the above passage, *le dédoublement,*[26] from his catch-phrase, ". . . le double dédouble ce qu'il redouble."[27] The reflection, the image, the *signifier,* the *double,* "the double splits what it doubles." We can begin to understand this assertion by considering the following. The signifier, conventionally understood to mirror the signified, really "doubles back" upon that signified, and *alters* the signified, so that one can really say (with argumentative parity) that the signified equally mirrors the so-called signifier.

Derrida begins with examples provided by Saussure himself (though Saussure, according to Derrida's reading, grieved over them since they had the wherewithal to dissolve his whole linguistic theory).[28] Saussure's examples are just of graphic signifiers which alter what are supposed to function as signifieds in this context, namely the appropriate phonic signs. Thus the French surname LeFèvre which originated when the graphs V and U were both written as the modern U, came to be read and vocalized by the less educated classes as LeFébure (and this latter form of the surname, along with the more authentic one, survives to this day). So a graph (signifier) had altered a phone (signified).[29] Likewise, the "t" of the French graphic sign for seven, *sept*, altered the phonic sign, which did not terminate in a "t" sound at all.[30] More important is the example that Derrida draws from Heidegger, since it offers a case wherein the sense (or idea) is altered by the utterance (whether phonic or graphic). Thus Heidegger points out that the word for "Being" in German is an infinitival form (*Sein*), rather than, say, a substantival form[31] and that the structure of this signifier necessarily affects, very determinately, the concept of being (the signified, in this context) as it is "thought" by German speakers. Another way Derrida tries to "get at" this notion of *dédoublement* is to involve the role of human forgetfulness.[32] A given concept (the signified) may be expressed, to use the conventional jargon, in a written signifier. This signifier, now released to the world and "loose in it," may be forgotten by the speaker, and the concept in the meantime may evolve (its attributes change, for example). If the written signifier is rediscovered by the speaker, it affects the concept; it may, for instance, change the concept, the signified, back to what it was. What is classically called the signified becomes the signifier of the graphic sign it has reencountered.[33]

Various sorts of "doubling back" akin to those mentioned above have been attracting the attention of academics more and more. In the field of literature *per se*, French and South American critics and writers have been plying this terrain for sometime already, and their work has been quite popular in the United States (Todorov's demonstration, for example, that the motifs of the fantastic, as signifiers, impose rigid controls on the "formulations," or signifieds, of the "fantastic" author; and Borges's "mirrorings" of a world where signifieds are first changed by signifiers and then become signifiers[34]); and for this reason, I pass on to what are perhaps for most of my readership more convincing zones of "evidence." Perhaps the most persuasive demonstration of *dédoublement,* at least in America, comes from the data proffered by scientists who research infant psychology. We have all heard of the mounting evidence to the effect that the ideas, conceptual linkings, and so on, which slowly develop in an infant's brain are imprinted[35] there, by, for example, the gestures and words of the parents. And the infant, when he/she expresses ideas by willfully "using" them, is really *mirroring* them. So, slowly the American youngster's idea of a "surgeon," for instance, comes to signify, at least so far as sexual gender is concerned, a male. And this because the grammatical usage has been to represent a "third person" non-sexually specific but human designate by a third person masculine pronoun. Thus, despite the circumlocutions (in the absence of an adequate English grammatical pronoun) suggested by the feminist movement, our society still produces sentences such as "When a surgeon in this hospital reports to the operation room, he must . . . ," and so on; whereas the Chinese language, in this instance, can employ a third person non-sexually specific pronoun (since the latter's reference function is not limited to nongendered designates).

What all this can reduce to, quite easily, is the claim that the signified and signifier paradigm, as conventionally understood, is too simple: each functions in some ways as a signified and in some ways as a signifier. In short, the exchange between sense and utterance is a complicated dialectic, or better yet—to borrow a term made current by Heideggerians—a *hermeneutical circle* of some kind. But Derrida intends a much more revolutionary thesis. *Le double dédouble ce qu'il redouble.* Indeed, *dédoubler* means "to split," "to cut in two," so that the so-called signifier can rebound (as we have seen in the above examples) and make "half" of the so-called signified into a signifier. The signified itself is thus distributed into two functions, signified and signifier, which it can perform in turn or simultaneously. Derrida intends, however, much more by *dédoubler*. *Dédoubler* can mean "to take out the lining" of something, which in terms of the tradition Derrida is attacking, a tradition dependent on the model of inside and outside, indicates that he wants to "tear the insides" out of the signified (the notion of the signified, that is!), to split and destroy the signified. Derrida wants to argue that if one takes the tradition "seriously" and doggedly works out the premises of the tradition to their bitter end, all so-called signs can only be *pure signifiers*, that is, *only* signifiers, through and through.

Derrida's *Of Grammatology*, in the very first chapter, puts it appropriately. I have amended the Spivak translation at several crucial points, where it departs from Derrida's original French version.[36] The passage proceeds as follows:

> Not that the word "writing" has ceased to designate the signifier of the signifier, but it appears, strange as it may seem, that "signifier of the signifier" no longer defines accidental doubling and fallen secondarity. "Signifier of the signifier" describes on the contrary the movement of language: in its origin to be sure, but one can already

suspect that an origin whose structure can be spelled as "signifier of the signifier" 'bolts off' and effaces itself in its own production. There the signified always already functions as a signifier. The secondarity that it seemed possible to ascribe to writing alone affects all signifieds in general, affects them always already, from the beginning of the game [*d'entrée de jeu*]. There is not a single signified that escapes (and if so, only to eventually succumb to) the play of signifying "referrings" that constitute language.

We shall have recourse to this rich passage again in the pages ahead, but now let us notice the part dealing specifically with the unmasking of the signified. If we resort to using the simplest of exponential signs for a moment, we can understand Derrida to mean that writing as the signifier^x of the signifier^o (no matter how far "up" the hierarchical model, or "into" the concentric model, one wants to move in order to reach signifier^o), i.e., writing even according to this old catch-phrase, can no longer be classified as an "accidental doubling and fallen secondarity" (i.e., a mere instrument). Signifier^x, in other words, is not an "accidental doubling or fallen secondarity" precisely because signifier^o is exactly that—a signifier *too,* and not a signified: "There the signified always already functions as a signifier." The status of signifier "that it seemed possible to ascribe to writing alone affects all signifieds in general, affects them always already, from the beginning of the game." Every so-called signified, since it is part of language, functions only as signifier.

Let us return to a practical example again. I very purposefully resort to an example of cultural difference which is a favorite of mine (which, indeed, I have used elsewhere),[37] precisely because it presents a "state of affairs" so uniquely alien to the modern occidental one. Let us see how Derrida could, if he wished, put it to work in order to demonstrate the pure signifier. The Japanese understanding of what a "vessel" or "container" is involves not what physically encloses space, but the enclosed space itself, which is where what is to be carried is to dwell. The empty space is what enables the vessel to be a vessel (though the vessel, of course, is surrounded and shaped by physical contours). A Japanese youngster growing up in such a culture bears a concept of vessel *inscribed* by this cultural play of signifiers. When one adds in, if you will, all the other usages which pertain to the Japanese concept of vessel, Derrida would want to argue that these many signifiers converge upon the concept vessel, a signified, from every direction and make it in *every way* a signifier, that is, *only* a signifier and *totally* a signifier.

The Japanese whose concept of vessel is "the empty space where content can dwell" holds to a concept of vessel that is a pure signifier. But the alleged signifieds, the acculturated terms such as "empty," and "space," and "dwelling," and so on, are themselves *utterances,* are themselves *signifiers*. If we were to pursue the value of the word "dwell," for instance, it would be for Japanese and non-

Japanese alike at zero degree of value, a non-function if you will, unless it were operative in a relationship of signifyings with other words. For example, horizontally (syntactically) it has relationship with the other words in its sentence (and beyond); and vertically (lexically) it has relationship with many cultural "definitions," each of the latter, of course, relating in turn to many other definitions, and so the semantic lines extending from even one word fan out further and further. Thus, in some contexts, the word "dwell" can relate to definitions such as to "fill up," to "sojourn in," to "remain," and "make a home." And each of these relates to a definition, to "make a home," for instance, relating in turn to the "bestowal of a qualitatively 'lived' ambience on a site" and many other semantic values. What is unorthodox about all this, though, a linguist may exclaim! Surely all words are signifiers! Indeed, the Saussurean current in linguistics emphasizes the *functional*, that is to say, the *relational* rather than static value of word signs. Signs are what we can call bivalent, so that they can function in one situation as signifier and in another as signified. All words can be signifiers! Yes indeed, Derrida answers, but none of them—if one is to logically analyze the evidence—can ever be a signified, no matter what its grammatical relation at the time, no matter what the circumstances. In sum, Derrida denies to words the bivalent function. Let us try to review how such a position can deploy itself. We shall consider how the sign functions (1) as the *nominans-nomen,* or reflexivity; (2) as the single word; and (3) as the word in relation to other words. In each of these three cases, we shall consider first a standard bivalent approach and then a "Derridean" approach (I place "Derridean" in quotation marks here, in the spirit of Derrida's performance of "crossing out," or "putting under erasure," which I shall explain later).

First we turn to reflexivity. If the notions of signifier and signified are applied to the constitution of personal self-identity, the "I-utterance," the expression, the *nomen,* is (for the tradition) the *signifier* which mirrors the *nominans* (the signified, what is mirrored). This formulation we have already seen. But Derrida's contribution at this point is to argue that the weight of evidence indicates the *nomen* imprints the *nominans.* What we have already said about signifiers in general applies in the most radical way to the *nominans-nomen.* Biogenetic properties, neurological impulses which precede the moment of self-identity: all of these do not issue from the *nominans* but provide "content" and "structure" for the uttered "I." And the uttered "I," thus "determined," in turn imprints the *nominans.* And—since many psychologists hold that self-relationship cannot occur without language of some kind—the nature of language, emanating after all from culture and not from the *nominans,* may likewise "determine" the *nomen,* which in turn imprints the *nominans.* That is to say, *nominans* is really the signifier: the *nominans* mirrors the alleged "expression," the "I." (Recall that, *in modo globo,* Derrida's chief target always remains the principle of personal self-identity: thus he can tell us he aims to dissolve the principle of "being as self-relationship"[38] and to dissolve "the self-presence of the cogito."[39])

Next we turn to the word sign itself. According to the Saussurean interpretation, the concept (idea) and voice "belong to each other" in a relationship of binary combination. The idea (signified) and voice (signifier) together constitute the word sign, but the signifier mirrors the signified ideas. Derrida casts this relationship *in modo reverso:* the idea is the mirror of the phone and the phonic form. By this time, at least, the first tremors of Derrida's upheaval should be rolling in. But the explosion, for most people, does not "hit home" until the target becomes everyday language, the linkage of words with words. The long-standing tradition (and it simply continues the format we have just seen operative in reflexivity, and in the single word) exhibits the following model. Let us utilize again the exemplary *lexis* we have been generating: "The vessel is the empty space where content can dwell." And (as we narrow in on one strand of this semantic web), "To dwell is 'to make a home.' " That is to say, "to make a home" is a *signifier,* a *mirror,* of "to dwell," which is the signified. If we pursue the semantic strand still further, "to make a home" is "to give a 'lived' ambience." And here the same model of course prevails. "To give a 'lived' ambience" is the signifier, the mirror, of "to make a home," *now become the signified* (whereas it just was, in the previous relationship, the *signifier*). It is crucial to notice how the conventional notion of bivalence has worked here. But the "Derridean" theory, here too in the domain of *lexis,* must cast the directional relation of signified and signifier *in modo reverso.* For Derrida (though recall, he does all this while "crossing out" the signified), "to dwell" is a mirror, a signifier of "to make a home," the signified; and "to make a home" is a signifier of "to give a 'lived' ambience." And so on, from definition to definition, further and further "outwards and away" from the "initial" word, and always for Derrida with signified and signifier *in modo reverso.*[40]

Let us continue our examination. According to the classic model, each word emits, like prismatic rays, many other words which are signifieds and function as "partial definitions" or "partial identifications." If one were to describe programmatically the whole linguistic spectacle, what appears is glorious radiation from center, origin, the signified, no matter where or how one wants to understand this signified. In terms of the lexis we have been using as an example, "to dwell" (signified) is "to make a home" (signifier); "to make a home" (signified) is "to give a 'lived' ambience" (signifier), and so on.[41] Now it is absolutely *essential* for the preservation of the whole model that the system be "closed." At some circumferential rim, though it be unknown, the "last" identifications of all the lexic chains are asserted, and the assertions end as they must with the directional mode of the conventional signified-signifier link, "y signified" is mirrored by "z signifier." Signifiers, not signifieds, must "ring the rim" of the traditional linguistic universe. Thus the signifieds (and remember that in this model, signifieds are necessarily "idea," "spirit," "concept") are on the inside, always on the "inner side" of each lexic link, and so on all the way back in. One can agree to follow back these links as far inside as one wants; but the necessary though implicit assumption, recognized or not, seems to be there is an "innermost" initial signified. The above model, Derrida would hold, is a requirement sine qua non of the "theory of signifieds and signifiers," though not all believers of the theory may "face so 'cosmic' a fact." In other words, Derrida maintains that if the traditional model dissolves, western metaphysics collapses. Why so? Recall that a Derridean "reading" of the bivalent lexis (if Derrida is to be faithful to his premises concerning reflexivity, the single word, and so on) places signifieds, of course "under erasure," around the rim of the linguistic universe: "z 'signifier' " is mirrored by "y 'signified,' " all the way out to the circumferential boundary. And the Derridean insists that he describes, in a *tentative* way, this alternate model because the weight of evidence gathered from within the metaphysical tradition itself "coerces," for one brave enough to look the facts squarely in the eye, such a consequence.

But we have just used the word "tentative" very advisedly. For the concentric model which supports the theory of signifieds and signifiers literally *implodes,* "turns inside out," and dissolves when signifieds rather than signifiers "ring the rim." Let us describe the scenario. If signifieds ring the rim and have been "outermost" in each link of the many chains leading to the rim, the innermost end of each link is a signifier; and more importantly, the *center* itself is a signifier. But such a situation is absurd! A signifier cannot be "center." First of all, how can an initial signifier "mirror," as it must by way of its specific function, the countless signifieds ringing the circumference? By definition a signified can be mirrored, or signified, by multiple signifiers; but by definition a signifier cannot mirror multiple signifieds.[42] For an initial signifier to do so is for it to fragment in all directions, to "explode and disperse." And at the circumferential rim, signifieds deprived of a "center" within, both implode (head towards the "natural locus" of a signified in the model) and "float loose." The linguistic model is no longer closed, but "spread," randomness, drift [*dérive*].

Second, bivalence depends on form, and idea, and logic, to be the signified. If, as *in the single word,* matter, sound and phonic form, and random mutation are the signified, then form, idea, and logic, as the signifier (the *mirror*), are at their "irrational" mercy. A kindred consideration is the following: namely, that the relation of *all* other language to the "initial word" at the center is, according to the tradition, the relation of sense to sound, but in *macrocosm.* To deconstruct this scenario, Derrida need only "buy into" it long enough to show that all "other language" is analogous to sound as *signified* in the single word, and the macrocosmic initial word is analogous to sound's mirror. Then, just as sound subverts idea, language subverts its central word. In the case of all these arguments, the linguistic universe, founded as it is on a *logocentric* model, collapses.[43] And the bivalence which controls word-to-word-to-word concatenations *also terminates,* whether the linkages be traditional or whether they be in Derridean *modo reverso.* That is to say, it is impossible to maintain a linguistic universe of the kind we saw a Derridean could propose—with the theory of signifieds and signifiers intact, but operating *in modo reverso.* Bivalence of any kind is impossible if the linguistic universe is not logocentric, not closed. And of course the Derridean, knowing this, makes his model "tentative." We shall examine how such a tactic "works" in detail later. Now it suffices to point out that the various arguments of *dédoublement* have dismantled the signifier-signified relationship, and that by definition, then, signifier and signified cannot coexist.[44] What possibilities remain? A language of "pure signifieds" (in the conventional sense of the logocentric, of "ideas," "concepts") approximates none of the features we have seen characterize "dispersion," but a language of "pure signifiers" does (the Derridean "signifieds" were [1] *in modo reverso* and [2] in the macrocosmic analogy drawn from the sense/sound relation of the Derridean single word, they played the role of "matter": thus, they are by rights, according to the conventional formula to which Derrida has in part reverted, "signifiers"). So Derrida resorts to the term *pure signifiers.* The random drift of these "pure signifiers," no longer operative in a closed universe, and their gradual "fanning out" to infinity, Derrida calls *dissémination.*[45]

Hypothetical relationships between signified and signifier can be summarized, with at least some show of adequacy, by the following diagram:

FORMAT	INWARDS	OUTWARDS
1	SIGNIFIED———————→	SIGNIFIER
2	SIGNIFIER ←———————	SIGNIFIED
3	SIGNIFIED/SIGNIFIER ←→	SIGNIFIED/SIGNIFIER
4 ←——— SIGNIFIER ←———————		SIGNIFIED ←⟨

The model with which we are concerned is what we have called "concentric," and again, "signified" and "signifier" can be understood as any two points on the linear sequence entailing movement between "innermost" and "outermost." However, my own focus right now—in terms of this summary—is precisely the reflexive act, the principle of self-identity. In the diagram above, format 1 represents the traditional relationship: the signified, the *nominans,* is mirrored by the signifier; the arrow indicates the "originating" function of the signified, which is most often understood to "express" itself by means of the signifier which mirrors it ("origination" need not mean, of course, a temporally identifiable "cause"; it can just as well mean an "ontological priority," or many other variants of "begetting").[46]

Format 2 indicates what would be the case if the Derridean argument became artificially fixated in its first phase. "Conclusive" evidence (even granting for the moment that such exists) showing the outer element, the alleged signifier, to be the real signified, the *nominans,* would indeed force a victory for environmental "determinism." But the format, while reversing roles, would still permit self-identity (though probably not free will)[47] and would still be founded on the paradigm of signified and signifier. Format 3 indicates that the innerwards and outerwards, the *nominans* and *nomen,* may really relate to each other in a very complex, "co-originative"[48] way. The "I utterance" *both* mirrors the originating factor *and* is mirrored by it. Many more moderate contemporary theories of psychology, etc., advance format 3 in one way or another when dealing with self-identity. Its extension to a general theory of identity and relationships among identities has not likewise flourished. Heidegger accomplishes this extension when the concept of the "hermeneutical circle" in his *Sein und Zeit* transmutes into the motif of "belonging together" in his later work. We shall soon study the implications of these, but now it suffices to observe the obvious: that late-phase Heideggerian thought as a "philosophy of life" is limited to a very small group of philosophers, poets, and their associates. Historically, it seems to me that among movements with a broad popular base, Taoism—at its finest—most consciously and universally applied format 3. Derrida's vigorous rejection of format 3 in favor of format 4 we shall appraise anon. Format 4, of course, indicates the impasse to which Derrida claims logic and empirical data inevitably lead us: the integrity of signified and signifier, or reflexivity itself, fragments. The *nomen* or outward element of format 2 is no more a "signified" than the inner element is a "signified": the outward element is a "signified" *sous rature,* since the model of language which it presumes can only "hold together" if it is a "signifier"; and even the inward element, lacking a signified with which it can link in binary combination, cannot "hold fast," but must "float."

The argument of *dédoublement* has led, then, to the "signified under erasure," since the logic of the linguistic model which founds "signifier and signified" only allows the "signified" and *all alleged signs* to be pure signifiers. But Derrida's crucial maneuver at this point, and it must occur precisely here in the overall argument, is to perform a second, more massive "crossing out." What Derrida does, in effect, is to simply "shake us out of it," if you will; that is, to exclaim: But how absurd our conclusion is! How can there be a pure signifier? Clearly the concept of signifier is logically paired with that of signified! *By definition* a signifier is a representation of a signified. So pure signifier too must come *sous rature*. And what has been the purpose of all our preceding argumentation, then? Derrida tells us straightforwardly:

> The 'primacy' or 'priority' [in the sense we have used "pure"] of the signifier would be an expression untenable and absurd to formulatě illogically within the very logic that it would legitimately destroy. The signifier will never by rights precede the signified, in which case it would no longer be a signifier and the 'signifying' signifier would no longer have a possible signified. The thought that is announced in this impossible formula without being successfully contained therein should therefore be stated in another way; . . .[49]

Derrida's enterprise, "strictly speaking, amounts to destroying the concept of 'sign' and its entire logic."[50] Far from being an exercise in futility, Derrida's enterprise has been to show that a persistent appraisal of the theory of signifier and signified (on which, after all, the concept of the sign is founded) leads inevitably to the conclusion that alleged "signs" are really "pure signifiers." *Invicem,* since pure signifiers are impossible, the whole theory of the "sign," of "signified and signifier"—whether it is functioning in the principle of identity, or in the principle of personal self-identity, or in formal linguistics itself—is null and void.

Recall, however, Derrida's observation concerning the pure signifier: "The thought that is announced in this impossible formula without being successfully contained therein should therefore be stated in another way. . . ." Derrida will have other ways of "stating" the thought, though necessarily none of them will be adequate. At this juncture, though, Derrida's other way of stating it is his resort to quotation marks, or better still, to the "crossing out." Under the mark of the X, the words "pure signifier" and the concept they represent can still be somehow apprehended. That is to say, the concept of "pure signifier" is somehow one of the closer approximations of "the way things really are"; the concept of "pure signifier," at least for the present, is the best we can do "within our order of thinking."[51] Like a palimpsest, the "erased" thought still shows some of its authentic markings. Also, as students for the moment of Derrida, we should observe carefully two features of his philosophical constatation (and I insist on this observation because the two features are widely disregarded). First, Derrida's argumentation is *primarily* a critique of *the way we think about* reality and not a judgment of reality. Thus the charge often brought against Derrida, that there is a hypocritical discrepancy between his "normal" lifestyle and his alleged philosophy of "non-logic," of "non-sense," is misplaced. Derrida is not condemning what is called "mundane behavior" in the technical sense, that is, ordinary participation in the life-world. He is critiquing how we think about such behavior, and especially, he is critiquing what we may perhaps call "meta-thoughts." To put it another way, his critique is lodged first of all against philosophy, man's "thinking about thinking," though no doubt the critique sees much everyday decision-making as warped, if you will, by erroneous meta-thoughts which have infiltrated everyday thought. Second, terms such as pure signifier, dissemination, and "supplementation" do not *name* the behavior of reality. Rather, these terms are the "impossible" (and therefore "crossed out") but necessary conclusions which derive from careful appraisal of logocentric thinking; at best, they are the *closest we can come* to understanding the behavior of reality. Some truth filters through the "cracks" in faulty word-thoughts, so that we sense we at least have achieved some "approximation" of reality (in addition to terms of this kind, there are words such as *différance* [spelled 'differance' in English] which, as we shall see, are not so much "X'd over conclusions" as they are "provisional names" for the unnameable. Because a name such as *différance* is provisional, in Derrida's usage it is employed interchangeably with other names, and the list of such names is open-ended, continually "supplemented," permutated).

A first essay to characterize Derrida's deconstructive method, properly speaking, discovers the following scenario. He regards the principle of personal self-identity and the principle of identity (and the correlate, the principle of contradiction) as founding all systematic thought (in other words, all systematic thought in our history has been logocentric). He proceeds to demonstrate, by various argumentative routes, that the aforesaid principles and their offspring, the significant theses of key thinkers throughout history (with special focus, for reasons of currency, on modern thinkers), are *self-contradictory;* that is, that their conclusions contradict their premises. Closer scrutiny of Derrida's practice shows that in some cases he tries to prove key conclusions of one thinker contradict their premises (*v.* Derrida's treatment of Saussure, for example, OG, pp. 44-45). At other times, Derrida attacks theories he considers universal, or at least common to many thinkers. In these cases he first describes each theory by constructing it from representative thinkers and then "deconstructing" it by showing that some *necessary* elements of the very same theory are self-contradictory, or contradicted by evidence introduced from "outside the formal presentation of the theory." To put it another way, Derrida sometimes attacks a conclusion by importing evidence from sources not used by the proponents of the theory, but judged accurate by other authorities (see, for example, Derrida, OG, pp. 88, 333, 334, where clinical data is used to subvert the older notion of the priority of the signified). It is quite clear, however, that Derrida's preferred approach, and the one he employs most often, is the former: the author under attack is used against himself, is shown to "be hoist on his own petard." And often, especially in the instance of modern thinkers, Derrida tries to show that the author in question recognizes, just for a moment or only implicitly, the self-contradictory nature of his own argument. For especially good specimens of Derrida's deconstruction of individual authors, the reader is encouraged to survey these treatments of Husserl (the whole of *La voix et le phénomène*), Valéry ("Qual Quelle" in *Marges*, pp. 325–63), Levinas ("Violence and Metaphysics" in *Writing and Difference*, pp. 79–153), Freud ("Freud and the Scene of Writing," *Writing and Difference*, pp. 196–231), and Hegel ("Le puits et la pyramide," *Marges*, pp. 79–127; and the whole of *Glas*, though here Derrida is already using a "later" Derridean style, which I shall discuss farther along in this chapter). For Derrida's treatment of authors whom he almost regards as prototypes of himself (in that they often catch "glimmers" of what shall be called *différance*), see his studies of Heidegger ("Ousia et grammè," *Marges*, pp. 31–78) and Nietzsche (the whole of *Eperons*).

What glimmers survive under the crossing out, what Derrida has to "say" about the unsayable situation called *différance*, we shall scrutinize anon. It suffices now to observe, and observe carefully, that for Derrida what survives under erasure is *not* the *logical contradictory* of the conclusion he has disqualified through deconstruction. In other words, he does not use *reductio ad absurdum* in the most technical sense. The rule of *reductio ad absurdum*, narrowly defined, is that we assume what we are to prove *not* so and demonstrate that the assumption is self-contradictory; *then* we feel justified in concluding that the contradictory of the assumption is true.[52] Because Derrida does not intend *reductio ad absurdum*, his demonstration that logocentrism, or the theory of "presence," is self-contradictory does not lead to an affirmation, on his part, of any theory of non-presence.[53] Even more to the point, Derrida's very use of the law of contradiction in order to show that the law of contradiction contradicts itself does not mean, for him, that he affirms the contradictory of the law of contradiction! And most to the point, in terms of the sequence we have just completed, the demonstration that the theory of "signified-signifier relation" is self-contradictory does not commit him to the contradictory of such a theory, viz., the whole domain of *non* "signified-signifier relations" (and clearly, that domain includes as possibilities a theory of pure signifiers, a theory of pure signifieds, a theory involving *no* signified and/or signifier whatsoever, and so on). Remember that even the concept of the "pure signifier" was "crossed out." All this leaves for our later consideration *how*, then, the "pure signifier" (rather than the "pure signified," say) undergoes the "privilege" of erasure. How can it be invalid but still some sort of "approximation"? And left for our later consideration too is the mystery of the *différance* which still glimmers, but which is not the contradictory of any proposition Derrida claims to have shown invalid.

iii

But there is a danger we are now "getting ahead" of ourselves. *Différance* should not be discussed except in the context of what Derrida calls *le mouvement* and *la trace,* and these are best understood in terms of the third grand argument Derrida levels against the "signified-signifier" relation. This third argument I shall call *l'effacement.*[54] In his celebrated essay, entitled "Differance,"[55] Derrida quotes from what he considers a pivotal passage of Saussure:

> The conceptual side of value is made up solely of relations and differences with respect to the other terms of language, and the same can be said of its material side. . . . Everything that has been said up to this point boils down to this: in language there are only differences. Even more important: a difference generally implies positive terms between which the difference is set up; but in language there are only differences *without positive terms.* Whether we take the signified or the signifier, language has neither ideas nor sounds that existed before the linguistic system, but only conceptual and phonic differences that have issued from the system. The idea or phonic substance that a sign contains is of less importance than the other signs that surround it.[56]

And Derrida goes on to paraphrase the above, saying "Within a language, within the *system* of language, there are only differences."[57] But, unlike Saussure, Derrida wants to push the critique to logical collapse. To do so he must, first, further radicalize the notion of definition by negative reference; and, second, he must deduce as a consequence of this radicalization the status of all alleged signs as pure signifiers. In sum, by a different route he hopes to again show that "sound thinking" necessarily reduces the sign to pure signifier *sous rature.*

A very important thesis of Saussure's passage, cited above, is that signifieds and signifiers do not function as positive terms, but are alike differentiated from other signifieds and signifiers by *negative reference.* If we recall conventionally a "self-identical element" such as a sign is understood to be temporally and spatially "present to itself," then a Saussurean critique of this notion (at least as adapted by Derrida) argues that "each element that is said to be 'present' . . . is called the present by this very relation to what it is not, to what it absolutely is not . . ." (the essay "Differance," in *Speech and Phenomena,* p. 143). The context where Derrida so argues for an "absolute" negative reference is one devoted to "the movement of signification," to the "trace," and "differance," —all provisional names for what somehow "constitutes" *that which survives* absolute negative reference; as we shall see, the "constituting" of *that which survives* does not involve an "origin"; nor does *that which survives* operate in the mode of signifier/signified or even existence/non-existence.

But my precise concern now, the thread I am now disengaging

from the web of Derrida's expository "fabric," so we can follow it with some accuracy, is Derrida's use of negative reference per se. To follow this thread, we must undertake a preliminary reconnaissance of *différance*, though not yet of *différance* as the "constituting" of *that which survives*. Derrida's fabrication of the neologism *différance*, the reason for his substitution of an "a" for the conventional "e" (of the conventional French word *différence*), and so on, occupy specifically pp. 129–33, 136, and 137 of his celebrated essay. The formulation of the neologism is properly clever and depends on the irregular "a" of *DifférAnce* (the internal capitalization is for illustrative purpose, and is mine). Our English word "difference" is spelled in the same way as the conventional French word *différence*, but the penultimate "e" in the French word is vocalized as the "a" in our word "father." But the substitution of a written "a" for the correct spelling "e"—so *différEnce* becomes *DifférAnce*—is undetectable when a Frenchman sounds the graphic sign *DifférAnce*. The upshot of all this is that when the graphic form *DifférAnce* is vocalized, a Frenchman (unless signalled otherwise by contextual "clues") *hears* the word *différEnce*. Thus the graphic notation "a" possesses here a strange status: it cannot, in and of itself, be heard. Besides the "side-skirmish" such an example carries off against the "naturalness" of sense-sound pairing, the "a" which is "lost" in the vocalization becomes a shadow, if you will, of all differences. That is to say, the difference between graphic "e" and "a" (and consequently the difference, too, between the "senses" of the two graphic forms, *différence* and *différance*, which are "differentiated" by these two graphs) cannot be *heard;* this "lack" is a shadow of the difference "as such" between graphic "e" and "a," for example, a difference which cannot be named; even the difference between the "senses" of *différence* and *différance* likewise cannot be *named*. In fact, when we say we "know" something, we know "it" only by differentiating from what "it" *is not*. (Even vocally this works out: what is the "name" of the "between," the "difference" between the sounds "a" and "ä"? Yet do we know either sound in any way besides its difference from the other sound and from the remaining range of possible sounds?)

We really "know" differences, and differences are not nameable, are not a *something*, not an "identity" that we can "point to." Differences *are not*. (Two cautions here: first, we are still choosing to focus on differEnce, on "definition" by negative reference—we are not yet focusing on the "constituting" of differEnces by Differance; second, we are obviously using terms, viz., "differEnces" and DifferAnce, to designate what are not "identities" and what are, therefore, not "nameable"[58]—these terms can be considered "crossed-out" names.)

To continue our pursuit of "negative reference," however, let us next play it off against the notion of a self-identical element as one which is spatially and temporally[59] present to itself. The verb *différer* in French can mean "to differ" (conventionally conceived as a spatial concept) and it can mean "to defer" (conventionally understood as a temporal concept). If negative reference is the only means of definition, then classical self-identity becomes Derridean self-difference! And self-difference in two senses which are to become inexorably entrammeled: self-deferring and self-differing. In his treatment of Husserl in *Speech and Phenomena*, Derrida denies the Husserlian distinction between retention and nonperception (and therefore the distinction between retention and nonpresence, in the context) and asserts:

> One then sees quickly that the presence of the perceived present can appear as such only inasmuch as it is *continuously compounded* with a nonpresence and nonperception, with primary memory and expectation, retention and protention.[60]

And since this "compounding" is for Derrida not organic but a relation of negative reference, he can go on to assert:

> As soon as we admit this continuity of the now and the not-now, perception and nonperception, in the zone of primordiality common to primordial impression and primordial retention, we admit the other into the self-identity of the *Augenblick;* nonpresence and nonevidence are admitted into the *blink of the instant.*[61]

If we were to plot the scenario programmatically, we could say the "now" only knows itself by the "not now," so self-identity (including personal self-identity) "self-defers." And it defers (negatively relates, "diachronically") to both the past (retentions, memories, etc.) and the future (protentions, expectations). What is more, "deferral" takes *time,* so that the so-called "present moment" never really "has its whole act together" at once: the so-called "present moment," on this count (pun!), must undergo still further mitosis. Thus Derrida attaches to the *blink of the instant* mentioned above an ominous coda: "There is a duration to the blink, and it closes the eye." Elsewhere, Derrida, echoing David Hume, reminds us that because of *retardement* (delay) the originating factor operative in classical self-identity can never really be reflected by the expression (*nomen*) which is its "mirror," for during the "time it takes" for the reflexive act to catch the originating factor, the latter has changed. And, it might be added, if self-identity were to be understood as the construction of a "present" *nomen* mirroring a "past but remembered" *nominans* (and this formula is fairly popular), then, Derrida would say, the construction cracks open under the same argument used against Husserl: the alleged "past but remembered" is a "not now," a nonpresence, inserted into, and thereby splitting, the so-called integral present moment (a fortiori, because the "present" *nomen,* cannot even define itself except as the *non-nominans,* and so on).

In the section of the essay "Differance" where "trace" receives its most thorough treatment, Derrida says self-differing and self-deferring are the problematic of "time's becoming spatial" (spatializ-

ing) and "space's becoming temporal" (temporalizing).[62] Again
taking care, in so far as we can, to disengage the thread of negative
reference from the more intricate refinements of "trace" (the latter
we shall study anon), let us try to clarify these two phrases involving
spatializing and temporalizing (i.e., differing and deferring). The relation of the "present" to the "past" and "future" is a negative relation, that is, the present is *not* the not-now. The relation, even if
negative, is a sort of shadowy "time's becoming spatial" (spacing); but
the relation becomes spatial only to self-differ, for the not-now, spatially and thus under erasure, is brought up alongside the now only
to differ from the now. And the now is nothing but the *not* not-now
which is functioning in the (crossed-out) same space. Likewise, the
relation is a "space's becoming temporal" (temporalizing) because the
not-now, when erasure is removed, defers from the now. The not-
now cannot be in the same space, and the now is nothing but the
temporally *not* not-now.

If we adjust our scopes again and broaden our language, we can see
that Derrida, in a very general way, is translating the workings of
negative theology to the "rational" but unconscious workings of
everyday mind. As negative theology defines God only by what God *is
not,* the human mind, for Derrida, always defines by negative reference and only by negative reference. And of course for Derrida, the
analysis of difference must a fortiori follow this negative way, though
negative reference necessarily "comes to the surface" and shows itself
as "reasoned" analysis, in so technical an attempt as discussion of
difference. "Already we had to note *that* difference *is not,* does not
exist, and is not any sort of being present . . . ," says Derrida, and he
adds, "we will have to point out everything *that* it *is not.* . . ."[63] Lest his
readers confuse difference with the telos of natural theology, however, Derrida here as always underscores the radical otherness of his
own endeavor. Though "the detours, phrases, and syntax that I shall
often have to resort to will resemble—will sometimes be practically
indiscernible from—those of negative theology," he reminds us,
" . . . difference is not theological, not even in the most negative order
of negative theology. . . . Not only is difference irreducible to every
ontological or theological—onto-theological—reappropriation, but it
opens up the very space in which onto-theology—philosophy—
produces its system and its history. It thus encompasses and irrevo-
cably surpasses onto-theology or philosophy."[64]

Derrida's negative reference, as we have already indicated and are
about to broach again, is *absolute.* Whereas Saussure considered the
"idea or phonic substance that a sign contains" to be "of less importance than the other signs that surround it,"[65] and thus implied a
self-identical nucleus of some kind, there is in Derrida no such concession. So surely, when "deconstructing" theology, Derrida corrodes
away any transcendental nucleus such as a Supreme Identity
(whereas negative theology obviously must grant a Transcendental

Nucleus to which all negative referents are the contradictory). All of this will become very exciting for our own work in the forthcoming fourth part, which, I believe, preserves Christian orthodoxy in its entirety yet consumes more of Derrida than he would ever expect possible. But clearly our present concern is Derrida's adaptation of negative reference from theology (among other sources), yet his firm rejection of a transcendental nucleus, or any nucleii at all. And of even greater relevance, because Derrida surely deems it the most likely "temptation" at this point, is his firm rejection of a supreme Nothing, be the Nothing a God of Western mysticism (as opposed to Western rational theology) or a great Void of centric Buddhism. Derrida's argument here is that a Nothing can only operate in dialectic with a non-Nothing (i.e., an Everything or Something), so that any theory of nothingness "buys into" a theory of presence. Absence is just the other side of the coin of presence, and it is this entire way of thinking that Derrida judges spurious. For Derrida, the history of thought consists of misguided efforts to recover origin, "wholeness," at any cost—at the dearest cost, in fact, that of repeated dissimulation. And the Void, for Derrida, is just another masked name for a center, a "whole."[66] To recapitulate, then, we can say Derrida radicalizes the process of defining by negative reference, and he does so by making negative reference absolute (i.e., no nucleus of identity survives the process; the nucleus is *effaced*). Perhaps the best way to affiliate this notion with a notion of the *pure* signifier is to "draw out" what is the already implied next step: any alleged sign is instead a *pure signifier* because *it only signifies what it is not.*[67]

One of my aspirations, however, is to render Derrida more understandable, and the above description may restate in clearer language what is Derrida's claim (so people can "mouth" the claim), but the description does not lead the reader, I do not think, to an intuition, an actual "seeing," of the way Derrida does his thinking here. So let us get down to the business of seeing what he sees (he, of course, would shrink with particular aversion from so "visual" a metaphor, but I shall have my own ways of reaffirming the mention of "vision"[68]) and of doing so without rhetorical extravagance. Easiest access to the problem comes by way of negative reference in its more temperate forms. The reader need just recall negation and its role in nineteenth-century German Idealism; and the popularity of Sartre's bizarre version of negative reference (where the *pour soi* negates the appearance of *en soi*); and the 'Analytic' and very domesticated version of J. L. Austin himself, who suggests that the "negative use wears the trousers" in words like "exists," "real," and "same."[69] But what does Derrida mean when he radicalizes the above? Let us give him as sympathetic a "try" as we can. Let each of us ask the following. If it were the case that I were completely alone from birth, and without eyes or any of the neurological components which involve vision, and if (very hypothetically!) I still matured, and then suddenly a whole "seeing" apparatus materialized, and I saw just "light," would I be able to know "light" at all? Or would "light" just be a "zero," a "neuter" to me? But then, if the "light" were to be extinguished, so I experienced "darkness," would I then for the first time "know" light? And if it were the case I for the first time knew "light," would not this be so because I knew "light" only by negative reference to the darkness? For if I knew the "light" *in itself,* if it had an identity or "nucleus" of its own, would not I have known it from the moment I had acquired the "seeing" faculty, and known it without necessary negative recourse to darkness? Apropos negative reference, Ludwig Wittgenstein's famous assertion can easily receive a Derridean reading: "If you went to Mars and men were spheres with sticks coming out, you wouldn't know what to look for."[70] That is, since a zone of comparison would be lacking, there would be no negative referents whereby one could "know" Martian men. Does the above account seem convincing? Derrida would think so, at least insofar as the argument from *effacement* is concerned. Now, in the steps of Derrida,[71] we are about to take the next turn and put the whole argument "under erasure," as we did with the argument from *dédoublement.* But let us leave the intact *effacement* argument by making a last general statement about it. Derrida's conclusion, at this stage, seems to be that everyday mind is so constituted that programmatically, like a quasi-instantaneous computer operation, it is secretly processing negative references all the time; and presenting naive "experience" with the "answers," the *faits accomplis:* "This is a chair. . . . This is a table . . . ," and so on.

The specific difficulty with the "conclusion" that all alleged signs *just* signify what they are not, and are on this account "pure," is that this conclusion contradicts other propositions which one must generate in order to explain why our thoughts *concatenate* in a *selective* way, and in accordance with what are at least quasi-determinate norms. That is to say, the mind does not move at random, but proceeds in everyday behavior from, say, interpreting a "knock" at the door, to the decision to ignore or to answer, and how to answer, the knock; and from this decision, if it is affirmative, "enabling" thoughts proceed whereby we can get up, walk to, and open the door. The everyday mind normally does not interpret a knock at the door as a green feather settling in a Brazilian jungle. However, pure, i.e., absolute negative reference, excludes ipso facto any *fil conducteur,* any connecting thoughts according to any "thread"[72] since every "thing" is in *absolutely no way* like any other.[73] Is there a way out of this impasse? Can, for example, purely negative signifiers somehow "link" by virtue of their very negativity? Say alleged thing A were like alleged thing B, in that both A and B signified *not being like* alleged things C to infinity. So alleged thing A would be different from alleged thing B only in that A also signifies not-B; and in turn, alleged thing B would be different from A only in that B signifies also not-A! Alas, Derrida's notion of negative reference is too absolute to accommodate such an escape! For if A also signifies not-B, this not-B must even exclude the possibility that A and B are alike in that they both negate C to infinity. To recapitulate, Derrida is claiming that the route of logic inevitably leads to a concept of purely negative reference, but that such a concept contradicts other premises which must perforce have a place in an overall argument concerning referentiality. Everyday mind works by purely negative reference yet everyday mind follows a "thread"! (Thinking about everyday mind will in short order present even a more obvious problem for Derrida: how can he invoke the "inevitable route of logic" when there are no routes!) Derrida must therefore, as he did in the *dédoublement* argument, again put the pure signifier under erasure; and again with the provision that the pure signifier—this time because of *effacement*—somehow "approximates" the "way things really are"[74] better than other alternatives do.

That Derrida "privileges" the pure signifier under erasure, and more specifically, that he toils to "account for" what we have momentarily called the "thread" (and we are about to investigate this accounting), all indicates his intriguing though indirect relationship to phenomenology. For Derrida's severe "rationalism" has opened up three possibilities. One is absurdism; a second is what we can call a Hindu monism; and a third is a "modified phenomenology." If one accepts Derrida's reasoning thus far, and what is more, if one chooses to be *only* a rationalist, it is eminently "rational" to be an absurdist in a "world" where contradictories reign: where each thing is *absolutely* unlike each other thing, yet where one can reach this very conclusion only by "thinking." And, Derrida would add, if one permits instead that the human mind's deceptive drive towards holism and the human psyche's need for security contribute their input, then it is understandable though wrong to be a monist. Under the pressure of these "natural" drives, a world where each thing is absolutely unlike each other thing can be interpreted, paradoxically, as a world of *sameness.* For all things become *alike* in that each of them is unlike the other. Absolute differentiation becomes absolute indifference. Absolute differentiation becomes, indeed, Supreme Identity. And it is this sort of leveling which allows certain kinds of Hinduism to regard individual things (i.e., individual identities which are in some ways like other things and in some ways unique) as an illusion, and to regard the "conductive threads" which link these things as an illusion. Rather, the only "real" becomes the Sameness, the one Identity which is the *contrary* of individual things. For Derrida, this Sameness—be it interpreted as Brahman, Yogacaric Nirvana, or whatever—is just the dissimulating substitution for Center, and equally spurious. The third possibility I have called a modified phenomenology, though Derrida would bristle at the term, since it represents for him the theory of presence *sans pareil,* namely Husserlianism; and it involves a formula of "experience" which, at least in its Husserlian manifestation, rests squarely on the principle of self-identity. My point nonetheless is that Derrida, though he may equate all experience with word-thoughts, nevertheless (at least in practice) gives experience priority over "logical conclusions." When faced with the self-contradictories which infect "logical" theories of meaning, he decides against absurdism and *in favor of experience* — in favor, for example, of the *fil conducteur,* though he will have to salvage this "thread" in a new, "crossed-out" manner. He decides, too, against Voidism, which he treats not only as illogical (as the other side of presence, voidism is as self-contradictory as presence), but as *unreduced*[75] *experience* (unreduced because infected by emotion): authentic experience is for him authentic Husserlian experience, that is, experience which is purified of emotional needs and bias, but which "takes the lead" (i.e., controls the phenomenological description). Derrida would deny almost all, if not all, of my above account of his thinking and its behavior. But how else can we explain his decision, for example, against Voidism (on the grounds it is illogical, *and also* emotional rather than experiential in the Husserlian sense) and his decision *in favor of* differance (on the grounds, as we shall see, that it is beyond logic, that it can be "approximated" by crossed-out logic, and that genuine experience will have it so, i.e., witness to it). In short, if Derrida were not a phenomenologist, he would not judge himself obliged to account for this "thread" which characterizes everyday thinking: he is obliged because experience testifies to this "conductive thread."

iv

The issue for Derrida becomes, then, how to account for the apparent "signals" and "enabling choices" whereby man interprets the knock at the door, and gets up, and opens the door. Because of the purely negative signifying which he considers the "function" of "alleged signs," Derrida must place any theory of *fil conducteur* per se under the firmest erasure. Since *that which survives* absolute negative erasure cannot be an identity, i.e., a "whole" constituted by signifier and signified, I shall call it the 'Derridean *else.*' The 'else' provides wherewithal so one can move in an other than random fashion from knock to the decision to open the door, and then on to the door, and so on (and Derrida takes great pains to explain the 'constitution' of this 'else'). In the essay "Differance," Derrida justifiably remarks that he is forced by the very nature of speech to resort to words, and these words are always already embedded in the tradition (the examples he here provides are "production," "constitution," and "history").[76] Derrida goes on to explain, "I only use these terms here, like many other concepts, out of strategic convenience and in order to prepare the deconstruction of the system they form at the point which is now most decisive."[77] The term "differance," he tells us, likewise "gets subjected, according to the context, to a certain number of nonsynonymic substitutions, . . . such concepts as 'reserve,' 'protowriting,' 'prototrace,' 'spacing,' indeed to 'supplement' or *pharmakon*, and, before long, to 'hymen,' etc."[78] As indicated in my own preface, future chapters will explain why I consider myself justified, indeed vindicated, in resorting to my own terms at times (terms which I keep *constant* in meaning), in order to "clarify" Derrida *while retaining* a faithful representation of his thought. By using the term the 'Derridean else,' for example, and using it in a functionally neologistic way, I wish to focus on *that which survives* purely negative reference, while taking care not to lose sight of pure negation. Derrida's vocabulary attempts much the same task, but he often uses the gestures of erasure or quotation marks (*en guillemets*) to "achieve" it, and he also prefers to "reenact" the implications of his thinking in his very employ of terms — so his ideas undergo quite steady "nonsynonymic substitutions." Derrida resorts to such techniques because each of them, in its own way, tends to undercut what he regards as the threat of reification, of a kind of hypostasis of ideas, and hence a deceptive recovery of a theory of identity. When he addresses the question posed by *that which survives* negative reference, he treats it within the purview of the word *trace*, though trace is permuted into supplement, *pharmakon*, hymen, and so on, in a supposedly continuous series of transformations. He takes care to tell us, however, that each of the above terms is "nonsynonymous," but used precisely within the field of its conventional context, in order to deconstruct that context. And the word *trace* is a case in point.[79] *La trace*, rendered into English, is "trace" or "track" or "trail." *La trace* suggests, then, (1) an absence (the "thing" as such being tracked is *not at all* there — an allusion, no doubt, to the absence effected by absolute negative reference), but also (2) a "direction" (if the "thing" is not at all present, it is still leaving a "trace," a *clue* which we can "track" and whereby we choose to move directionally), and (3) a "movement" (the "thing" is moving ahead of us, or once moved; and we are moving along its "trail"). Derrida's "work of deconstruction," in this context, as we shall see, is precisely to eliminate the "thing as such" yet somehow preserve the rest.

We can begin with Derrida's splendid essay, "Edmond Jabès and the Question of the Book," which appears as chapter 3 in *Writing and Difference*. Derrida regards Edmond Jabès, the French-language poet and writer whose subject-matter is so often Jewishness and poetic vocation, as among those privileged ones who have stumbled upon the hole in the road, i.e., who have surmised differance. In any case, Jabès is "reread" by Derrida, so that overtly and covertly Jabès's literature allegorizes and reenacts differance.[80] Since our present enterprise is discussion of the trace, we can start with the *thématisation* of trace in Jabès, and specifically with his phrase, "Do not forget

that you are the nucleus [*le noyau*] of a rupture."[81] According to
Derrida, those who have found the fatal crack in logocentrism, those
who are the people of *écriture,* and especially those who are Jews
(people of the Book become writing, people of exile), must recognize
and never forget they are the "nucleus of a rupture." Strange talk
this, for it retains the term "nucleus" we have seen effaced, but explains the effacement by constituting the nucleus through rupture
rather than identity. In terms of Jewish theology, as "read" by Jabès
and "reread" by Derrida, the beginning of "history" is the "rupture"
within God whereby God chooses not to continue His "speech," but
to "write" (to write the Tables of the Law). The implications of all
this for what can become a very intriguing discussion not only of the
Jewish concept of Yahweh, but of the Christian concept of Trinity, I
shall develop in the last part, but it suffices now to remark that the
"writing" of the Tablets by Yahweh is already a departure from the
"conventionally formulated" unity of God, whose Being and Voice
are one. Writing is God "at a remove." (For a while, God—by allow-
ing Moses to break the tablets—even puts Himself at a "double remove".) It is precisely the "remove," the "silence" of God's voice, this
interval, this *difference* (in the sense of differance!) which *constitutes*
the writing whereby we "know" Him, but this writing *is not* God. This
writing is "trace," a "directional," if I may gloss Derrida's term with
my own (a "directional" because it is not an "entity," i.e., a binary
unity of signifier-signified,[82] yet it is a trail which provides "direc-
tives" and "direction").[83]

And Derrida goes on to apply the Pentateuch's imagery further, so
that the Jewish people exiled in the desert "articulate" the whole
human condition: the desert is the interval, the differance, the "between" which both negates the presence of Canaan but also *constitutes*
it; that is, because of the desert the land of Canaan is not in their
possession, but also because of the desert, the land of Canaan is a
"direction" and is "blessed and promised." Only in the cities of
Egypt, where "letters" are weeds between the cobblestones, and in
the desert, where letters are patches of scrub, can writing flourish at
all; for "in the garden" there would be no need of writing—there
would be God's Voice. Because one follows the "directional" which is
trace, there is "movement," "pathway," *passage, procession, parcours.*
Derrida's further suggestion, however, is that the Jewish people as
the avant-garde, but the human race as a whole, is only now recognizing the full import of Genesis and Exodus: the Jews as the
"people of the Bible," the "people of the Book," are only now coming
to realize the Book is Writing, i.e., the Text is not God having a
"modified presence" in words, but God *infinitely* postponed by
graphic signs. Signs are trace, are direction, but there is neither
Terminus nor Telos (no final Where or What). The desert, *différance,*
"absolutely negates" presence but constitutes the crossed-out *fil conducteur,* the crossed-out "nucleus," the trace. In suchwise, Derrida

salvages *that which survives,* the else, so we can proceed from knock to door to a decision about opening the door. Life, in his words, "does not negate itself any more than it affirms itself: it differs from itself, defers itself and writes itself as *différance.*"[84]

The above has just been a parable under erasure, however, and surely more clarification of the Derridean else would be helpful. Perhaps we can begin to clarify by drawing a very dangerous analogy. The analogy is to the concept of substitution. What Derrida is implying is that all alleged signs are "substitutions," but "substitutions" which are *not* self-identities (since they are not combinations of signifiers and signifieds); nor do these "substitutions" originate in origins (again, self-identities). Thus the word "substitution" (Latin etymology: that which "is or stands under, in place of"), dependent as it so obviously is on logocentric theory, is most inappropriate. As we have already seen, alleged signs are not really self-identities; and as we shall see in some detail, alleged signs are constituted (and, as we already know, *purely negated*) by intervals rather than origins or self-identities. Thus, sign is trace. But the analogy to "substitution" is serviceable if we retain its connotation of "postponement," of *movement:* the reader of traces too is "passed on" from trace to trace, because no trace is the "thing." Both the trace and conventional sign-as-substitute are understood to leave clues so we can move directionally (though for trace, direction never comes to a "rest"). Much of this explication Derrida develops masterfully in his essay "White Mythology,"[85] where he argues that logocentrists—to be consistent—must somehow escape from the "slide" of endless and radical "metaphoricity," but cannot. If we were to catch ourselves up short right now, for example, and examine each and every word in the preceding sentence, we would find each and every word is "metaphorical"; it is not structured to be equivalent to something, but is structured to be "like" somethings, which in turn pass us on to still other "things," and so on ad infinitum. For instance, the very word "consistent" in that preceding sentence is founded on the sense "to stand firmly," so to be "consistent" is to be *like* someone standing firmly (but clearly the word "consistent" is not equivalent to "standing firmly"—we do not mean logocentrists are assuming the physical posture of "standing"—so why can we not ever say what we mean, Derrida would exclaim!)[86] What is more, the word "consistent," even in context, has several senses, i.e., is reducible to several metaphors: to be *like* "one standing still," or to be like "one causing (an entity) to stand still," are two others. And these senses are divergent, and of course are, all of them, reducible still further. Thus the disconcerting issue of undecidability, of which we will in due course hear more, also intervenes. As the next step, Derrida argues that even the philosophy of metaphor must be ousted, since "likeness" cannot be predicated of two elements that are never "present" as such to the metaphor-maker. So Derrida's own thesis of "radical metaphoricity" operates under erasure. But my concern now is to pursue the skein of trace, as it were, and for this it suffices for us to gather up, as we have just done, the notions of postponement and of "tracking" (i.e., even with the "undecidabilities" that cause "breaks," "mutations," in the "journey"—there is still, in Derrida's own words, a *"journey"*).[87]

In his essay on Jabès, Derrida spoke of the *between,* which is the desert, and the *between's* "simultaneous" negation and constitution of the trace, the promised land. In the section of "La Double Séance" of *La Dissémination,* Derrida offers a programmatic motto for his notion of the between. Because the context this time speaks of Stéphane Mallarmé, and Jean-Pierre Richard's "logocentric" interpretation of him, Derridean trace must again undergo contextual transformation, and this time the imagery is *Mallarméiste* and sexual.[88] Trace becomes "hymen," and the programmatic inscription reads, "Hymen,—it is the structure of *and/or* between *and/or*."[89] According to Derrida, Richard emphasizes the "marital" denotation of Mallarmé's imagery of the "hymen" (the conventional "poetic usage"), and thus interprets hymen as "one of those 'beneficient figures' in which 'the opposition of the closed and the open can come to an end,' and 'at the interior of which these two contradictory needs can both be satisfied, simultaneously or successively' "[90] (other such figures, for Richard, are the image of the dancer, the book, the fan). Such an interpretation is "logocentric," of course, and in terms of our own discussion, specifically 'Taoist', in that it resolves opposites.

Derrida's reading, as is to be expected, breaks the resolution, or—to go along with Derrida's pun—puts a crease in the fold. His reading is at once ingenious and more graphic, though it moves, be assured, far beyond jocularity.[91] The hymen, as a biologically discontinuous membrane, is an "and/or," and it is an "and/or" *between* a fold, or second "and/or." Trace is a Derridean constitution/negation *between* conventional constitution/negation. The latter conventional sort of constituting and negating, Derrida has already dispatched: a "word" is not a binary formation which is at once a unity (an "and") of signifier and signified and an opposition (an "or") of signifier and signified. Derrida has also explained, already, the Derridean negation which is trace and which is performed by the between. The so-called sign is *absolutely* negated by *purely* negative reference. We now develop further the Derridean constitution of trace, the "that which survives" of trace, and the constitutive role of the between (that is to say, of differance). To do so, we take up again the problematic of "time's becoming space," and "space's becoming time,"[92] but on this occasion we must cite the whole relevant passage from the essay, "Differance"[93]:

> Differance is what makes the movement of signification possible only if each element called "present," appearing on the stage of presence, is related to something other than itself, but is retaining [*gardant en lui*] the mark of the past element and is already letting itself be hol-

lowed out [*se laissant déja creuser*] by the mark of its relation to the future element,—the trace relating no less to what is called the future than to what is called the past, and constituting [*constituant*] what is called the present by this very relation to what it is not, to what it absolutely is not; that is, not even to a past or a future considered as a modified present. In order for it[94] to be, an interval [*un intervalle*] must separate it from what it is not; but this interval that constitutes it [*qui le constitue*] in the present must also, with one and the same stroke [*du même coup*], divide the present in itself, thus dividing, along with the present, everything that can be conceived on its basis, that is, every being,—in particular, for our metaphysical language, the substance or subject. This interval, dynamically constituting and dividing itself [*se constituant, se divisant dynamiquement*], is what could be called *spacing* [*espacement*], time's becoming-spatial [*devenir-espace du temps*]—or space's becoming-temporal (*temporalizing*) [*devenir-temps de l'espace* (*temporalisation*)]. And it is this constitution [*constitution*] of the present, as an 'originating' and irreducibly nonsimple [*non-simple*], and therefore, in the strict sense, non-originating, synthesis of marks[95] [*de marques*], of retention's and protention's traces [*de traces de rétentions et de protentions*] (to reproduce here, analogically and provisionally, a phenomenological and transcendental language that will presently be revealed as inadequate) that I propose to call protowriting, prototrace, or differance [*archi-écriture, archi-trace ou différance*].[96]

The "irreducibly nonsimple" which Derrida evokes above can only be understood over and against the simple, i.e., the conventional model of "presence"; or, to be more "precise" in our phrasing, the "irreducibly nonsimple" can only be understood as functioning *between* conventional and/or. The conventional model (and Derrida clearly assumes that it, and its dialectical variants, are the only viable alternatives to his "nonsimple") must posit a "present" which is *composed* of three qualitatively different "presents." There is (1) the *immediately perceived present;* and it must contrast itself with at least the chronologically preceding moment, so there "arises" a remembrance which is (2) the *past as present;* and there must be a contrast as well with the expected future moment, which appears on the scene of presence as (3) a *future as present.* In a nutshell, the present (as opposed to just "sensation," say) cannot exist unless it is qualitatively three presences in one (though, to condense the discussion a bit, we can just designate the non-immediate presences as "modified presences"). What is more, the three presences must somehow "adhere" in order to compose one presence, and many philosophers have argued the only way to explain such adhesion is to posit a Present (presence) which is somehow "other" than mundane presence, a Present which is not located within ordinary experiential limits and thus can elude the nature of ordinary time—and, most importantly, which because of this transcendence can "support" the unity of the three experiential presents.

The conventional *and/or,* the *and/or* belonging to the above model,

is traditionally portrayed as follows: the likenesses between immediate present and modified presents (and the likenesses usually
proceed from the sublatent or transcendental, though the theory
does not seem to *compel* this) are the *"and,"* and the differences between them are the *"or."* But Derrida, as we have seen, already
believes he has proven there are no "likenesses" (and therefore no
conventional *"and"*): the "present" is absolutely negated by the
"modified presences," because the latter are *not* presences *at all* (they
are not even "qualitatively different" presences);[97] and consequently,
Derrida adds, there is neither need nor reason for a transcendental
Present. Just as vengefully does Derrida's wrath descend on the conventional *"or,"* because neither are there differences of the conventional kind between (and this is a conventional "between")
immediate and modified presences. The key to his critique here is
that absolute negation destroys the possibilities of "things" as such,
i.e., self-identical *entities*. So likeness (meaning the possession of like
substances, or perhaps like *qualities,* dependent on the logocentric
theory involved) are ipso facto impossible; and just as impossible are
unlike substances, unlike qualities, etc. (the conventional *"or"*). Finally, the conventional *between* as the movement of *comparison* between conventionally "different" or "like" things, becomes an impossible function. The grand questions, of course, are how the Derridean *and* distinguishes itself from conventional *and,* plus how the
Derridean *and* survives absolute negation (the Derridean *or*). And it
is here that we find limned the lines of the Derridean quandary, a
quandary about which he will sometimes sound apocalyptic, both
terrified and exuberant.[98] Recall that Derrida has placed his
enterprise under the sign of logic (though in order to destroy logic
through its self-contradictions). Recall he has also acted in a way that
legitimates the testimony of empirical data—scientific information
can be absorbed and used by the workings of his logic. And finally
he has, at least by his choice of concerns, deemed his logic account-
able to experience in a phenomenological or half-phenomenological
sense.[99] (Ordinary experience—though keep in mind that for Derrida it is always experience which is in word-thoughts, in
language—testifies to the conductive thread under erasure; without
constitutive activity, Derridean absolute difference would lead to an
absolute indifference which destroys the thread.)

But now, face to face with the grand questions, what does he do?
If we survey his above passage on *différance* and constituting trace,
what is most striking is that we do not find "answers." Derrida, in this
treatment of *différance* and in his many other treatments (which, despite their frequency, are transformations of this one), does not give
affirmative answers in the sense of logical proofs that establish a
"truth." Indeed, his message is that there should not be any more
answers of this kind. His mission, we must recall, has been to show
logically that each logical system self-destructs (so when he was doing

this, the logical demonstration of self-contradiction was the 'answer', if you will). But the conclusion he reached which undid the logical system in question (and the conclusion was always the contradictory of what the system had traditionally concluded) was not an 'answer' either.[100] For it came under automatic erasure. Absolute negative reference, like the pure signifier in general, undoes presence, but it is also under erasure. It is under erasure not only because it is self-contradictory, but because as a concept it violates the witness of ordinary experience, the latter's phenomenological display of conductive thread. Yet absolute negative reference is under erasure as *approximate*. That is to say, to be under erasure means that the crossed-out concept gives some glimpse at the real state of affairs (though the real state of affairs is always in language[101]). The "glimpse," of course, is not an answer in the logical sense, not a "logical demonstration." To recapitulate, the following *points de repère* characterize Derridean method. Any philosophy of presence can be disproven. The contradictory which unseats the conclusion of a philosophy of presence is also illogical. But it apparently belongs to "another order" of thought as well, and as such it "approximates" the real state of affairs. This privileged status is indicated by the sign of the crossing-out (placement under erasure). To this last we can add the following. A survey of Derrida's quotation on differance — and it is "typical" — shows recourse to description and to brief sequences of logical reasoning. Thus the last *point de repère*. The *sous rature* cannot be logically proven, but insights into the *sous rature* can be *evoked*[102] by phenomenological description[103] and by some isolated postulates and truncated sequences of logic. Alas, the lines of dilemma vector out nonetheless from this agenda and its associations. If Derrida takes seriously his concession that all language is founded on the theory of presence, on signifier and signified, and takes seriously his disproof of this theory, then his logical demonstrations, and even his "descriptions" of differance, his snatches of logic, indeed every word he utters — they are all absurd. How match this absurdity up with an 'approximation' of the real-in-language, especially if you are befuddled by the future of man's thought and if you eschew mysticism? This dilemma will occupy us soon enough, but now we resume consideration of the excerpt from "Differance," this time forewarned that systematic and affirmative logical answers are not what we shall find.

What then do we find? We find the "element called 'present'" (presence *sous rature*) retains the "mark" of the past, and that there is too a "mark" of the reference towards future. We already know the marks, or trace, cannot be substances or qualities, things or even thing-like. Most importantly, in terms of our discussion, the marks, or trace, are a *constitution* (as we are told several times in the excerpt) as well as a negation. Absolute negative reference (relation to what the crossed-out present "absolutely is not") does not only absolutely negate (this we already know from foregoing treatment), but also constitutes, and "with one and the same stroke." And this absolute negative reference is the "interval," the between. Mind boggling, of course. How can reference functioning as pure *is not* still "put in gears" the wherewithal for *that which survives?* Derrida is suggesting, surely, that this dilemma arises in part from an enslavement on our part to logocentrism, or thing-oriented thought. That which survives, the conductive thread under erasure, is not a thing-like remnant, but in Derrida's words, a "movement of signification," a movement which at the same stroke negates! The motif of trace or trail as absence and as directional pathway still holds good. "The interval, dynamically constituting and dividing itself, is what could be called spacing, time's becoming-spatial or space's becoming-temporal (temporalizing)," the crucial sentence of the excerpt reads. If we amplify our previous "gloss,"[104] we can say that the crossed-out moment when we *assemble* the three presences (the "shadowy 'time's being-spatial,' " we called it) is "with one and the same stroke" a moment of division. It is a moment of division in two ways. The shadow of synchronic formation *differs* (i.e., the shadowy "present" is only the *not this, not that* of the crossed-out synchronic field: as a pure signifier, it signifies only that it is not the other "elements" in the "same" field). And the crossed-out moment is also a moment of division because it *defers* ("space's becoming-temporal"). The result is that no moment (no presence) as such "happens" at all! In the previous gloss, we stressed that absolute negation defers, but "with one and the same stroke" it *assembles*. And "to assemble"[105] is "to constitute." (And, to turn to differing again, instead of deferring, perhaps Derrida even means this shadow of synchronic formation, the formation which—while it is disassembling through *not this, not that*, is also assembling—to be a kind of *constitution*.) If we wish to draft a *mot d'ordre*, an appropriate one at this point would perhaps be,—there can be no present or presence because instead there is constitution/deconstitution. Recourse to the figure of the sounds *a* and *ä*[106] can help us with the above notions and with the Derridean "interval" or between. Not by virtue of thingness, of self-identity, but by virtue of "their" interval do the sounds *a* and *ä* "trace."[107] What *constitutes* the sounds *a* and *ä*? Only the *difference (differance!)* between them, which both negates and constitutes "them." Since the interval is not a self-identity, a binary combination of signifier and signified, "it" is unnameable ("differance" is just a "provisional" name, Derrida avers). And since "it" perpetually alters,[108] as ongoing constitutions and negations, it is "an 'originating' and irreducibly nonsimple, and therefore, in the strict sense, non-originating. . . ." If we keep in mind the perpetual slide of the non-simple, we avoid—Derrida would say—a steamy metaphysical seduction, that of fixing constitution/deconstitution as a formal center of some kind.[109]

The "milieu of the between has nothing to do with a center,"[110]

Derrida repeats in another *mise en scène,* so the "else" is a "trail" constituted by way of negative *referring:* thus we can proceed from the knock at the door to a decision about the knock, to an opening of the door. An analogy I find more perspicuous than most is that Derridean "constitution" is like "slipping forward diagonally" between oncoming ranks—a *vertiginous* experience which almost seems coerced by what Derrida so often calls the *jeu,* the play of differance. Is it so strange that one grasps for poetic description, when even Derrida can really offer us at this point only description and some logical links? And is it strange that one does so despite Derrida's frequent disavowal of "feelings," or at least of their appropriateness in this context? In terms of constitution and the "else" which saves differance from absolute randomness, Derridean thought can achieve two more successes, and I mention these just as codicils of sorts. Just as the work of "constitution" attained at least descriptive success within the argument from *effacement* (for the sequence just concluded drew all its "reasons" from there), so too can it achieve some descriptive merit in the context of *dédoublement* and the argument from *l'arbitraire.* In the latter context, the explicatory scenario displays signifiers which "spread" and "overwhelm" [*débordent*] the signifieds, so the signifieds too are arbitrary, and thus signifiers: this movement of *débordement*[111] evokes "negation" (the Derridean *or*); but the signifiers do not collapse into an indifferent field—each exhibits alterity and "directionality": this movement of *altérité* evokes "constitution" (the Derridean *and*). In terms of the argument from *dédoublement,* that the bivalent function lingers though signified and signifier operate *in modo reverso,*[112] evokes "constitution" (the Derridean *and*); that the lingering function *in modo reverso* is always "under erasure" evokes "negation" (the Derridean *or*). How is all the above not just a devious way of reinstating the old signifier-signified relationship? The obvious Derridean riposte is that the concept of "thing," of a closed binary relation which is a self-identity, has been successfully circumvented, or, to choose a more apposite phrase, has been "given the slip" (a "Derridean slip"!).[113] Perhaps the mind best gains purchase of this deconstruction if it considers the following: the negating and constituting are not "quantitative," i.e., not a question of "one half" of an activity being negation and "one half" of an activity being constitution—so a "whole" of some kind is formed. Rather, there is *absolute* negation (and, by implication, *absolute* constitution), and both, amazingly enough, are accomplished by *purely* negative reference: these notions together preempt the possibility of a spatial or temporal "whole." Absolute negation and constitution exclude any theoretical correlating of these activities with a philosophy of presence (the *pairing* of signifying and signified), or with Taoism (which here would have to be the "mutual implication" of *two halves,* constitution and negation), or with Voidism (which here would be absolute negation without constitution).[114]

Another problem too must be broached, that of the respective roles played by undecidability and constitution in Derridean "theory," and the relationship of both to "directionality." Indeed it must be said that Derridean constitution provides the "wherewithal" for directionality, but surely does not explain Derridean directionality itself. Our everyday "choices" concerning the knock at the door, the interpretation and decision, the walking to and opening of the door, and so on, are movements "constituted" while "negated," but how does Derrida account for such "directional" behavior? Clearly he does not deny "trace-as-directional." He does not yield to the theoretics of pure randomness, despite the readiness of literary theorists and critics in particular to "explicate" him thus. Actually, Derrida's adept use of the word "trace" leaves a track here too: for one who is "tracking" often makes a "false start," and then, even along the "way," must often "back up and restart," must "retrack," and so on. In short, "tracking" is *discontinuous* and functions as a kind of crossed-out figure for the "immotivations," "mutations," and the like, which characterize human behavior. No doubt, Derrida denies causality, teleology, purposefulness, decidability, as logocentric theory[115] "originates" and explicates them: for Derrida, the track, while mysteriously "directional," has no "beginning" and no direction East or West, no *Telos.* Even history is not "coming from somewhere" and "going somewhere" in a logocentric sense. Nonetheless, when Derrida staves open (or better, "un-limits" the "margins" of) the logocentric Book, so it becomes Writing, he is by no means proclaiming pure randomness! The elaborate *jeux* for which he is justifiably famous: the splicings, exergues, prefaces, prefaces to prefaces, the postfaces, marginalia, commentaries on commentaries on commentaries—all of these ingenious figures work to "reenact," and of course to reenact "non-synonymously," what can only be called a kind of Derridean "purpose under erasure."

I think Derrida comes closest to a "description" (and it is no more than that) of purpose under erasure at the end of his essay, "Form and Meaning,"[116] where he first shows that logocentrism (and Husserlian phenomenology in particular) defines presence in terms of "form" and the "sense of being" (*"le sens de l'être,"* but intended here to mean the "feel," the "sensing," of being, as opposed to the intellectualizing [formalizing] of it)—so presence is the formal relation of beings to each other; and where, deconstructing this formula and coming to its contradictory (which is of course put under immediate erasure), he is then able to say:

> Form (presence, evidence) would not be the final recourse, the last instance, to which every possible sign would refer—the *arché* or the *telos:* but rather, in a perhaps unheard-of way, the *morphé, arché,* and *telos* would still turn out to be signs. In a sense—or a non-sense—that metaphysics would have excluded from its field, while nonetheless being secretly and incessantly related to it, the form would

already and in itself be the *trace* (*ichnos*) of a certain non-presence, the vestige of the formless [*in-forme*],[117] announcing and recalling [*annonçant-rappelant*] its other to the whole of metaphysics—as Plotinus perhaps said.[118]

This new "approximation," which you will note is cast gram-matically in the conditional, has consequence for the "history" of metaphysics: "The closure of metaphysics would crack [*fissurerait*] the structure and history of this field, by *organically* inscribing and sys-tematically *articulating* from within the traces of the *before*, the *after*, and the *outside* of metaphysics."[119] And then arrives a most remark-able description of "historical" permutation, a kind of causality or purpose under firm erasure, and the problem is discussed in terms of the formalizing and the sensing of being. Derrida proclaims that our task is "to reflect on the circularity which makes the one pass into the other indefinitely. And, by strictly repeating this *circle* in its own historical possibility, we allow the production of some *elliptical* change of site, within the difference involved in repetition; this dis-placement is no doubt deficient, but with a deficiency that is not yet, or is already no longer, absence, negativity, nonbeing, lack, silence. Neither matter nor form, it is nothing that any philosopheme, that is, any dialectic, however determinate, can capture. It is an ellipsis of both meaning and form; it is neither plenary speech nor perfectly circular. More or less, neither more nor less—it is perhaps an entirely different question."[120] It seems that historical movement, and for that matter, the individual movement from knock to deci-sion to door,[121] are not, for Derrida, the *plenary speech* of decidability; and they are not, for Derrida, the *perfect* (and vicious) *circle* of fatalism, be the fatalism that of pure randomness, or that of deter-minism. Purposefulness, "elliptical change," "this displacement," is "more and less, neither more nor less" than these two: decidability and fatalism. Purposefulness is perhaps an entirely different ques-tion from this logocentric opposition. Purposefulness is in between and crossed-out. This is not to say, of course, that we should give up interpreting knocks at doors and deciding whether to open them. Derrida himself obviously keeps up his everyday thinking, and think-ing about thinking, and keeps publishing the latter. The status of Derrida's own "thinking about thinking" we will take up anon. What Derrida is proposing is that our metaphysical theories called "causal-ity," "teleology," "free will," "determinism," and so on, are technically invalid, and that they are "false" indicators of the phenomenal world (the way things "are").

Given the nature of *sous rature*, however, it is no wonder that Der-rida turns to literary enactment as a way of "approximating" the "approximations" which are just descriptions under erasure! My ap-pendix on deconstructionist literary techniques will explore some strategies of enactment, among others, but for now I offer an example; and I do so because it enables us to observe Derrida "living

out," or better "half/showing" (or better, "off/showing" [*dé-montrant!*])
the tenuous track or trail or trace which wends between (1) decidability and (2) the fatalism of randomness or determinism. Ten pages
into the dazzling *séance* (session, meeting, sitting) which is the "essai"
entitled "LA DOUBLE SEANCE,"[122] the reader is told to pronounce
three times, without writing down, the following (for non-French
language readers, I have inserted English translations to the right of
the vertical bar):

L' ANTRE DE MALLARME	CAVE [cavern, den] OF MALLARME
autrement dit L' "ENTRE" DE MALLARME	THE "BETWEEN" [spatial interval, or temporal interval] of MALLARME
autrement dit L'ENTRE-DEUX MALLARME	THE SPACE INBETWEEN [the insertion (of lace, etc.); the trough (between waves); the embroidered edge; the "toss up" ("jump ball" in basketball)] [named after—] MALLARME

Clearly, the different senses indicated by the graphs can "get lost" in
their vocalizations, since in French the three phrases sound like each
other (hence, we have here "shadows" which mimic the function of
différance as "shadow," when *différance* is vocalized).[123] The whiteness
of the page, in an off/like way, is the interval which constitutes and
negates the "words," the traces. Though the free-flotations and off/
filiations which characterize the three phrases at hand, even excised
as they are from their elaborate "con-texts," are already *de trop* in a
Derridean sort of way, let us content ourselves with one "elliptical
change," the oblique movement of one trace between decidability
and fatalism. "L'ENTRE-DEUX 'MALLARME'" disperses in
undecidability (randomness): the phrase can mean, among other
things, "insertion," "trough," "embroidered edge," "toss up," etc.,
named after Mallarmé. The disparate senses defy a holistic interpretation, a synthesis. One could attempt a synthesis, indeed, but there
would be an *excess* of senses which would be "left over," and these
latter could stave "open" the "closed" synthesis (so even the sense
"insertion," above, off/allegorizes how texts "deconstruct"). However,
if we unravel one "errant" (wandering) thread, let us say
"L'ENTRE-DEUX 'MALLARME'" as "TROUGH," and recognize that it
evokes, or is off/like "L' 'ENTRE' DE MALLARME" as the "BETWEEN of

spatial interval" (the off/like relation is not causal, but seems more like a crossed-out analogy); and if we "track" the tenuous skein to "BETWEEN as temporal interval" (here "trough" becomes an off/ image of the temporal trough which is Derridean "deferring"); and if "BETWEEN as temporal interval" is a "directional" for "L'ANTRE DE MALLARME," or the "CAVERN" of Mallarmé, so " 'ENTRE' " evokes "ANTRE," (Mallarmé's use of negative reference, i.e., reference as cavernous, historically foreruns Derridean negation)—then we have perhaps enacted the "movement" of the *else*, of "that which survives." (Reader, please forgive so truncated an example! The *jeu* of these three phrases can go on and on: Mallarmé's cave evokes difference/ ance in off/relation to Plato's Cave, of course, especially since the "philosophies" of both men are at stake in the "con-texts," and so on, and on, and on . . .).

Difference is the *"sameness* which is not identical."[124] The *-ance* of difference indicates it is "neither simply active nor simply passive. . . . it announces or rather recalls something like the middle voice."[125] The middle. The between in between conventional betweens. The interval of perpetual yet discontinuous drift (*dérive*). The pure interval by virtue of which there is constituting/ negating—trace which is directional without Direction. But all these programmatic descriptions are just palimpsest—writing through which one gets a glimpse at the glimmer, at the "under-writing" which is difference. So the programmatic descriptions are crossed-out. But the greater danger, warns Derrida, is not that we mistake formulae as adequate for difference, but rather, that we hypostatize, that we "name" the "glimmer" we cannot formulate, and thus behaviorally treat the under-writing not as writing but as Logos. Perpetual drift becomes a mystical Ineffable. For to "name" means to frame within the relational presence of a signifier and signified, and thereby assuage man's psychic need for control of the mysterious. The temptation is for man to worship what he does not know. In the case at hand, through some Freudian mechanism of condensation or whatever, the temptation is to label and surcharge with awe between which is after all, in Derrida's words, an *errance* (a "wandering").[126] Thus Derrida's many earnest appeals: use the word "difference" only provisionally, and do not capitalize it.[127] Even provisional use is seductive: Christians use the name "God" only "provisionally," yet the word is treated as sacred and what it "provisionally" represents is taken logocentrically. So Derrida's appeals continue. Keep changing the "provisional" names for difference, since a forever altering difference should be "reenacted" by forever altering names, functions, and contexts.[128] Difference is the *jeu* (play) beyond opposition.[129] Difference "has neither existence nor essence. It belongs to no category of being, present or absent."[130] Difference, the word and the concept,[131] is crossed-out.

V

Derrida has proceeded from logocentric theory to its contradictory, and then has necessarily cast this contradictory conclusion *sous rature*. He has rejected absurdism and monism, and we have inferred he has done so because of the "testimony" of "experience."[132] Experience has vouched for *that which survives,* a "constituting" which—along with negating—he "describes" in terms of differance. Differance, though, must also be crossed-out both as a name and a concept. But Derrida leaves no doubt that there is an enigmatic experience which shines from under erasure, and he insists on this despite his necessary discomforture with the name and concept of "experience." Clearly, "experience" as a concept depends on a philosophy of presence and, as a name, runs the same risk that the name differance does, viz., it is a "constant" name which cannot do justice to a forever altering movement.[133] But the altering movement is "going on," as it were, and Derrida is "appreciating" it, though he must even draw a scratch-line through the words and concepts of "going on" and "appreciating" (and through all the words in this sentence, and every sentence, for that matter—but more of this predicament later). What interests us now, rather, is that Derrida resorts nonetheless to the name and concept of experience, though crossed-out, when he wants to talk about "what goes on." Thus, when describing differance, he reports "that it is in the specific zone of this imprint and this trace, in the temporalization of a *lived experience* which is neither *in* the world nor *in* 'another world,' which is not more sonorous than luminous, not more *in* time than *in* space, that differences appear among the elements or rather produce them, make them emerge as such and constitute the *texts,* the chains, and the systems of traces."[134] Likewise, what Derrida calls the "inadequation" of scientific and popular attitudes towards the alphabet "had always already begun to make its presence felt" . . . and "today something lets it *appear* as such, allows it a kind of takeover without our being able to translate this novelty into clear cut notions of mutation, explicitation, accumulation, revolution, or tradition."[135] And likewise what Derrida calls the "eclipse" of logos by writing should "itself *appear* in a different" way.[136]

That Derrida chooses the terms he does, *living experience* and *appearance*, even though they are under erasure,[137] establishes that he is undergoing an "appreciation" of what is "going on." For function under erasure, in some circumstances, is not only a cancellation, let us recall, but a privileging too: that which survives under the crossing-out is a glimmer of the "way things are." By choosing, and choosing so selectively terms which indicate an "appreciation," a "contact," even, with what is "going on," Derrida manifests a phenomenological behavior of sorts (as we've already indicated[138]): a phenomenologist, after all, "describes" what "appears." We have also indicated[139] that Derrida (and here he is unlike Husserl) understands all "appearance," all "experience," to be "in language." As a consequence, Derrida's awe-ful predicament ventures forward—the one he accedes to and anoints unceasingly. If all language is logocentric, and all experience is language, and experience is all that "goes on" for "us," then how does Derrida "appreciate" difference? To say he appreciates it *under erasure,* to say he appreciates the glimmer that shines beneath the crossing-out, is no answer. No answer because he has rejected both feelings[140] and any "third" mode of appreciating, so we are left only with *reason,* with *Ratio!* And reason, as Derrida has indefatigably toiled to prove, is absolutely logocentric. Reason *absolutely* depends on the law of contradiction. Precisely because of dependence, Derrida has been compelled to the repeated crossing-out operations. Reason in no way accounts for the glimmer. Nor is it just the case that reason has not learned to cope yet with difference, that the laws of logic need revision; nor is it even the case that there are *other* ways of "knowing," ways yet to be evolved. On the contrary, Derrida tells us the "thought of the trace" is "a perfectly neutral name, the blank part of the text, the necessarily indeterminate index of a future epoch of difference. *In a certain sense, 'thought' means nothing.* . . . This thought has no weight."[141] And in *Speech and Phenomena,* Derrida asserts that the concept of difference "opens neither upon knowledge nor upon some nonknowledge which is a knowledge to come. In the opening of the question [i.e., of the 'unheard-of question' about the 'concept of differing'] we no longer know."[142] Nonetheless, as we have observed, Derrida is admitting to contact with a "going on." In the same passage from *Of Grammatology* cited earlier, Derrida says too that the thought of trace "must also point beyond the field of the epistémè [i.e., of the epistemological stance, or epistémè, characterizing logocentrism]."[143] A few pages before, in the same book, he speaks of the "meta-rationality or the meta-scientificity announced within the meditation upon writing";[144] and in *Speech and Phenomena,* he poses difference "beyond the order of understanding."[145] What Derrida seems to be suggesting is that difference is totally "other" (though one must scratch a line through this concept, too, since "other" only functions in binary combination with "non-other"). That Derrida associates "knowledge" per se exclusively with the signifier-signified doublet—which, no matter where one "closes" its *com-prehension* in the technical sense, is by nature absolute—becomes very clear when the passage quoted above on knowledge and nonknowledge is examined in full:

> As for what 'begins' then—'beyond' absolute knowledge—*unheard-of* thoughts are required, sought for across the memory of old signs. As long as we ask if the concept of differing should be conceived on the basis of presence or antecedent to it, it remains one of these old signs, enjoining us to continue indefinitely to question presence within the closure of knowledge. It must indeed be so understood,

but also understood differently: it is to be heard in the openness of
an unheard-of question that opens neither upon knowledge nor
upon some nonknowledge which is a knowledge to come. In the
opening of this question *we no longer know*. This does not mean that
we know nothing but that we are beyond absolute knowledge (and its
ethical, aesthetic, or religious system), approaching that on the basis
of which its closure is announced and decided. Such a question will
legitimately be understood as *meaning* nothing, as no longer belonging to the system of meaning.[146]

So absolute [from the Latin: "to be cut away from," hence, "to be
complete"] knowledge—knowledge which comprehends its beginning and end or at least is conceived in terms of an ideal beginning
and end, that is to say, all *reasoning* whatsoever—is at a close.[147] And
"meaning," the enclosure which is signifier and signified, is at a close.
Likewise, "nonknowledge," taken as the dialectical opposite of
knowledge, is hereby excluded. But for "what 'begins' then—
'beyond' absolute knowledge," in short, for that crossed-out "beginning" which is differance, "*unheard-of* thoughts are required." And
Derrida augments this puzzling phrase with another: "*we no longer
know*," but this "does not mean that we know nothing." Derrida can
only mean we are approaching an "appreciation," an *awareness*,
which bears no comparison with rationality (or non-rationality).
Once we have deconstructed reason and the theory of presence
within their own logical domain (which Derrida does by proving *ratio*
self-contradictory), once, in sum, we are left with the pure signifier
under erasure—and the concept of differance "must indeed be so
understood" within the closure of demolished logocentrism—*then*
the concept of differance must be "also understood differently." The
glimmer beneath the pure signifier *sous rature* requires "*unheard-of*
thoughts" which have no bearing on rationality.

A curious quandary for Derrida, nonetheless! Any reader of
Derrida's work is familiar enough with his recurrent and heated protestations against "mysticism"; yet here he is, driven to the wall both
by his own relentless reasoning and by his "lived experience" (which,
in his words already cited, "is neither in the world nor in 'another
world' "), so that he must speak of "meta-rationality" and the
"unheard-of thoughts" which are " 'beyond' absolute knowledge."
Too much the rationalist to grant that a mysticism can announce, can
indeed be intimate[148] with and frequent the movement of
"unheard-of thoughts," Derrida instead narrows the definition of
mysticism so that it means only the Absolute Present and/or the
Absolute Void (i.e., the doctrine of presence/absence in any of its
formulations). Is it that Derrida mistakes some logocentrist
philosophies of mysticism for all "announcements" of mysticism? I
shall argue in a forthcoming chapter that his mistake is precisely this,
and that differance has already been *announced* and frequented in
past but recent "epochs," and is now still announced, and "true" to
his surmise but in a way "different" from his erased expectation—is

to "break over" the world soon, in new and perhaps invigorating dispersal. The point I wish to make now, however, is just that Derrida's taboo-feelings in reference to mysticism have apparently blunted his research into the "history" of mysticism, or at least into his interpretation of (i.e., his "going through and between," his working through) past "mysticisms." His apprehensions in the face of other-than-rational knowing, in other words, coupled with an extravagant rationalism, have limited his options. He is, to sum up, *enfeebled* where there can be vigor and "unheard-of" well-being *sous rature*. A Derridean may object that, take it or leave it, insecurity is what is "going on," is what differance uncovers and Derrida anoints. My answer shall be that *security* (from the Latin, *se-cura*, "without anxiety") is what is "going on" and that people had best be "with it."

The next two matters I wish to address also relate to Derrida's predicament, a predicament I know he does not deny but laves and anoints—a predicament which we would nonetheless opt to avoid if we could, and my message is *we can*. First, recall that earlier we observed Derrida has excluded all forms of knowing and non-knowing, and add to this our more recent observation that he has not excluded a beyond-knowing (why does he think, by the way, all mysticisms involve knowing/non-knowing and exclude beyond-knowing?). Recall we also concluded that differance is for Derrida totally "other" (and he says as much many times). How then can he ever, even by way of an opening "beyond knowledge," approach differance? Indeed, and this may be one of the few contradictions in his own thought he has not recognized, how is he *already* aware—as he apparently is—there is a "going on" at all? That pure signifier *sous rature*, despite all its defects as a formulation, is a better "approximation" than many other erased formulae? Derrida cannot say, not-say, or beyond-say the opening (I shall argue this opening has been already beyond-said). Let us read his lavish description of language functioning in, or more precisely functioning *as* the historico-metaphysical epoch, *our* closing epoch:

> This inflation of the sign "language" is the inflation of the sign itself, absolute inflation, inflation itself. Yet, by one of its aspects or shadows, it is itself still a sign: this crisis is also a symptom. It indicates, as if in spite of itself, that a historico-metaphysical epoch *must* finally determine as language the totality of its problematic horizon. It must do so not only because all that desire had wished to wrest from the play of language finds itself recaptured within that play but also because, for the same reason, language itself is menaced in its very life, helpless, adrift in the threat of limitlessness, brought back to its own finitude at the very moment when its limits seem to disappear, when it ceases to be self-assured, contained, and *guaranteed* by the infinite signified which seemed to exceed it.[149]

Derrida is correct, of course, at least in proportion to the actual mastery logocentrism has had over our epoch (I shall deny, in due course, the universality of this domination). But I wish to underscore the predicament in which Derrida is mired. According to Derrida, language has at last discovered that language is all there is, so language is now in the process of self-cancelling, as it were (let us recall that Derrida accedes to a strict signifier-signified formulaic: whatever "language" there is at all is signifier-signified language, and it is now cancelling itself). Language "menaced in its very life, helpless, adrift in the threat of limitlessness" (a limitlessness which is limitless "finitude" in that it drifts forever, but falls forever short of logocentric infinity[150]) is "language" recognizing itself as Derridean "writing." But the predicament arises because there is, according to Derrida, no "language" available *at all* but logocentric language. Even language-become-writing, which is a grander way of saying word-as-sign become pure signifier *sous rature,* is a *concept* operative entirely as logocentric language. How then is Derrida already aware of difference, at least aware to the extent he can privilege certain phrases as "palimpsests," if there is for him—at least at this time, and as he openly acknowledges—still no awareness outside of "language" (be the "language" logocentric, or that "writing" which remains at this point in history still just an unorthodox *concept,* and thus structurally logocentric[151])?

The modes of discourse Derrida studies and practices pose some complications, and perhaps some "sorting out" would be helpful here. From what we have already determined, it follows that "thinking about theories of thinking" is a discursive mode Derrida practices and Derrida studies, though he would not want to designate this mode generically. "Thinking about theories of thinking" is Derrida's strong suit: it is here that he demonstrates the self-contradiction of logocentrism; the irony, of course, is that he must accomplish this demonstration by operating from "within" logocentrism itself. Because he is necessarily "within," all his resorts to non-synonymous terms for ever-altering difference are more gestural than "successful" in terms of his declared purpose.[152] That is, the charade of names for difference—*réserve, proto-trace, pharmakon,* etc., each functioning in an altered context—"act out" in an off/allegorical way, the *concept* of a forever-altering difference, but in fact certain predications (for example, difference as absolute negating and constituting) remain "common" to all the specimens of differance offered us. And such must be the case precisely because Derrida's "thinking about the crisis of thinking" must itself be logocentric. What about Derrida's turn from the formal and systematic logic used *against* logocentrism to the "descriptive mode" used *on behalf of différance?* We saw that Derrida assembles a collage of techniques to "evoke" difference: isolated postulates and brief sequences of logic are linked to "description," that is, to programmatic accounts (seemingly) of the erased appearance (accounts which provide more "what" than logical "how"—laws of causality are not invoked) and to metaphor.[153] When Derrida's recourse to metaphor,

and to literary tropes he much prefers to metaphor,[154] come together into a scenario, we can safely speak of a "rhetorical mode of
discourse," and we have already instantiated it.[155] In both the descriptive and rhetorical modes, though, the language used to evoke
differance remains logocentric: the structure of the individual
words, the syntax, even the assumptions of referentiality, are
founded directly or indirectly on a theory of presence. Even the ar-
cane off/likeness of "ENTRE" and "ANTRE," as we saw it, depends on
the self-identity of ENTRE as a word (affiliated sound and senses, in
closed combinations), and the self-identity of ANTRE as a word (a-
gain, affiliated sound and senses, in closed combinations), and the
repetition (of identity) of their represented phones. (I might add,
parenthetically, that Derrida has little recourse to the poetic mode
per se, because of his severe rationalism: even his study of Mallarmé,
and other poets, is of their rhetorical games rather than their non-
rational poetic affectivity—affectivity, you will recall, smacks too
much of "another way of knowing." A fortiori, nonsense verse,
perhaps even sequences of sound unassociated with sense [that is,
unassociated with rational concepts], are ostracized, because they
appeal to affectivity and/or emotion *and also* because they cannot reenact the constituting behavior of differance, what we have called
the Derridean *else*, the directionality, the *fil conducteur* under erasure.) Of course, all the foregoing renders the whole notion of *evocation*, whereby Derrida somehow approximates the approximation
of differance, very problematical indeed. Derrida has left himself no
way of talking about evocation, nor even justifying such activity.
Another *gravamen* to weigh into his quandary.

We have observed some implications of the Derridean meta-
language which is (1) systematic and logical, and which treats
logocentric theories of thinking (which treats, by way of systematic
and logical language, logocentric languages about language, is another way of putting it). And we have observed the implications of
two more Derridean meta-languages, which are (2) descriptive and
(3) rhetorical languages respectively. But, when representing
Derrida's purpose—a deconstructive critique of theories about
everyday thinking (languages about everyday language)—we noted
that it is not his intention to deconstruct everyday behavior.[156] It is
not his intention, that is, to claim that everyday thinking (everyday
language) does not work, and that consequently we should no longer
think, no longer speak, no longer calculate decisions. Rather, Derrida wants to show how our theorizing about these activities is self-
contradictory. But there is a quandary involved, and Derrida knows
it. Thus, when discussing the "idea of the sign" (and its inseparability
from the logocentric notion of "inside and outside"), Derrida says
"our entire world and language would collapse" if the sign col-
lapsed.[157] The quandary, simply put, is that logocentrism characterizes, and seemingly motivates, our *everyday* thinking as well as

our thinking about thinking. In what is a carefully choreographed assault on the principle of cause and effect, Derrida says differance "speaks of an operation which is not an operation, which cannot be thought of either as a passion or as an action of a subject upon an object, as starting from a patient. . . ."[158] But is not the very idea of sign that saturates all our behavior, is not our everyday decision-making, inextricably entrammeled in just the conventional notion of causality that Derrida rejects? When I make a mundane decision, do I not judge that *if* as subject I do such and such, *then* such and such will be the effect on the object; that if I rise, walk to the door, turn the knob, and pull in, the door will open? And so on? Do I not normally initiate and construe behavior in terms of questions involving "why," "how," "because," and the like? And if these referential landmarks, these questions, are misfounded, how can I keep on thinking, saying, deciding? Why *should* I? How *could* I? Especially if, with Derrida, I exclude the possibility of other kinds of knowing and reasoning per se? With the collapse of the sign, "our entire world and language would collapse," Derrida asserts. What has he actually provided us, once he has deconstructed *ratio*, to prevent this collapse?

Derrida's sometimes expressed hope is that we are on the edge of a 'beyond knowing', a 'beyond knowing' which will understand " 'historical geneology' in a new way,"[159] *but* which will not necessitate a "move on to something else."[160] One senses Derrida is indeed *on the verge* (from Latin, *vergere:* to bend, to be at the turn) of *someway* else, if not a something else, but surely he has not yet broken out of the turn. Derrida is in the turn of language, but he has logically demonstrated language to be not a turn but a labyrinth. Thus, appropriating and reinterpreting a passage from Husserl, he proclaims:

> Everything has, no doubt, begun in the following way—
>
>> "A name on being mentioned reminds us of the Dresden gallery. . . . We wander through the rooms. . . . A painting by Teniers . . . represents a gallery of paintings. . . . The paintings of this gallery would represent in their turn paintings, which on their part exhibited readable inscriptions and so forth" (*Ideas* I, 100; ET, p. 293, modified).
>
> Certainly nothing has preceded this situation. Assuredly nothing will suspend it. It is not *comprehended,* as Husserl would want it, by intuitions or presentations. Of the broad daylight of presence, outside the gallery, no perception is given us or assuredly promised us. The gallery is the labyrinth which includes in itself its own exits: we have never come upon it as upon a particular *case* of experience—that which Husserl believes he is describing.
>
> It remains then for us to *speak*, to make our voices *resonate*[161] throughout the corridors in order to make up for [*suppléer*] the breakup of presence.[162]

Any persistent reader of Derrida's work awakens sooner or later, I think, to what is Derrida's own repressed vacillation: his vacillation between the fastness of labyrinth and the awesomeness of breaking out of the turn.

Thus, it is along the curious Derridean "version" of breaking out or uncovering that we now wend our way. Despite Derrida's frequent insistence that linear time, and all discussions of "antecedent" and "subsequent," are founded on logocentrism,[163] he must of course—and he concedes (or off/concedes) this—resort to temporal notions. As we shall see in our chapter on the Blessed Trinity, Derrida poses *dispersion* "temporally" *before* the "epoch" of Logos in our history, so that Origin abdicates in favor of a pre-origin which is perpetual drift (and which he provisionally calls the "originary"). About the crossed-out "future," Derrida vacillates a great deal; and though I can imagine him summoning man to accept and celebrate this very vacillation (such a summons would be characteristic), it is a clear indication to me that he has not *attained*. "The age of the sign is essentially theological" and "perhaps it will never *end*," he says to us, although "its historical *closure* is, however, outlined."[164] But he also tells us the "opening" is the "indeterminate index of a future epoch of differance."[165] There is a vacillation here, and also the off/recognition that perhaps resonating through the labyrinth is not enough. Notice the apocalyptic strain in Derrida's description of our "task":

> Within the closure, by an oblique and always perilous movement, constantly risking falling back within what is being deconstructed, it is necessary to surround the critical concepts with a careful and thorough discourse—to mark the conditions, the medium, and the limits of their effectiveness and to designate rigorously their intimate relationship to the machine whose deconstruction they permit; and, in the same process, the crevice [*la faille*] through which the yet unnameable glimmer beyond the closure can be glimpsed [*par laquelle se laisse entrevoir, encore innommable, la lueur de l'outre-clôture*].[166]

If one assembles the apocalyptic passages in Derrida, the scenario is a sort of erased eschatology: mankind is on the flatland and overhead the vaulted dome of the metaphysical heavens is cracking; mankind is on *this side* of the opening, so his "thought" of differance is "blank"—the face that is open to view is the opening on the inside of the closure and is thus "a necessarily indeterminate index."[167]

While I do not wish to indulge in the sensationalisms of what some scholar-scientists deprecatingly call "pop science" (and I do not have the qualifications in mathematics and the natural sciences to do better than "popularize"), I still think some reference to the current situation in astronomy, and so on, begs mention. Derrida speaks of the "juncture—rather than the summation—of what has been most decisively inscribed in the thought of what is conveniently called our 'epoch': the difference of forces in Nietzsche, Saussure's principle of semiological difference, differing as the possibility of [neurone] facilitation, impression and delayed effect in Freud, difference as the irreducibility of the trace of the other in Levinas, and the onto-theological difference in Heidegger."[168] Is it legitimate for us, in passing, to supplement juncture with some other names, drawn from physics, mathematics, and so on? Niels Bohr, Albert Einstein, Werner Heisenberg, Kurt Gödel, as well as some of the more and most recent contemporary scholars in astronomy? Is Derrida's *la faille,* the fissure or crevice at the metaphysical closure, analogous to astronomy's own vaunted "black hole," the black hole which because it opens on *this side* of science's closure, is for the astronomer a "necessarily indeterminate index"? As Heidegger and Derrida, in their own ways, "undid" the "space and time" formulae of classical philosophy, Heisenberg and the others undid Euclidean geometry. Over the last decades, and with ever gathering momentum, mathematicians and physicists have been making leap after radical leap— rethinkings and newthinkings which leave behind in the dust concepts of matter, energy, origin, infinity and the finite, and so on, considered à la mode just a short time before. When Derrida avers that knowing and non-knowing are at closure and then speaks hesitatingly of a possible 'beyond knowing', is he falling short of the triumphant progress, and the impressive results of this progress, that physicists and mathematicians seem able to display? I leave, by necessity, this delicate adjudication to the labors of interdisciplinarians in science and humanities. But I do think I can at least broach some intuitions. I sense that among the scientists one finds the same problematic we shall shortly meet in Taoism and Zen. Simply put, it is this: even though "conventional" laws of our "physical universe" (Euclidean space and time, for example) and classical laws of logic (the principle of non-contradiction, for example) are rejected (and/ or "superseded"), some principle of organization, some holism— even if it be a "holism" comprising alterities—survives.[169]

Derrida's intention at least is to demolish *all* theories of holism, yet through the process of deconstruction to *preserve* directionality. Unlike both the scientist and the Zen master, he does not want to be kerygmatic—he is not delivering good tidings. There is in Derrida neither the Roshi's claim to "another way of knowing" nor the scientist's confidence in the intellect. When Derrida sketches out (in the faintest of strokes, as we saw) the *intervalle* which is absolute "negation," but which can accomplish "constitution" nevertheless, is this imprecision just a blind stumbling about where the scientist can (either now or in the future) provide precision and rational answers? If the scientist can achieve where Derrida stumbles, Derrida is ap-

parently wrong about the inadequacy of all knowing. But remember
that Derrida uses his claim about the inadequacy of knowing to justify the imprecision of his own "descriptions." Derrida's claim is that
any scientific formulation—invented in the past, present, or
future—insofar as it is rational, is linked directly or indirectly to
self-contradictory postulates and thus must come under erasure. Is
Derrida anomalous in that he clings tenaciously to so "classical" a law
as the principle of non-contradiction just so he might destroy the
efficacy of reason itself? Whatever one's assessment of where Derrida really stands in relation to contemporary thought, clearly his
conviction is that he is at the closure of all *ratio*, of *logos*, and that all
scientific closures (insofar as they remain "rational") and all mystical
closures (insofar as they remain "non-rational") are fixed deeper
"within" the dome over the flatland and quite some remove from the
vertiginous crack, *la faille!*

Back now to the Derridean eschatology of *sous rature*, the eschatology of the crack! As happens often in Derrida, his description here
mutates Husserlian and Heideggerian terms: by way of a clue (Husserl's *Leitfaden*, or "hints of paths"; here, the self-contradictory nature of a logical proposition), Derrida tracks the trace, the *pathway*
(the *parcours*,[170] Heidegger's *Weg*), and this pathway leads to the "closure which shall 'crack' the structure and history of the field. . . ."[171]
The pathway, of course, is the Derridean track which is absence and
directionality, the movement of "scissions." Individual men may "discover" the pathway for themselves and possibly others. The whole
"epoch," too, is moving along the pathway. If we remember our
prior discussion of Derridean *errance* and crossed-out purposefulness,[172] Derrida's hesitant prognostication seems to be the following:
mankind, by his individual purposes *sous rature*—be the purposes at
a given "moment" to open a door or to kiss a baby or to write a
"book," but especially if the decision is to intentionally track the
pathway[173]—makes for an *errance* of the whole epoch, so that the
whole epoch moves *directionally towards* the closure (neither individual men nor mankind are "at random"). What affectivities invest Derrida as he speaks of the *errance*, the elliptical change of site "towards
the closure/opening"? There is of course the memorable passage
towards the very end of his essay "Differance," a passage replete with
nuances the reader can identify with the existentialism of a Camus as
well as the exhilaration of a William Gass:

> There will be no unique name, not even the name of Being. It [dif-
> ferance] must be conceived without nostalgia; that is, it must be con-
> ceived outside the myth of the purely maternal or paternal language
> belonging to the lost fatherland of thought. On the contrary, we

must *affirm* it—in the sense that Neitzsche brings affirmation into play—with a certain laughter and with a certain dance.

After this laughter and dance, after this affirmation that is foreign to any dialectic, the question arises as to the other side of nostalgia which I will call Heideggerian *hope*. I am not unaware that this term may be somewhat shocking.[174]

"I venture it [the term, hope] all the same," continues Derrida, and he produces a short excerpt from Heidegger's "Der Spruch des Anaximander" wherein Heidegger perseveres in the search for the "unique word" of Being. But when read in the light of the whole last section of the essay "Differance," a section where Derrida deconstructs the Heideggerian pathway to a "unique word," it is very apparent Derrida is just ending the essay with a formal recapitulation: Heidegger's version of pathway is self-contradictory, but by working one's way *between*, that is, inside its inside and outside its outside, one can glimpse *la lueur,* the glimmer. The "close" of Derrida's essay, in other words, represents no new "advance" (or retrogression!) in his thinking. The "hope," while poignant, remains utterly enigmatic and is more than counterbalanced by expressions elsewhere of malaise, if not foreboding. To be at the closure is to be where "Death strolls,"[175] to be where all is "perilous"[176] and a "monstrosity."[177] No doubt these expressions are laced with a sort of off/irony, even off/parody: the "peril" is to the security of logos, the "death" is to "presence," the "monstrosity" is the demise of "normality," and so on. Derrida is perhaps more French than generally recognized in his labors to be passion-less, to be *impassible.* But the irony has an edge to it, and the edge can still make a reader wince. The collapse of the universe is no "small matter," and even Derrida is shifting apprehensively in his shoes.

The Derridean strain of "death to presence," as one would expect, can trigger political and social reverberations, a cry of "death to the old order." Indeed, reverberations of this kind are occurring and are already shaking establishments and institutions, including the "literary establishment," and more specifically, literary theory and literary criticism. Actually, Derrida's work of deconstruction depends on a thorough mastery of logocentrism, of the Western tradition—philosophical, historical, and literary. One must know it through and through, and work all the way through it, in order to be inside its inside and outside its outside. Derrida is the first to repudiate abuses of his thought: the derision of the past which some graduate students indulge, all in the name of Derridean theory; and, what is worse, their refusal to even *learn* the tradition, because it is already proven, in Derrida's argumentation, to be *dépassé!* Still, there are sequences in Derrida which do fuel the fire. *Of Grammatology* tells us that because the written sign (logocentrism) "assures the sacred power of keeping existence operative within the trace, and of knowing the general structure of the universe," it is the case that "all clergies, exercising political power or not, were constituted at the same time, as writing; . . . that strategy, ballistics, diplomacy, agriculture, fiscality, and penal law are linked" to the "constitution of writing"; that "the possibility of capitalization and of politico-administrative organization had always passed through the hands of scribes who laid down the terms of many wars,"[178] and so on. In short, logocentrism here and elsewhere in Derrida is identified with power.[179] Derrida's claim, of course, is that history could not have unfolded in any other wise, and his implication is that "at the closure" new social arrangements may deploy. When Derrida affiliates logocentrism with the European ethnocentric drive, and even with Europe's cultural expansionism in the Third World, as he does in "White Mythology," for example, his work can become an arsenal for revolutionary fervor.[180] My purpose is not at all to study the political and social effects of Derrida's writing, nor even its effects on the institution of belles lettres as such in the American (or European) university. I do make the observation, however, that many literary critics—and here they are in proper conformity with Derrida, I believe—do judge that traditional literary theory and criticism are no longer viable.[181] And if Derrida is right, their judgment is correct: literary theory and criticism at the closure must work their way through the Tradition by way of deconstruction, and not just by way of the "logocentric" approaches.

In what is one of his darker apocalypses, Derrida offers the following declaration:

> The future can only be anticipated in the form of an absolute danger. It is that which breaks absolutely with constituted normality and can only be proclaimed, *presented*, as a sort of monstrosity. For that future world and for that within it which will have put into question the values of sign, word, and writing, for that which guides our future anterior, there is as yet no exergue.[182]

Exergue in French means an inscription at the beginning of a book, or on the face of a coin near where the coin's date is engraved. *Exergue* also functions in the phrase *mettre en exergue*, "to put in evidence," "to bring to the fore," "to display."[183] In the above citation, and in "White Mythology," one of the *exergue*'s most important roles is to be the "scene of interchange" ("*la scène de l'échange*"), the "place of crossing-over" ("*le lieu de croisement*").[184] Derrida does not know that there is already an *exergue*. Perhaps one way of describing the poststructuralist quandary is to say Derridean deconstruction can "cross-out" (i.e., it can place even the best of conclusions *sous rature*), but it cannot "cross-over," or better, "cross back-and-forth" BETWEEN the comportments of presence and alterity. I shall soon argue that Derrida's longed-for *exergue* is the ancient *tathatā* of Nagarjunist Buddhism, and the "keines schrittes breit" of Christian differential mysticism. However, for several reasons it is important that we first step back very squarely into logocentric interpretation. And justice, at least, demands we encounter logocentrism at its most sophisticated—not the "all or nothing" of more simplistic systems, but the majestic pluralism that can be elaborated from the early and late phases of Heideggerian thought.

a/Mid the Tao:
Heideggerian Centrism

i

Derrida wends/rends the off-way, the anguished off-rationalism of the natural man. It shall be my claim that there is a mystical off-rationalism, an off-rationalism which comports a security and liberation, and even enables—at will—a transaction between the differential and the logocentric. Our investigation of mysticism shall be graduated and methodic. Since one of our main concerns is theory of interpretation, especially literary interpretation, we begin this part 2 with a practicum involving what is, in Derridean terms, logocentric rationalism. That is to say, we shall begin with specimens of two monologic interpretations—two interpretations which are disparate (and even contradictory) and which claim, each of them, to be solely in the right. Then we shall have recourse to a theory of *pluralistic* interpretation—one, in other words, which justifies the simultaneous validity of several monologic readings. While pluralist theories can be purely rational, I shall be advancing a Heideggerian theory of pluralism: Heideggerian pluralism, as a redaction of Heidegger's early and late phases, is mystical *in radice* and thus can accommodate even contradictory interpretations (as long as the latter are not "fanciful," a provision we shall discuss shortly). Heidegger's notion of *Verstand,* as we shall see, and of *Sein,* constitute a logocentric (or 'centric') mysticism. In Derridean terms, there are, you will recall, three kinds of mysticism: mysticism of (1) *plenum,* (2) void, and (3) the unity of opposites (what we are calling Taoism). Manifestly, Heidegger's *Sein* belongs to this third kind, and Derrida himself so classifies it[1] (the "post-structuralist Heideggerianism" now quite popular is really the result of a deconstruction of Heidegger[2]). Derrida argues, of course, that the three mysticisms are just as logocentric (i.e., focused, framed, centered) in their non-rational, or 'affective' way, as rationalism is in its logical way. Before my contravention that there is a differential mysticism which is off-rational and *sui generis,* we now take up Heideggerian thought—Derrida's "prajñapti"[3] and, ironically, our own as well.

We commence, then, by way of praxis. Examples from the

ambiguous writing of Cervantes, Nietzsche, or Kafka are usually adduced here (the immediate controversy has a long history), but our practicum, though serving the same purpose, will be a different and therefore possibly a more refreshing one. Our "case in point" will be Flannery O'Connor's story "The River."[4] O'Connor's compacted plot recounts less than two days in the life of a child named Harry, who is "four or five" years of age. His mother and father party in their apartment and send him off to baby-sitters. As the story opens, a Christian woman named Mrs. Connin is about to assume charge of Harry for the day. On the way to her home, she announces she will take Harry and her own family to a healing service, where the Reverend Bevel Summers will preside. When she asks Harry his own name, the boy lies, declaring his name is Bevel. Mrs. Connin is astonished that the boy's name is the same as the preacher's. At her home, she introduces Harry to Christianity. Immediately afterwards, her own children maltreat the boy. Then the whole entourage attends the healing service, conducted at water's edge. The preacher seems to identify the earthly river and the "river of Jesus' Blood." Throughout, a heckler named Mr. Paradise jeers at the proceedings. At Mrs. Connin's behest, the preacher then baptizes Harry, immersing him in the river water. When the boy returns home, he finds another party in progress. The next morning he goes to the river, intending "not to fool with preachers any more but to Baptize himself" (50). Mr. Paradise, who lives near the river's edge, sees the boy headed for the water. Hoping to offer Harry a peppermint stick, he follows. The boy wades far into the water and is soon sucked under. As the story closes, Mr. Paradise emerges from the water, his attempt at rescue thwarted. Little Harry has drowned.

O'Connor's "The River" permits variant interpretations, two of which are clearly contradictory. "The River" can be read as a vindication of secularism, and it can be read as a testament to Christian redemption. I propose to use this situation as a model for a whole congeries of hermeneutical problems. For Heidegger, do the norms of validity permit variant interpretations? Or must one and only one exegesis be adjudicated as "correct"? If one argues for multiple validity, does such a position lapse into relativism, or is there a middle-ground between absolutism and relativity? What if the interpretations are not only variant but contradictory, a problematic that applies to "The River"? And finally, what if variant interpretations unfold diachronically, so a given literary epoch interprets a work in one way and a later epoch in a different way? Does the literary work itself change?[5] The practicum offers substance from which the above questions can be evolved. After this we can try to bring forth solutions, and these are founded on section 32 (entitled "Understanding and Interpretation") of Heidegger's *Being and Time*.[6] The solutions proposed appear in the last chapter of my earlier book, *Phenomenology and Literature*,[7] but in the present format enjoy the advantages of emendation. The critical feedback which follows upon publication of a book has apprised me of the arguments which have needed elaboration or clarification.

A Secular Interpretation

In a society that is absurd and malicious, the only hope is to trust in the radically human—to trust in human instincts and the virtues they evoke. Grandiose belief in 'another world' which puts all things aright is a dangerous illusion. Religion distorts the personality and comports death. Thus the story accompanies Mrs. Connin with the imagery of death: she is a "skeleton" (34) and has a "skeleton's appearance." Christianity has lubricated Mrs. Connin's pride, so she engages in the most egregious habit of the religionist: she sits in righteous judgment over the worth of others. She criticizes her husband's lack of faith and disdains the alcoholic mother of Harry. Well indoctrinated in Christianity, Mrs. Connin's children give Harry a cold welcome: "They looked at him silently, not smiling" (34). In order to embarrass the boy, they seduce him into releasing the bottom board of the pig sty, so the pig escapes. Consistently, Mrs. Connin and her family exhibit uncharitableness, a sad comment on the religion they represent. As the Connins set out for the healing service, the death motif resurfaces: the whole contingent looks "like the skeleton of an old boat" (37). At the service, the believers are grotesques, bearing in their bodies the sign of inner deformity. An old woman "with flapping arms whose head wobbled as if it might fall off any second" (41): she is the archetypal Christian. Indeed, the name of the preacher itself is symbolic. "Bevel" as a noun means "slant," and the clergyman is "slanted," biased, warped because of religiosity. And Harry, in assimilating the name, assimilates the self-destructive impulse. As for Harry's own baptism, it is repugnant to his instinctive nature—his body resists immersion, and he rises from the water with eyes "closed and half-closed" (44). The surprising end to "The River" is a specimen of black humor without compare. The river which is supposed to be the "River of Life" draws Harry to gruesome death. Significantly, the one heroic gesture of the story is executed by Mr. Paradise, the secularist who scoffs at the healing service. His name is of course ironical: the only true paradise is a kind of grim existentialism. In sharp contrast to the rarefied imagery associated with religion, Mr. Paradise appears as primordial earth: he is a "humped stone" (42) and an "old boulder" (50). The old man struggles in desperation to save the boy, but all for nought. Cadaverous Christianity has triumphed.

A Christian Interpretation

Harry had lived in a household where "everything was a joke" (43). After baptism "you'll count" (43), the preacher promises the boy. With its message of redemptive love, Christianity brings meaning to an otherwise absurd world. Harry is destined to be an "old sheep" (32) of the Lord, so Mrs. Connin introduces him to Christ. She reads from *The Life of Jesus Christ for Readers Under Twelve* and displays the illustrations. One shows Christ "the carpenter driving a crowd of pigs out of a man" (38). Mrs. Connin is herself a disagreeable person, but the process of exorcism lasts a lifetime. The Kingdom of Christ does incessant battle with the pettiness of earth— Christ does not achieve absolute victory until the Parousia. Even in the Elect of the world, good and evil stand side by side.

As for Harry, he is from the start driven by grace to seek the kingdom. When Harry reports his name is Bevel, the name of the preacher, he expresses an innate desire to identify with the Christian message. It is significant that the narrative of the story itself affirms this subterfuge, and thereafter designates the boy by his new name. There is symbolic import in Harry's words, "Will he [the preacher] heal me? . . . I'm hungry" (33, 34). After Mrs. Connin shows the boy *The Life of Jesus,* he steals the book, but even this should be seen as an attempt to assimilate the Kingdom. The image of the sun likewise functions as a symbol of Harry's spiritual desire. On the way to the service, the child wants to "snatch the sun" (39). Indeed, throughout the story the sun appears and disappears: when Christ's love is triumphant, the sun shines; when human resistance thwarts the movement of grace, the sun is hidden in mist. Before reaching the river, Harry passes through dark woods and the sun vanishes. The woods are a "strange country" (39) where the boy has difficulty keeping afoot. The episode symbolizes the dark night of temptation, a combination of Dante's dark Wood and Bunyan's Slough of Despond. Harry even meets the Devil, "two frozen green-gold eyes enclosed in the darkness of a tree hole." When the boy emerges from the forest, the "sun . . . set like a diamond" is awaiting him.

Then the preacher begins his sermon, proclaiming the "River of Life, made out of Jesus' Blood" (40). Here the color red, the color of the precious Blood, assumes importance as a motif. "Red light reflected from the river" (79) bathes the preacher's face, and later his face "burned redder" (41). He baptizes Harry, announcing "You won't be the same again. . . . You'll count" (43). The preacher's name is "Bevel," which bears the lexic significations "incline" or "ascent." The preacher builds the "incline" whereby Harry mounts to salvation; paradoxically, as Saint Paul says, by immersion in the saving waters he rises to new life. The next morning, Harry goes back to the river. The salvific sun, "pale yellow and hot and high" (49), follows him. At this point the symbolism of the story permits only one reading—the waters are not an earthly river, but the flow of Christ's grace. In the beginning Harry's body refuses to submerge, indicating the resistance human life offers to salvation. At the end, the "River of Life" prevails, catching the boy "like a long gentle hand, and pulling him swiftly forward and down" (50).

Salvation foils the mysterious Mr. Paradise, who can only be an inverse paradise—Satan himself. Clues to the old man's identity had begun much earlier when he had derided the preacher at the healing service. Staring for a moment at Mr. Paradise, Harry had instinctively recoiled: "Bevel [Harry] stared at him once and then moved into the folds of Mrs. Connin's coat and hid himself" (42). The preacher had glanced at Paradise and then cried to the crowd, "Believe Jesus or the Devil. . . . Testify to one or the other!" (42). At the end of the story, when the old man tries to balk Providence, he is called "a giant pig." Earlier, the illustration in *The Life of Christ* had pictured Christ "driving a crowd of pigs [devils] out of a man." The equation is self-evident: Mr. Paradise is really the Satanic force, prowling to destroy souls. In sum, the tale "The River" is a kind of *Märchen,* replete with symbols of God and the Devil, goodness and evil. And in it, Christianity wrests an innocent soul from destruction and absorbs that soul into the life of grace.

ii

Is "The River" a call for religious extrapolation, that is, the *Aufhebung* of mundane life into the supernatural? Or is the story a summons to retrenchment, so that man should confide in human nature alone? Is the skeletal imagery just *prima facie* portraiture—as a Christian reading would argue—or does this imagery connote more sinister meanings? Are the "foreign green-gold eyes" in the tree hole a symbol of Satan, or are they a simple description of an owl—as a secularist reading could maintain? Within the frame of logocentric rationalism, Christian and secularist interpreters can go on and on, arguing their respective cases. One alternative in such a situation is to insist that only one of the 'cases' can be 'correct', that is

to say, 'true'. And this is so even if the debate is prolonged or seemingly insoluble. There is a correct meaning even if it be forever unknown.[8] Another alternative is to argue that the reader can accept
both of the conflicting interpretations as equally correct, and that he
can accept many others as well. Indeed, this alternative is Heidegger's
special claim[9] and characterizes what I call logocentric mysticism.

We shall now work our way through section 32 of *Being and Time*,[10]
adjusting its more universal applications so they apply to literature as
such. The start of the hermeneutical process, begins Heidegger, is
the projection of *Dasein* (the human person) towards the possibilities
"laid open" by a text. That is, the "aspects"[11] of a given text are open
to the sight of the interpreter, and each of these aspects has the
potential to participate in meaning—as long as the interpreter goes
on to "meet" the aspect in question appropriately. The aspects, then,
present "possibilities" for engagement in meaning. Significantly,
"these possibilities, as disclosed, exert their own counter-thrust
[*Rückschlag*] upon *Dasein*" (188). This counter-thrust collaborates in
the mutual implication of interpreter and literary work, so that both
belong to the same ontological field (that is, they share the same
being).[12] For Heidegger, in the first stage of hermeneutical activity,
the critic is *at-one-with* a text. (We shall treat the words "a text" and "a
work" synonymously, and we shall mean by them a composite of
verbal signs[13] and relations among verbal signs, identified by a society as a literary entity, distinguishable from other literary entities
and all other entities.)

Next Heidegger says that the "development of the understanding
[*Verstehen*]" is "interpretation [*Auslegung*]" proper. Though he will
shortly describe the development more clearly, it suffices now to
point out that by "understanding" he means the unitary ensemble
wherein critic and text are one; and by "interpretation" he means a
phenomenological description[14] of this understanding. Heidegger
attaches an admonition: "Nor is interpretation the acquiring of information about what is understood; it is rather the working-out of
possibilities projected in understanding" (188, 189). By all of this, he
intends to place the origin (of what becomes hermeneutical activity)
at the level of understanding (which is the level of primal Being[15]),
and not at the level of "assertion" (*Aussage*) or even interpretation
(*Auslegung*). To rephrase it, Heidegger maintains that philosophy
should become meditative "Thought about Being," philosophy
should take as its main concern how entities are the same, not how
entities are different from each other. In so far as entities are the
same, they share the same being—they are, indeed, one and the
same! Ultimately, all entities are alike in one respect, all are

"grounded" in a "one and the same." And this "one and the same" bears none of the triviality associated with a term such as "lowest common denominator": rather, the "one and the same" is a *vis primitiva activa*,[16] an "active primordial power," a dynamic. This dynamic is the origin[17] of individualities, of particularities, if you will. The formula here is manifestly logocentric, and logocentric in what Derrida calls a "mystical" sense. And it is in various forms of the Heideggerian *vis primitiva activa* that Derrida finds his fissure — since Heidegger on the one hand argues all knowing is conditioned by vantage-point, yet on the other hand argues that his intuition of Being is *complete*. (If his knowing is not complete, he cannot posit or describe the *vis primitiva activa!*)[18] The *vis primitiva activa* "originates" meaning; or, to employ even more abstruse Heideggerian terminology, *Deutung* is the "impulsion which (working through the engagement of interpreter and aspect) will become meaning [*Sinn*]."[19] Interpretation (*Auslegung*), what we called "phenomenological description," is literally a "laying-out" of *Deutung* so the latter is apparent. Assertion (*Aussage*), in and of itself, is propositional thinking: it deals with "information" and, therefore, with individual Things-in-being (*Seienden*) instead of Being (*Sein*).

For Heidegger, hermeneutics is ontology (description of Being, the matrix of all beings) and not just ontic study (description of individual entities which particularize themselves within the matrix). Assertion, as we shall see, divides the more holistic configuration which is interpretation into mutually distinct and isolable "subject" and "object," and then utters "truth-statements" which are measured by how well they "match" subject and object.[20] Heidegger laments the epistemological tradition which insists that philosophizing, from beginning through end, must operate on the level of assertion. Assertion is often necessary, says Heidegger, but should be at the service of interpretation and understanding. Otherwise, thinking effectively cuts itself off from the source of meaning. (This is indeed a logocentric mysticism!)

Heidegger next attempts to ascertain what is common to all interpretation. Interpretation is the second level of hermeneutical activity, and is descriptive (thus, phenomenological) rather than propositional (assertional):

> In interpreting, we do not, so to speak, throw a 'signification' over some naked thing which is present-at-hand, we do not stick a value on it; but when something within-the-world is encountered as such, the thing in question already has an involvement which is disclosed in our understanding of the world, and this involvement is one which gets laid out by the interpretation. (190, 191)

In his section 32, Heidegger's greatest contribution is a phenomenology of a phenomenology (i.e., a concrete description of the second level, which is itself a description of understanding). He finds
that interpretative activity manifests three functions: the "As-
question" (what we may call the "interpretative question"), the "As-
which" (or "textual aspect"), and the "As-structure" (or
"interpretation" proper, which—as we shall see—is equivalent to
"meaning").[21] Regarding the "interpretative question," Heidegger
simply means that an interpreter is never neutral, but always
approaches a text with an implicit or explicit question, so that the
answer given is shaped by the question asked:

> As the appropriation of understanding, the interpretation operates
> in Being towards a totality of involvements which is already
> understood—a being which understands. When something is
> understood but is still veiled, it becomes unveiled by an act of appro-
> priation, and this is always done under the guidance of a point of
> view, which fixes that with regard to which what is understood is to
> be interpreted. (191)

The next function of interpretative operation is the "textual aspect"
which the text proffers in answer to the question:

> That which is disclosed in understanding—that which is under-
> stood—is always accessible in such a way that its 'as which' can be
> made to stand out explicitly. (189)

Any given interpretative question should select and illuminate its
affiliated textual aspect (if one exists),[22] an aspect which is "there" in
the text and which is appropriate to the question.[23] In a narrative
such as O'Connor's "The River," the plot and its mythemes, the images, prose rhythm, phonemes (and even their interstitial silences),
and so on, all constitute aspects. The third function of hermeneutical
knowing is the "As-structure," the taking of "something-as-
something" (189). The As-structure is the Articulation (*Artikulation:*
literally, "exercising of the joints"), or description, of the "joining
together" of interpretative question and textual aspect. The As-
structure is the interpretation (or Articulation) proper:

> That which is understood gets Articulated when the entity to be
> understood is brought close interpretatively by taking as our clue the
> "something as something"; and this Articulation lies before [*liegt vor*]
> our making any thematic assertion about it. (190)

The Christian reader may ask religious questions of "The River,"
and if the story displays affiliated aspects, an As-structure or
interpretation solidifes—the text AS a Christian document. If there
are aspects relevant to each set of questions, they are real aspects,
parts of the real text. But what about the case of equivocal verbal

signs, for example, signs which contain two or more denotative or connotative significations? A case in point is the noun "Bevel" in "The River." The noun "bevel" is lexically defined as a "slant" or "incline." While the denotative significations of these two may be more or less the same, their connotative significations are very different. The secularist interpreter can choose the signification "slant" (negative qualities), and the Christian interpreter the signification "incline" (positive qualities). My point here is that within the logocentric frame of reference the verbal sign "bevel" has two real aspects (and many more, of course, with which we are not now concerned), and both of these are part of the text: one aspect is the "typical phonic form" of "bevel" plus the signification "slant" (with its negative qualities), and another aspect is the "typical phonic form" of "bevel" plus the signification "incline" (with its positive qualities).

To recapitulate, then, understanding is a prereflective at-oneness of critic and text; interpretation is the phenomenological description of understanding and consists of an As-structure which is the articulated "hold" an interpretative question has on a textual aspect, and *vice versa;*[24] and finally, assertion is the logical language which abstracts from interpretation and classifies interpretation into concepts (it therefore breaks interpretation all the way down into subject and object).

We can proceed now to Heidegger's next observation, that of "fore-structure" (*Vor-Struktur*). When using the word "fore," he means (1) that a kind of structure[25] antedates encounter with text, and in part determines how the text will be understood; and (2) that the structure meshes with a text before the interpreter even knows this is the case.[26] Fore-structure is characterized by three kinds of fore-awareness, namely, (1) fore-having (*Vorhabe*), (2) fore-sight (*Vorsicht*), and (3) fore-conception (*Vorgriff*). Fore-having equates with the first grasp a critic has on a problem at the level of understanding (and it occurs before he consciously knows it has). Recalling that interpretation is grounded in understanding, Heidegger tells us "interpretation is grounded in something we have in advance—in a fore-having" (191). Fore-seeing adequates to the first interpretative grasp that the second level has on the first, so that "This fore-sight 'takes the first cut' out of what has been taken into fore-having, and it does so with a view to a definite way in which this [this understanding] can be interpreted" (191). Fore-sight occurs before the interpreter knows he has seen anything, and is shaped by the way of seeing his environment has encouraged. As you will notice, Heidegger's earlier treatment of the interpretative question anticipated much of what he says about fore-sight. Finally, there occurs in some instances a fore-conception, which is a set of pre-reflexive ideas that eventually become reflexive and assume logical form. Fore-conception works upon the material of interpretation and transmutes it into concepts. Heidegger says "Anything understood which is held in our fore-having and towards which we set our sights 'fore-sightedly' becomes conceptualizable through the interpretation" (191). To rephrase it, fore-conception begins the process whereby the level of assertion conceptualizes the descriptive level.

Heidegger next takes up the question of "meaning" (*Sinn*) and the related percept of the hermeneutical circle. Keeping in mind that Articulation for Heidegger refers to the activity of the second stratum of awareness, we can conclude from the following that meaning is precisely that dimension of understood Being which can be "described":

> Meaning is that wherein the intelligibility [*Verständlichkeit*] of something maintains itself. That which can be Articulated in a disclosure by which we understand, we call 'meaning.' The concept of meaning embraces the formal existential framework of what necessarily belongs to that which an understanding interpretation Articulates. (193)

Meaning, in other words, is an As-structure—and this aperçu functions as the pivot for the whole of section 32. Whereas meaning for the early Husserl is appropriated from a pool of ideal significations and incorporated into the *intending act*;[27] whereas meaning for Mikel Dufrenne (whose theory of meaning is the opposite of Husserl's) is situated squarely in the *intended object*;[28] for Heidegger, meaning is the *holistic formation* constituted together by interpretative question and proper textual aspect.

As for Heidegger's famous "hermeneutical circle,"[29] in this context it refers to the circular movement from understanding to interpretation and back again: "Any interpretation which is to contribute understanding must already have understood what is to be interpreted" (194). Heidegger grants that the hermeneutical circle is indeed circular, and that "according to the most elementary rules of logic, this circle is a *circulus viciosus*." Why so? Because in both traditional logic and "scientific proof, we may not presuppose what it is our task to provide grounds for." In his iconoclastic way, Heidegger continues, ". . . if we see this circle as a vicious one, and look for ways of avoiding it, even if we just 'sense' it as an inevitable imperfection, then the art of understanding has been misunderstood from the ground up." The understanding, or first stratum of awareness, operates on the pre-objective level; and interpretation as such Articulates the understanding: this relationship is what Heidegger means when in the quotation cited earlier above he says that "any interpretation which is to contribute understanding must have already understood what is to be interpreted." Interpretation pre-supposes understanding, but through the very process of Articulating, interpretation provides grounds for understanding. That is, interpretation is vitalized by understanding alone, but in turn "circles back," so it reveals the "how" and "what" of understanding, and indeed, constitutes the exclusive agency whereby understanding manifests itself.

Heidegger concludes section 32 with a very important discussion of "authentic" (*eigentliche*)[30] interpretation, and he of course takes great care to distinguish the latter from mere "fancy" (*Einfall*). Heidegger's treatment of "authenticity" comprises the same range of issues subsumed under the notion of "validity" in English, though he eschews the literal German word for "validity" (namely, *Geltung*), because the term *Geltung* conjures up for him the antiquated methodology of positivism (I, however, shall use the English words "validity" and "authenticity" interchangeably). To understand the Heideggerian norms of validity, one must begin again with the notion of fore-structure. Recall that according to the first sense of this term, fore-structure is the psychological apparatus the individual brings to the text: for example, he may think in terms of English language syntax, he may be a Freudian, he may be an Archetypalist. Heidegger argues that without fore-structure, interpretation of any kind is impossible. That is, unless a person has the wherewithal to understand a phenomenon, it can make no sense to him whatsoever.

To use an analogy, unless a person has a vantage-point, he cannot look at something else (because he is simply un-situated, or "not there"). The vantage-point is at once enabling and blinding. It enables him to see some profiles of the something else, but not other profiles. The vantage-point helps to "structure" the character of his "view"; and, chances are, people standing next to him and looking in the same direction will have much the same experience of the something else. But those on the other side of the something else may "see" profiles that are very different, or even contrary. Ethics, linguistics, philosophy, and other elements of fore-structure are psychological vantage-points, as it were.

So fore-structure is essential to interpretation. But if fore-structures which illuminate a text differ from one another, how can interpretations ever be "invalid"? *Da capo*, let it be said that Heidegger most emphatically does not deny the possibility of invalid interpretations. Again, the crucial stratum is the interpretative stratum, which falls midway between the pre-objective awareness of the first stratum, and the objective awareness of the third. The second stratum, in other words, does not dichotomize experience into subject and object as the assertive level does, but neither is it as unitary a phenomenon as the level of understanding. After all, as soon as one talks of an As-question issuing from the interpreter and of an As-which offered by the text, one is talking in terms of a dichotomy. But the second level, in its *essential* construct, does *remain*

true to the experiential unity found in understanding: the interpretation strictly defined, that is, the As-structure, is precisely the
mutual engagement of critic and text (and by engagement, we do
not just mean the interface of critic and text, but the holistic formation which includes the relevant elements of critical fore-structure
and the text). The interpretation is constituted simultaneously by an
interpretative question and a textual aspect, and thereby bridges the
dichotomy of subject and object. The As-structure, in short, is a
unitary phenomenon.

Regarding authenticity, Heidegger says the following:

> To be sure, we genuinely take hold of this possibility [primordial
> knowing] only when, in our interpretation, we have understood that
> our first, last, and constant task is never to allow our fore-having,
> fore-sight, and fore-conception to be presented to us by fancies and
> popular conceptions, but rather to make the scientific theme secure
> by working out these fore-structures in terms of the things them-
> selves. (195)

Notice, this structure applies not only to the interpretative level, but
to contact between all three strata of fore-structure on the one hand,
and texts on the other. In fact, earlier Heidegger spoke of the same
requirement in regard to conceptualization (fore-conception), warning the thinker not to "force the entity into concepts to which it is
opposed in its manner of Being." Heidegger is saying that the particular As-questions appropriate to the phenomena at hand (and not
inappropriate As-questions, "fancies and popular conceptions"
which do not suit the phenomena) are essential for validity. Or, to
approach the matter from the other direction, Heidegger is saying
that As-questions must grasp textual aspects that are *really there* in
the phenomena. When such contact occurs, a *valid* interpretation,
and therefore a *correct* interpretation, materializes. Otherwise, there
remains a merely fanciful, or pseudo-interpretation. Since Being
exhibits itself precisely in and through meaning, and meaning (as we
have seen) is interpretation, a valid interpretation is by necessity *true*.
To have several valid interpretations of a text, then, is to have several
true interpretations, each of them determinate and self-identical
(that is to say, each exegesis discloses a different aspect of a literary
work which by nature has many aspects, and each combination of
question and relevant aspect is a "truth"). The issue that next sur-
faces, of course, concerns criteriology. How does one determine
what are apposite As-questions? How does one demonstrate that the
textual aspects alleged are "really there"? Clearly, a literary critic
must convince his peers of the appropriateness of his interrogation;
clearly he must "show" the presence of the textual aspects he claims;
and clearly, he must demonstrate how his interpretative questions
engage the aspects. I shall address the conditions which characterize
the "making of a case" for an interpretation. And I shall, within the
Heideggerian purview, defend Heidegger, as long as one grants his

broader premises, from accusations of relativism. Heidegger is customarily attacked for the wrong reasons, in other words, and Derrida's deconstruction of Heideggerian 'Tao' comes elsewhere.[31] First,
though, some remarks on "authorial intent" are in order. And I wish
also at some length to consider the matter of contradictory interpretations, and how they are accommodated by the Taoism of logocentric mysticism.

You will notice that throughout section 32 Heidegger ignores the
relevance of authorial intentionality, that is, the significations[32] the
author related to a text when he created it.[33] Hans-Georg Gadamer,
Heidegger's disciple, goes on to strictly exclude the relevance of
these significations. In *Truth and Method*, Gadamer says "The *mens
auctoris* is not admissible as a yardstick for the meaning of a work of
art."[34] And in another book, he repudiates the tradition of "objective
hermeneutics" and its quest for the author's significations: ". . . all
that Schleiermacher and Romanticism report to us on the subjective
factors of comprehension seems to us unconvincing. When we
understand a text we do not put ourselves in the place of another,
and it is not a question of penetrating the spiritual activity of the
author. . . ."[35] Since in his practical exegesis of literary writers and
others,[36] Heidegger often does involve the author's "willed
significations" for a word or passage, it seems safe to conclude that
Heidegger's position is more inclusive than Gadamer's: a critic may
ask an "authorial" As-question, but he *need not.* Much depends on
the critic's purpose. A critic may try to approximate (through biographical or other means) the author's fore-structure, and a textual
aspect which accommodates it, so the meaning that arises is similar to
the author's meaning. Or a critic may investigate the medieval
significations available to a medieval poet, say, and encounter the
poem in that light. But again, the attached provision is that such a
maneuver is by no means requisite. *In nuce,* O'Connor's own deep
Christian commitment need not deter an atheist or anyone else from
a secular reading of "The River." Biographical and historical critics
incorporate their researched data into fore-structures and bring
these structures to bear on aspects of a work. Conventional Christian, Jungian, and other critics operative within logocentrism exercise their own distinctive options, dependent on other values and
other kinds of research.

At this juncture I call to the reader's attention that throughout this
stage of our study the way I have "laid out" (*ausgelegt*) the above
issues—the structure of hermeneutical activity, and so on—is itself
Heideggerian and phenomenological. Obviously I have not tried to
argue in the way a "logical atomist" does, or a "logical positivist"
does. Rather, with the aid of Heideggerian As-questions, I have described what one "sees" if he collates the practical criticism of many
reputable critics identified with many critical schools. He invariably
sees fore-structures and textual aspects in collusion or attempted col-

lusion. What we have called the authorial As-question, or an attempt
to read a text in terms of the author's fore-structure, is a variable:
sometimes it plays a role in a given critique and sometimes it does
not. What Derrida will do is reject phenomenology as practiced in
this mode and operate instead as a pure rationalist, on the level of
"assertion," and he will find that on the assertive level Heidegger's
account has "cracks." Derrida abstracts phenomenology, but—
having uncovered the vulnerability of abstraction—is caught at the
crack's "opening,"[37] and cannot *passer outre*.

As I have already indicated, I shall treat anon the functions of
verification used by logocentric critics. Concerning the principle of
verification, in advancing a whole phenomenology of the hermeneutic act, I see operative in this mode a traditional maxim of
phenomenology: "Corroborative description is the only verification."
In other words, phenomenology is ultimately a communal activity: it
checks its conclusions against multiple concrete experiences of what
is common to the subject at hand—in this case, critical practice. With
many phenomenologists over a long period of time, I have tried to
experience and then describe interpretative activity. *Sic feliciter
evenit!* The reader is invited to attempt at this stage the
phenomenological mode and do likewise.

The reader may further ask what is the status of this very essay of
mine? First, I call to your attention that this sequence manifests the
"aspects" of an "assertive" paper (as Heidegger would say). It operates primarily on the level of assertion, so it is not just *Auslegung* (in
this case, description of hermeneutical activity) but *Aussage* ("explaining," or "the making of a case" for the embedded description). And I
usually choose to "make the case" by the phenomenological means: I
provide examples of representative critical activity and explain
them.[38] I ask the reader to consult the examples, and any others he
pleases. Expository assertion, the kind of *Aussage* of which this
undertaking purports to be a kind, is by nature concerned with
authorial intent, in this case, the significations Heidegger attached to
section 32 of *Sein und Zeit*. So I consistently ask the authorial As-
question. But for that matter, part 2 of this book is far from true
philosophizing in the Heideggerian sense, the deep "Meditation on
Being," and hopes to perform just a humbler, ancillary service.

The contrast of secular and Christian readings of "The River"
exemplifies a special kind of multiple interpretation: the readings in
question are not only variant but contradictory. In my first book, I
state that a sequence from Heidegger's essay "What Are Poets For?"
can provide the wherewithal to justify, within the Heideggerian
compass, the simultaneous validity of contradictory interpretations[39]
(indeed, I could have adduced many other similar passages from the
late-phase Heidegger). Heidegger's turn in his later career towards
Oriental thought is well-known (though as early as 1929 he already
resorts to phraseology which is Orientalist, even if it may come by

way of Oriental motifs long miscegenated with nineteenth-century German idealism: witness the passage in his *Vom Wesen des Grundes,* "The self can yield up the 'I' in order to achieve its true self"[40]). Heidegger's "A Dialogue on Language" originated in 1953/54, on the occasion of a visit by Professor Tezuka from Japan, and the "Dialogue" demonstrates the affinities of Heideggerian and Japanese attitudes towards poetic language. Moreover, the very respected Chang Chung-yuan, whose earlier work on Chinese philosophy, poetry, and art moved Heidegger to express his admiration, has written a new translation of the *Tao Tê Ching,* accompanied by commentaries which draw extensive comparisons to Heideggerian thought.[41]

Let us begin with the quotation cited originally in my book from Heidegger's "What Are Poets For?":

> If Being is what is unique to beings, by what can Being still be surpassed? Only by itself, only by its own, and indeed by expressly entering into its own. Then Being would be the unique which wholly surpasses itself (the *transcendens* pure and simple). But this surpassing, this transcending does not go up and over into something else: it comes up to its own self and back into the very nature of its truth. Being itself traverses this going over and is itself its dimension.
>
> When we think on this, we experience within Being itself that there lies in it something "more" belonging to it, and thus the possibility that there too, where Being is thought of as venture, something more daring may prevail than even Being itself, so far as we commonly conceive Being in terms of particular beings. Being, as itself, spans its own province, which is marked off (*temnein, tempus*) by Being's being present in the word. Language is the precinct (*templum*), that is, the house of Being.[42]

A really substantive grasp of the above passage can only be had in the light of Heidegger's treatise *The Question of Being,*[43] which with his other late treatise *Identity and Difference*[44] sum up Heidegger's last appraisal of Being. And the reader is urged to read these two treatises (both quite short). The passage quoted above first attests to the "surplus" which characterizes Being (indeed, Heidegger's phraseology throughout the two paragraphs recalls the medieval notion of *bonum diffusivum sibi*[45]). Yet we know individual beings—on the level treated by *Aussagen*—are often contradictory. Nonetheless "Being is what is unique to beings," argues Heidegger, so each being shares in the transcendent Being (the *transcendens* pure and simple) which is at one and the same time immanent in the individual being.

The "surpassing" which is overarching Being still "enters into its own." Thus as early as *Sein und Zeit*[46] Heidegger repudiates inquiries into Being which are *tiefsinnig* (deep); that is, *tiefsinnig* in the sense that they *deduce* or *speculate* about Being because they fail to recognize Being is at-work and to-be-experienced. But the Being which enters "into its own" also "surpasses," with the enormous conse-

quence that the "more" which is universal Being subsumes all contradiction into itself. What are logical contradictions on the level of
Aussage are organized into a holistic formation (what Heidegger earlier called "the one and the same") at the primal level of understanding. As a result, contradicting elements (as unique entities) can be
simultaneously valid—since they are emanations, if you will, of the
one Being. This paradox, furthermore, finds its privileged locus "in
the word."[47] Being "ventures" language, and language becomes the
"house of Being."

In the face of interpretative questions which produce contradictory readings, Anglo-American critics often praise "ambiguity."
These critics are in fact affirming the mystery of which Heidegger
speaks—when two or more readings argue solid but irreconcilable
cases, these critics rest in awe before the spectacle, confident that at a
deeper level of experience the interpretations bespeak the *one and the
same*. I say "deeper level of experience" advisedly, because as Chang
Chung-yuan testifies—and as even I and some of my colleagues can
testify—this oneness can be *experienced* on the level of logocentric
mysticism. And within this experience, the interpreter circles from
the phenomenal contradictories to phenomenological oneness, and
back again. And the "aesthetic" (that which involves beauty) tensions
as well as ontological tensions which arise from all this interplay are
dazzling indeed! On the phenomenal level, contradicting interpretations both lure and elude each other, like coquettes fixated in hyp-
notic dance. Yet at the phenomenological center, this dance—which
Roman Ingarden so beautifully calls "Opalescent Multiplicity"[48]—
dissolves in the *one and the same*. As Heidegger would put it, there is
a kind of "homecoming." The ontic becomes ontological. The *Seienden* become *Sein*.

As demonstrated at length in my earlier book,[49] Heidegger's
theoretical writing on literary texts gives short shrift to the relevance
of the author's personality. Poetic language summons the "World" of
Dasein, a world where the primordial powers of Sky, Earth,
Divinities, and Mortals intersect; and this World is "mutually impli-
cated" with the realm of *Things-as-things*.[50] In and through the
simultaneous tension and intimacy of World and Thing, language
"presences" Being. But why is poetic language, which Heidegger so
often deprives of its authorial filiations, somehow privileged? And so
gloriously privileged that it is for all practical purposes a secular sac-
rament, "a symbol which makes present what it symbolizes"? The
answer for Heidegger lies in the understanding of *Dichtung* (poetic
language), its genesis and nature. According to Heidegger, *Dichtung*
(and meditative philosophy is a kind of *Dichtung* and vice versa) is
the most human of all activities; *Dichtung* is at once bodily and
spiritual, concrete and intellectual—*Dichtung* brings us home to
Being and Being home to us. Nor does Heidegger normally invoke
the romantic image of the seer, who transmits his inspired vision of

Being. Rather, Heidegger says "the artist remains inconsequential as compared with the work, almost like a passageway that destroys itself in the creative process for the work to emerge."[51] Heideggerian thought sees *Dichtung* as quintessentially human, which is to say, quintessentially communal[52] (remember, Heidegger is not the isolated existentialist, but the ontologist—even at times, I dare say, the cultural anthropologist). Being "be-ings" itself in the human being, since human being "gathers" the World and Things. And the quintessential display of communal human being, and therefore of Being, is *Dichtung*.

Heidegger's attitude towards contradictories approximates the essence of Zen described by the famous Orientalist R. H. Blyth: "We live supposedly in a world of opposites, of white against black, of here versus there. But beneath this level of opposition lies a sea of tranquillity in which all things are complementary rather than contradictory." And Blyth quotes the ancient Buddhist dictum:

> On the sea of death and life,
> The diver's boat is freighted
> With "Is" and "Is not";
> But if the bottom is broken through,
> "Is" and "Is not" disappear.[53]

A kindred example that comes to my mind at once is from Seng Ts'an, third Ch'an patriarch in China (c. 600 A.D.):

> At the least thought of "Is" and "Is not,"
> There is chaos and the mind is lost . . .
> In its essence the Great Way is all-embracing.[54]

Many other passages in both Taoist and Buddhist tradition make it clear that so monist a vision is not intended to undermine the particularities and even the contradictions of the phenomenal world; indeed anyone familiar with Japanese art knows that Zen, for example, celebrates uniqueness, but the uniqueness is "measured out" in its relation to the *oneness*. And this is precisely Heidegger's idea too.[55] It is crucial to keep in mind, however, that the Zen which parallels Heidegger is what I call centric Zen (as opposed to the differential Zen treated in my part 3[56]) and that Nagarjunist Buddhism is not logocentric at all.[57]

But perhaps some further clarification is in order. Though Taoism and centric Buddhism both preach the complementarity of opposites, so that each event, say, has a "happy" quality and a "sad" quality, and these should be harmonized so the human being achieves stasis—it is not this principle as such which concerns us here. For this principle would have as its analogy the phenomenon of multiple (or "variant," or "disparate" literary interpretations), where textual event may, conceivably, profile various "complementary" aspects— an event may be simultaneously erotic in a Freudian way, politically aggressive in a Marxist way, and still esthetically "holistic" in an

American New Critical way. Many of the "complementary" opposi-
tions can be what are technically called contraries, as "happy" quality
and "sad" quality attributed to the same textual event can function as
logical contraries.

But I have been maintaining that Heidegger does much more
than approximate the law of complementary contraries, as found in
most Eastern philosophy and indeed some Western philosophy. I
have been maintaining that he approximates a more radical Taoist
and centric Buddhist principle, called by Lao Tzu "the unification of
affirmation and negation,"[58] and illustrated by Lao Tzu's phrase,
"Great white is as if it is black."[59] That is, not only contraries (e.g.,
one literary event sad in one way and happy in another way) but also
contradictories (one literary event sad and non-sad in the same way)
can be simultaneously valid. Perhaps a rationale of this can be that
for Heideggerian Being, all time is ultimately *one and the same,* all
experience ultimately *one and the same,* so *sub specie aeternitatis* all real
contraries reduce into real contradictories, and all real contradictories into oneness. Yet again, up from the oneness "se jaillissent" the
glorious multiplicities. (Notice that I use the word "real" above
advisedly, because for Heidegger not all contradictories are simultaneously valid—in many cases, one interpretation is simply true and
its contradictory is false—but more of this later.) Of the many relevant Heideggerian passages cited by Chang, I quote here a line from
Heidegger's "The Origin of the Work of Art": "This rift carries the
opponents into the source of their unity by virtue of their common
ground."[60] And Chang adds in his own words, "The source of the
unity of opposites maintained by Heidegger is what Taoists call the
Tao."[61] If one recalls that thinking (as consciousness or *pour-soi* in
European philosophy) is the contradictory of Being (or *être-en-soi*
according to European philosophy), then Chang is correct in recognizing the iconoclasm of Heidegger's reinterpretation: "Different
things, thinking and Being, are here thought of as the same . . .
Thinking and Being belong together in the same and by virtue of
this same."[62] Recall that conventionally, thinking and Being are considered not just contraries, but contradictories—thinking is the contradictory of non-thinking, and non-thinking is Being. In the cited
passage, in other words, Heidegger is affirming the identity of these
contradictories. For much further evidence from Chang, see the
footnoted references.[63] The superb irony, of course, is that here we
see Heidegger deconstructing the first phase, logocentric rationalism; and in part 3 we shall see the Heideggerian sort of logocentrism likewise deconstructed!

iii

Now let us face the issue of validity. If one reviews the panoramic
history of logocentric criticism (if he does a "phenomenology" of the

situation, if you will, seeking out the concrete essential structures), the following becomes readily apparent. Privately, the critic adjudicates for himself the validity of his own interpretation (his norms may resemble or differ markedly from those of his contemporaries). Publicly, if he wants to convince others his interpretation is valid, the critic must accept the norms of his audience, and try to show his interpretation suits these norms; or he must convert his audience to new norms, and demonstrate his interpretation suits the latter. Even if a critic maintains the "author's meaning" is the only valid meaning, the critic must obviously convince his peers that such a norm is justified and, indeed, that his interpretation really coincides with the author's meaning. The role of critical audience leads at once, of course, to the concomitant issue of intersubjectivity. That is, norms which are publicly operable are shared among a community of subjects (eighteenth-century neo-classicists, for example, were a body of subjects who agreed on many hermeneutical norms; so are American New Critics today, or Marxists, or Freudians, and so on).

A further description of literary history reveals that the meanings which various logocentric groups accept as valid can differ because of two different reasons. One reason is that the "work" or "text," which when regarded in a Heideggerian way we have already defined as a literary composite of verbal signs and relations among verbal signs, is in fact a different work to different audiences. Recall that the meanings of a work, for Heidegger, are engagements of interpretative questions and textual aspects. If we suspend for the moment the factor of variable interpretative questions and deal only with textual aspects, we find the following. Textual aspects are appearances of verbal signs and relations among verbal signs, and these appearances are really "in and of the text." Now if the verbal signs of a "work" change, it follows that the work itself changes. And some of the aspects or appearances of the work, since they are "in and of the work," likewise change. If we recall that for Heidegger meanings are engagements of interpretative questions and textual aspects, the conclusion is inescapable: meanings can differ because textual aspects have changed. Sometimes these changes are synchronic: for example, different dialectical groups may attach different significations (lexic values) to a given word sound.

Most changes, however, are diachronic. A famous instance is provided by René Wellek in his *Theory of Literature*.[64] In the seventeenth century, Andrew Marvell's phrase "vegetable love" signified what today could be called "vegetative love." That is, the signification, or lexic value, of "vegetable" was about the same as today's "vegetative." And according to the scholar Louis Teeter (quoted by Wellek), the usual *qualitative value* (something like "connotation") imparted by the expression "vegetable love" at the time was "life-giving principle." But in the twentieth century, "vegetable" signifies "edible plant," and this signification opens the way to a new qualitative value: "vegetable love" connotes "torpidity," or "slow and stifled love" (love as an "erotic cabbage," as Teeter says). In short, the word sound "vegetable" has taken on a new signification, so that we can indeed have a new verbal sign (and to that extent, a new "work" or "text"). In terms of the concept "textual aspect" or "textual appearance" (and there are, for phenomenology, all kinds of textual aspects or textual appearances), the word sound "vegetable" signifying "vegetative" is an "aspect"; the word sound "vegetable" signifying "edible plant" is another aspect. The verbal signs "vegetable love" (the word sounds plus the significations vegetative and love) connoting the qualitative value "life-giving principle" are an "aspect." The verbal signs "vegetable love" (here, the work sounds plus the significations edible plant and love) connoting the qualitative value "torpidity" are an "aspect."

In the story "The River," perhaps at some future time the significations of "skeleton" will change; and with these mutations, the qualitative values contingent upon "skeleton" will change, and these permutations of aspect will to such an extent change the literary work per se. In any case, it is crucial to recognize that changes in verbal sign are effected by the language-group which constitutes a work's audience at any given time. Signification, and qualitative values dependent on signification, are conferred by the language-community; individual interpreters and even whole "schools" of criticism naturally accept the lexic values, multiple as they may be, which a *langue* confers on word sounds so that verbal signs can occur. In this sense, and to this extent, the reader is merely a mechanism whereby *langue* vivifies word sounds: Freudian, Marxist, Christian—one and all will normally accept that the word sound indicated by "triangle" bears the lexic values attributed to it by the *langue* which is English.

We can submit the notion of *langue* to further examination, by putting our conclusions to the test of the "extreme case." Here we can assume the original significations of a text have been lost completely. In other words, the *langue* has been lost. In terms of the twentieth-century interpreters and their culture, the text may then make no sense or perhaps some sense—the latter through chance alone. The marks on the page happen to make sense in a language known by the interpreters, even though their language is different from the language of the author (and the author's culture). Let us turn the screw another spiral. Through a fortuitous happening, the text makes complete sense in the second language. Surely one cannot appeal to the author's sense now! Yet by chance perhaps an exquisite poem has arisen. Whence come the significations? They can only come from the language of the interpreter's culture.

An entirely different matter is change in meaning which arises because interpretative questions differ. In the latter case, the work and its aspects remain constant; that is, a given language culture at a given time makes available one or several significations for a word sound. Since a literary work is the totality of verbal signs (word sounds plus significations) made possible by the circumambient culture, different As-questions can contact different aspects of the one work. Such changes are initiated on the side of the individual interrogator, but the meaning as a whole changes, since meaning is the mutual engagement of As-question and relevant textual aspect. Notice that in such cases the literary work itself has not changed, only meanings have changed. In sum, the meanings which various groups accept as valid can differ because of two reasons: the work itself can change, so it is indeed a different work; or, while the work remains the same, the interpretative questions—assuming they are valid—can differ (the latter is often a synchronic phenomenon). Again, however, we must remind ourselves the foregoing is a "solution" that "works" only within the criteria mutually accepted by logocentrists—rational or mystic. Derrida's attack is on the underpinning of diachrony itself.

In his famous work *Validity in Interpretation*,[65] E. D. Hirsch argues that formulations of the above kind are relativistic. Though Hirsch has modified his position somewhat in a second book, *The Aims of Interpretation*,[66] his first book remains the classic logocentric/rationalist attack on Heideggerian thought. Hirsch assails Heideggerian "relativism," and his arguments in that first book are still upheld by many theorists. So I turn to what can be, I think, a Heideggerian *riposte*. In *Validity in Interpretation*, Hirsch discusses Wellek's example out of Marvell, mentioned earlier. (Before we begin, however, I interject a provisional statement. In that the significations of "vegetable" have changed, historically, a Heideggerian can say that to such an extent the work has changed. So a comparison of "valid meanings" is here in a way inappropriate. It is really a matter of two different literary passages, each participating in several possible meanings.) However, since the work as a whole (the poem "To His Coy Mistress") has not changed (i.e., most of its words retain the same significations they had in the seventeenth century), we can make the practical choice of considering it the one and the same work which existed in the seventeenth century. (Actually, a more suitable ground on which to argue all this would be a modern text that bears contradicting significations, with each signification alive in the *langue* today: but the example out of Marvell has been sanctified by usage—Wellek's, Hirsch's, and mine—so I shall stay with it.) We proceed to hear Hirsch's case. Hirsch advances the following argument. Wellek's very thesis, that the modern interpretation is also valid, assumes the distinction between the author's "sense" (what we have called "signification") and subsequent "senses" (significations, again). In order to avoid a relativism, a chaotic flux of meanings, it is absolutely essential to distinguish between an author's "willed" significations and other possible significations. Thus the necessary distinction, says Hirsch, between "meaning" (which is Hirsch's term for the author's willed signification) and "significance"[67] (Hirsch's term for the relation of authorial meaning to the reader's other meanings, emotions, etc.).

Heidegger would answer that he too sees distinctions among significations (how could he not?). However, he refuses to attribute an exclusivity to the author's willed significations. When one does a concrete phenomenology of any hermeneutical experience, one plainly sees that what Hirsch calls "meaning" and what Hirsch calls "significance" both arise from a live contact of an As-question and textual aspect. *In situ,* there is absolutely no difference in their functional nexus. Thus the same validity obtains for both. Hirsch's As-question can be: Did the author intend such and such a qualitative value for this verbal sign? A critic identified with the New Hermeneutics may ask: Can an archetypalist, say, intend such and such a qualitative value for this verbal sign? And, I might add, much excitement in exegesis arises from the dazzling interplays of As-questions and textual aspects, as various combinations complement and contradict each other, converge upon and tug away from each other.

Remember that Heidegger proposes there are a plural number of aspects in texts, but that each of these aspects is determinate and self-identical (whether the author "willed" them there or not). To invert Hirsch, the work—in the grasp of various As-questions—means *many things* in particular. Hirsch's perception of a text is remarkably flat: a text cannot have more than one facet (our analogy for "aspect"). The author's chosen signification excludes all others. Thus *Validity in Interpretation* announces categorically: "It may be asserted as a general rule that whenever a reader confronts two interpretations which impose different emphases on similar meaning components, at least one of the interpretations must be wrong."[68] But why must this be the case? The often-used analogy with a diamond is appropriate here. Our interpretative glance at the diamond can contact one or more facets (aspects), and each is really part of the diamond. But let us take a verbal example—the word *cleave,* which has two opposing definitions. *Cleave* can mean *to separate* or *to adhere.*[69] Let us say a given text describes a God who descends in blinding theophany and utters to his hushed disciples, "Men and women, cleave!" Let us assume furthermore that the verbal context is of no help. But, and this is of utmost importance, let us take it as given that all authorial evidence points to one interpretation as the author's own—that he willed, let's say, "cleave" to mean "separate." Does this authorial data make the alternative interpretation, that to "cleave" is to "adhere," less determinate and self-identical? Both significations (to "separate" and to "adhere") are held firm by the syntax and lexic of the *langue,* which gives them shareability and particularity. What further determinacy is needed? For a Heideggerian, Hirsch's argument remains ineffectual.

That many interpretative questions can be axiologically sound does not by any means deny the importance of historical criticism and the reactions of some past interlocutors of mine seem to require of me an addendum of this kind. Heidegger, especially in his re-valuation of the past history of metaphysics, has repeatedly asked "the historical question"—to put it another way, he has asked what significations were attached to verbal signs by given historical periods. And he has also asked "authorial questions"—what significations a given author intended for given word sounds. Heidegger has often stressed the importance of "sedimentation," whereby word sounds accumulate significance historically.[70] And much depends, as I have previously suggested, on the kind of lan-guage under study—be it *Aussage,* for example, which involves inter-locution of several kinds between authors and listeners; or *Dichtung,* which in a deeper and richer sense communicates Being without re-gard for the historical author.[71] But my point here is that in the case of *Dichtung,* or literary language, modern interpretative questions and modern significations can be just as valid and, indeed, fruitful as historical or authorial readings. Hirsch's rejoinder is that such a proposition reduces to pure relativism. In answer, I postulate there is a constancy adduced by Heideggerian theory—the constancy im-parted by intersubjectivism. The differentialist may be able to gain-say it, but the logocentrist cannot.

We can begin with an example. In Henry James's novella *The Turn of the Screw,* a governess struggles to protect her two young charges against diabolical ghosts. It so happens that nineteenth-century crit-ics brought a traditional Christian fore-structure to the text and saw the governess *as* an integrated and wholesome personality, fighting the war of a Christian heroine against Satan. Freudian critics of the twentieth century have seen the governess as a neurotic personality, perverting the children through her malign fantasies. If we were to perform a phenomenology of critical dialogue, we would find each critic trying to "make a case" for his own interpretation (of course, this does not preclude learning from others as well). Each critic would try to "convince" the others. But "convincing" can take place only to the extent that the critics share values in common. In the above example, Freudians could convince both those already sym-pathetic to Freudianism and those converted to Freudian insights by the vigor of the Freudian argument in this case. Of course, the "making of the case" would require much more than beliefs-held-in-common. The Freudian interpreter would have to show that, in terms of Freudianism, the precise questions they have asked are appropriate. The interpreter would also have to show that the tex-tual aspects he espies are "really there."

That, for example, in the story "The River," Bevel exhibits the behavior of a young child who is rejected by his parents, and who, rebounding from this hurt, is subconsciously driven to suicide—a motive he must consciously disguise as holy and beneficent, viz., as self-baptism. In this case, the Freudian critic would be showing an engagement of As-question and textual aspect: Bevel-as-delusive-and-suicidal. Obviously, the traits of repression, self-delusion, and so on, are seen as "really there" in the events of the story only by readers who believe repression and self-delusion of this kind can possibly occur, either in reality or in fiction. I add that important second phrase, "in fiction," because a reader may accept repression and self-delusion as possible ways of presenting behavior in fiction, even if they are not (for the reader) a correct way of explaining behavior in the real world.

But another reader, say a devout Fundamentalist Christian, logocentric to the core, may pose other questions of "The River" and "see" other textual aspects "really there" in the work. Because of the fore-structure this interpreter brings to the text, he does not see repression and self-delusion. Yet he can "make a case" for his Christian audience that the meaning, or As-structure, he advances is appropriate: As-questions meet textual aspects according to norms intersubjective among his peers. Even if he is told the historical author of "The River" intended a Freudian interpretation (which, incidentally, is probably not the case, but for our purposes makes no difference), he can with perfect legitimacy answer that consultation of authorial intent is unnatural and inappropriate for *Dichtung*. After all, the Christian critic, from a formal perspective, is doing here no more and no less than other critics, including critics asking the "authorial question." For example, the critic asking the authorial question attaches a Freudian qualitative value to a verbal sign because the author did. The Christian critic attaches a Christian qualitative value to the same verbal sign because the Bible does.

The Christian critic is asking questions vital to his group; he is showing to this group's satisfaction that textual aspects answer to these questions. Surely, on the side of the work and its aspects, he must adhere to couplings of signification and word sound permitted by the language-community's *langue*. (If he and his group do not, they are bespeaking a new and different work.) But at any given time in history, several significations and even more qualitative values are available through culture and its *langue* to a given word sound, and a fortiori, to the work as a whole. The literary work, as we have said, is within the logocentric purview an organon comprising all of these synchronic significations and qualitative values. Practically speaking, all interpretations contact only some facets of a multi-faceted work. The Christian critic in the foregoing case is "finding" in the work significations and qualitative values the Freudian is not finding. The Freudian is finding other significations and qualitative values. But the collective language of our culture (which includes, indeed, many subcultures) comprises both sets of lexic and qualitative values—the Freudian, Christian, and many, many more.

A critique that has been leveled at my account of Heidegger is that it would, in effect, validate, say, both an astrological (Ptolemaic) and astronomical description of the heavens, though the whole civilized world surely "knows" the astronomical description is the "correct" one. The conventional answer the European hermeneutical tradition would give to this argument is that hermeneutics concerns the realm of *Geist,* or human spirit, and not physical matter. Thus, examples drawn from science do not apply to aesthetics, the liberal arts, social sciences, and other human activities and constructs. Scientific laws, and the certainty they provide, apply to matter alone; a great fallacy of the empirical tradition has been to apply physical laws to human spiritual activity.[72] Attacking empiricism even more earnestly, existentialists and others can even argue here that astrology presents a "truth" of its own kind, just as valid in its own way as the astronomical truth. The heavens can and indeed have "appeared" to many perceivers in a way which Ptolemaic description satisfies—just as ocean water has a molecular structure, say, which empirical science discovers and claims to be "true," and also an array of other characteristics—archetypal values of motherhood, death, and so on, which the *sciences humaines* discover in ocean water and claim to be "true" (and claim to be more important, in terms of the human psyche, than mere "physical facts" about "matter").

The fact remains, however, that the astrologers, in their heyday, claimed to be asserting specifically scientific truth. My own stand on these matters is perhaps more radical than that of others who oppose an over-extended empiricism. It seems to me that if one wants to represent a consistent Heideggerianism, then one must claim that truth of all kinds, including scientific as well as *geistliche* truth, must be adjudicated by the group. Medieval scientists judged astrological theories true, and by their norms the theories were true. Today's empirical scientists consider the conclusions of astronomy true, and these scientists are believed by all those who accept the normative constants identified with empiricism, namely, at this point in history, the 'scientific method' and its corollaries.[73] But obviously astronomical 'certainties' are certain only for those who accept the scientific method. That virtually all civilized people, at this point in history, accept the scientific method's suitability for the investigation of material objects is in a way deceptive. Just as the majority of people once accepted astrology as a valid science, and then succeeding generations lost that conviction, so too are there indications that the 'scientific method' will cede in time to other 'scientific' norms which will in turn become 'intersubjective constants' for a relative chronological period. But, as we shall see, all this does not despoil the empirical scientist, for example, of the right to declare the astrologer dead wrong, and a fool at that. Likewise, it does not despoil the Hindu swami, and thousands of his devotees, of the equal right to deny the efficacy of the scientific method, even in relation to physical matter.

Relativism is the absence of truth conditions. But in the Heideggerian system at least, the collective *langue* vouches for the presence of determinate significations and qualitative values in the work. And each logocentric school accepts as a prerequisite the engagement of As-questions and textual aspects and establishes norms-held-in-common to "test" whether the engagement is achieved. Thus Heidegger establishes what he deems a universal truth condition for the function of validity (namely, the formation of mutual implication, as already described) and upholds as a truth condition the necessity of group norms whereby this function can be evaluated (though he obviously affirms a plurality of norms and leaves the determination of these various sets of norms to the various critical subcultures which appoint them).

But the further objection can be raised: perhaps Heidegger's formulation is not solipsistic relativism, but it does suggest a kind of peer-group relativism (similar to Dilthey's and others'). My answer is that the logocentrist simply cannot hold Heidegger guilty of this. Group relativism would "found" its truths on the beliefs of the group pure and simple. But Heidegger says, "That which is 'shared' is our *Being towards* what has been pointed out—a Being in which we see it in common. One must keep in mind that this Being-towards is Being-in-the-world, and that from out of this very world what has been pointed out gets encountered."[74] The validity of a meaning requires implication of As-question and As-which, but whenever this implication really occurs, Being is manifested. Validity, and the truth that consecrates validity, is at bottom founded not on subcultures or "critical schools," but on Being; truth is only mediated through subcultures and critical schools. For Heidegger, different critical schools can reflect different facets of Being.

Nor does Heidegger imply that one must accept every critical school that emerges in history. One may be convinced a given school, with its own distinguishing norms and so on, does not reflect Being. It may just produce *Einfall*, or fancy. And what about a perverted author who produces textual aspects which bespeak hatred? A reader may (and indeed, for my part, I think should decide) that the proper As-questions for such aspects would be questions which display the plot, qualitative values, and so on, of the work *as* evil and perverted. Then the As-structure or meaning of the work appears *properly*; Being ultimately is "the ways things really are," and the interpretation here would show evil to be evil. So again, Heidegger is not advocating an "anything goes" criticism. But he is saying that if we wish we can simultaneously affirm some contradictory schools and interpretations, and that we can do so without ontological embarrassment.

Starting from a base in O'Connor's own marvelous work, we have attempted to describe the structure of literary experience (including interpreter and interpreted) as logocentric mysticism regards it. We have described the nature of Heideggerian meaning, and the function of validity and principles of literary transformation which issue therefrom. Heidegger's perception, especially in his last phase, is rooted in what the Scholastics called *admiratio* and what O'Connor herself calls so often a "sense of Mystery."[75] *Admiratio* pauses in awe before the "multiple unity" of Reality. If, in O'Connor's words, fiction pushes "its own limits towards the limits of mystery,"[76] the horizon of this mystery—for Heidegger—is that Reality can mean several things at the same time, and still be radically one. Within ("amid") the Tao, the most critical turn in the argument is the last— that the poetic language of a Flannery O'Connor, and of others like her, utters *sans pareil* the mystery which is Being. Though Derrida's deconstructing arguments of *dédoublement* and *effacement* crack the holism of Heidegger's "holy saying [*Sagen*] of Being," there are other means for reinstating this holism, and these we shall develop most thoroughly in part 4.[77] We must first advance "all the way across the gap," and to do so we are compelled to what is indeed a most unexpected "going on"—the differential mysticism of Nagarjunism, a lesser-known (and indeed ancient) school of Indian Buddhism. Derrida is often touted by his disciples (even if inaccurately) as the herald of the "post-modern" age. The practitioners of Nagarjunism are often called the "Middle-Mosters,"[78] because they argue that to be the *most* "in the between" is to sidestep the logocentric between. Following their extravagant rhetorical lead, we can perhaps say (may the reader forgive!) that in advocating differential mysticism, we shall become at once the Post-Mosters and Post-Leasters.

Part 3

Across the Tao: Buddhist Differentialism (Athwart the a/Mid and Between, I)

The juncture of "our epoch," and Derrida's own sustained task, is "meditation," cautious and concentrated, on what he has called the "and/or" *between* "and/or." Nagarjuna, an Indian thinker who flourished in the second century after Christ and developed the Madhyamikan approach in Buddhism, tells us the following: "In the Katyayanavavada-Sutra the Lord [Buddha], who had the right insight into both *bhāva* [existing] and *abhāva* [non-existing], rejected both the extreme alternatives of 'is.' "[1] And Theodor Stcherbatsky, the pioneering Buddhologist, explains that for Nagarjuna the *madhyamā pratipad* ([Buddha's] Middle Path) is not "a mean between the two [i.e., between existence and non-existence],"[2] but a slipping between and away from the binary categories of existence and non-existence. Nagarjuna's Madhyamika 'philosophy',[3] as we shall see, teaches the "and/or" which is *between* the "and/or" of existence and non-existence, identity and non-identity, causality and non-causality.[4] I shall argue in this chapter that Nagarjuna's Middle Path, the Way of the Between,[5] tracks the Derridean trace, and goes "beyond Derrida" in that it frequents the "unheard-of thought," and also, "with one and the same stroke," allows the reinstatement of the logocentric too. (As we shall see, we can "have it both ways," and the two ways are a non-paradoxical, ever altering and wayward way; as we shall see, "*saṃsāra* is *nirvāna*.")

At the very outset of this discussion, however, I wish to dispel two vitiating suspicions—one suspicion which is rooted in a covert bigotry but is nonetheless commonplace among Western intellectuals who are not Orientalists, and another suspicion which is at least respectable, indeed, arguable, but which proves to be nonetheless vacuous. The first suspicion would have it that the principles of Buddhist thought in general are too 'escapist', too 'other worldly' in the pejorative sense of the term, too preposterously removed from the real, to be worthy of attention, and consequently, that any comparison of Derrida and Nagarjuna can only result in miscarriage; or, in a variation which is little more generous, that Buddhist thought is too alien to Western sensibilities, and on this count well nigh irrecuperable, so that a putative comparison of these two thinkers is de facto meaningless. Let me assure such suspicious ones that Buddhist thought, and the Hindu thought which chronologically

87

precedes and accompanies it, are as spectacularly diverse and profound and rigorous and challenging and indeed *relevant* as European thought; that the activity of Greek pre-Socratic schools found their counterpart in the intense metaphysical debates of the early and middle Upanishadic periods—that Indian philosophy divided into materialist, evolutionist, atomistic, idealist, and other schools; that Aristotelian and scholastic logic were matched by the elaborate Indian Nyāya and the Chinese "canons of Mo Tzu"; and that the Western medieval and renaissance periods were also tenures of breathtaking esthetic, philosophic, and religious activity in the East.[6] What is more, traditional Oriental thought is experiencing revival and new growth in contemporary times, especially in the non-Marxist Orient and in large part through fertile dialogue with Western specialists: Chinese logicians with German logicians, Indian philosophers with American philosophers, Buddhist monks with Catholic monks, Japanese poets with Brazilian poets, and so on.[7] All the above is not to deny that ideological consensus, the 'weight' of sophisticated opinion in the Orient, has often gravitated elsewhere on the spectrum of philosophical possibilities than it has in the West; but my point is that the spectrum has been the same for all of us, Eastern and Western, and has been the same precisely because we are all human, all likewise human. Indeed, a future turn of my argument, in the context of our quite specialized discussion, will involve the uncovering of very similar intuitions between Madhyamika and some past masters of Occidental thought.

The second suspicion I wish to allay is on the face of it reputable, but results from hasty generalization. The suspicion in question leads one to expect from Nagarjuna's Madhyamika the same 'Voidism' (non-presence) or at least 'Taoism' (interdependence of presence and non-presence)[8] that supposedly represent the whole of Oriental philosophy. As we have remarked, Derrida's own characterization of Eastern thought charges that the East offers no more than variations of logocentrism. But Derrida's cursory judgment is, in short, egregiously misinformed. In the *Mūlamadhyamakakārikās*, Nagarjuna declares: " 'It is' is a notion of eternity. 'It is not' is a nihilistic view. Therefore one who is wise does not have recourse to 'being' or 'non-being.' "[9] We shall see that Nagarjuna takes as his specific task the deconstruction of the principle of identity; and that to accomplish this, he employs the same logical strategy, and often the very same arguments, as Derrida. Like Derrida, he recognizes that the concept of eternality (and infinitism) is a consequence of logocentrism, of the "It is," in other words; that nihilism (including Voidism), the "It is not," is a dialectical variation of logocentrism; and that both alternatives, and any metaphysical 'compromises' mediating them, must be ousted in favor of a 'beyond knowing'.[10] As we shall discover, for Nagarjuna[11] the 'beyond knowing' allows for logocentric, i.e., language-bound knowing (in a way which frees him from Derrida's quandary concerning entrapment in language); and still Nagarjuna's 'beyond knowing' is not itself logocentric. I shall argue that Nagarjuna's *śūnyatā* ("devoidness") is Derrida's *différance*, and is the absolute negation which absolutely deconstitutes but which constitutes directional trace. In fact, I have selected out "devoidness"[12] from the several renderings of *śūnyatā* suggested by translators simply because it renders so well the kind of 'working' which is *śūnyatā*. "Devoidness" as a translation evokes negation (the Latin prefix *de* meaning "completely," so we have "devoid," or "completely void"); and "devoidness" also evokes constitution (the Latin prefix *de* meaning "away from," so we have "devoid," or "away from voidness"). Nagarjuna, in other words, does not want to do away with our hearing the knock, making the decision, getting up, and opening the door.[13] *Śūnyatā* is not 'indifference' as we have already defined it, nor is *śūnyatā* a random kind of drift. As we shall also determine, to live authentic devoidness is to recognize the phenomenological can be bliss, the "quenching"[14] (*saṃsāra* is *nirvāṇa*). In short, Buddhists in the Nagarjunist tradition can function as productive, often outstanding members of society (no undisciplined idling here, none of the pseudo-Orientalism that has so misrepresented Buddhism in the West). They can savor and create the exquisitely esthetic (think of Zen[15] painting, ceramics, gardens, poetry); yet, I argue, they are doing all this *as* trace, as indeed, Derridean trace!

A main point to be established, of course, is that Nagarjuna's *śūnyatā*, his *madhyamā pratipad*[16]—and of course he treats the terms as only 'provisional'[17]—is not logocentric, neither in the sense of logos nor as a dialectical variation of logos such as the "void." In short order I shall state my case, which will require as well the 'ideological' placement of Nagarjuna in relation to his immediate historical predecessors, contemporaries, and successors. Let us first, however, accomplish several discriminations which might otherwise cause the non-specialist some confusion. In this regard it must be said that the dominant forms of Hinduism, Buddhism, Taoism, and Confucianism which have occupied the Orient from near the historical beginnings to the present *are* logocentric in the Derridean sense, though in very sophisticated ways that Westerners seldom appreciate, but which sometimes strongly encourage engagement in "the world" and sometimes do not (depending on whatever variant of these four philosophies is in question, its stage of historical evolution, and so on). Let us recall that for Derrida logocentrism is any *identity* at all that one conceives, or even "feels," and then "labels" or perhaps "behaves towards" as if it were an "idea." And the structure of an identity, for Derrida, is necessarily a binary unit—factor and expression, signifier and signified. As we have already demonstrated, after a good many logical turns Derrida is able to produce this consequence: every experience interpreted as holistic, every 'naming' whatsoever, every formulation which coincides space and time, every notion of entitative causality—all of these modulations and more are logocentric. In terms of philosophico-religious systems, every notion of an 'absolute' as Origin, as End, as Center, as Circumference; or even every paradoxical[18] variation of these, such as God as Center and Circumference, the absolute as presence and absence, and so on; in short, every 'sense' of an absolute as the 'frame' which contains or accounts for 'everything else', be the latter taken as real, illusory, or whatever, is for Derrida logocentric. In this regard, to say God is ineffable, for example, is for the Derridean simply to formulate an identity which is declared 'beyond naming', and which, by this very declaration, is ironically 'reified' in a philosophical sense, or, if you will, 'focused'. (Derrida's own remarks in regard to 'beyond knowing' come perilously close to this, of course, but Derrida's very strength is that he knows such is his peril and dilemma. . . . Our own task at present is, with Nagarjuna, to escape the quandary.) If we are to discriminate Oriental philosophico-religions, then, in terms of logocentrism, we must apply the above to the characterizations Oriental specialists provide concerning their ideological terrain. Derrida's norm being as inclusive as it is, application is fairly easy to achieve as long as we attach the proviso we are talking of *dominant* forms. In other words, there are anticipations and recurrences of what we can call the Nagarjunist attitude scattered throughout the Orient, in several 'schools' belonging to various 'religions', and these are not logocentric.

We now take up application and begin with Hinduism, which in its Vedic period is largely henotheistic and in its Upanishadic period monist.[19] The Vedanta, be it judged monadic, or monist, modified dualist, and dualist,[20] is quite clearly logocentric, in that it accounts for 'everything' in terms of an organic whole. Confucianism, in effect the most 'worldly' of all major philosophico-religions, has also the most elaborate 'theory of presence', with each and every member of society related to each other and to Heaven, the Supreme Reality, in one glorious architectonic.[21] If a circle of presence[22] perhaps best describes Confucianism, and an empty circle, the Void, can represent much of Hinduism, the Taoist symbol—red and blue halves enfolded in mutual implication, 'belonging together' so a full circle is the result—surely stands as an adroit representation of Lao Tzu and his Tao.[23] "For Lao Tzu," Chang Chung-yuan tells us, "the return to Tao itself" is "the union of opposites on the higher level of non-differentiation."[24] One must step delicately here! The above characterization is clearly logocentric, based as it is on a resolution of opposites, but how convenient it would be for us to adapt the following from Lao Tzu and interpret it in Derridean fashion: "To be aware of the positive, yet to abide in the negative is to be the abyss of the universe, and to be aware of the white yet to abide in the black is to be the chasm of the universe."[25] Why, Lao Tzu's wiseman, the "abyss" and "chasm," would become Derridean *la faille*, the "fissure," and even *différance!* Lao Tzu's "positive" and "white" would represent Derridean 'constitution', or even a constitution given new security, so it could also reinstate the logocentric world and give us escape from Derrida's dilemma![26] But the fact remains that scholars just about everywhere agree that the Tao of Taoism has always represented, in one formulation or another, the union of opposites. In the excerpt from Lao Tzu just cited, the "black" is the unified field of non-differentiation and the "white" is the differentiated and empirical world, and in the case of Taoism these two opposites relate as a binary unity. To identify or even find analogous the classical Tao and Derridean thought would be dishonest. Taoism in its characteristic form from the beginnings down to contemporary times has been logocentric.[27] The remarkable similarities between Heidegger's "thinking about Being" and various registers of logocentric Oriental thought, especially Taoism and what we shall call logocentric Zen,[28] I have adverted to elsewhere.

An evaluation of Buddhism in its various forms, and their relationships to logocentrism, is an intimidating task. According to the earliest Buddhist scriptures, Buddha (c. 563–483 B.C.) taught that all existence is marked by *Duḥkha* (turmoil); that turmoil rises from ignorant desire; that there is freedom from turmoil; and that freedom is the Middle Path (a term subject to much Buddhist interpretation over the centuries: Nagarjuna's interpretation, for example, is very different from Abhidharmic interpretations).[29] Buddha rejects the Hindu notions of soul and matter and of transmigrating eternal selves, and speaks instead of *anitya* (impermanence) and the doctrine of *anātma* (no soul). Early Buddhism accounts for the continuity of one moment to the next by the notion of *pratītya samutpāda* (dependent co-arising).[30] There are no essences or substances but 'phenomena', including the 'apparent' self, arise through the interaction of *dharmas* ('elements' in English, as long as we understand they are not 'objective'[31]) which form momentary configurations, configurations which are orderly but in continual flux. The Abhidharmic schools, while preserving Buddha's notion of 'no self', usually *do* treat as real the five *skandhas* (components)[32] that configure the appearance of self, and this Nagarjuna is to regard as a lapse into identity-theory. Nagarjuna, who writes about seven centuries after the life of Buddha, undertakes the integration of Abhidharmic analysis and what had become the Prajnaparamitan tradition. The Abhidharmic thinkers, very active in Nagarjuna's time, were scholastic: they defined and catalogued the *dharmas,* and taught that *nirvāṇa* (for them, the cessation of *āsravas,* i.e., of 'defiling residues' which are mental, emotional) could be attained by analyzing how the *dharmas* arise and dissipate.[33] The Prajnaparamita tradition, on the other hand, discarded theories of origination and cessation of elements, and holding to the doctrine of 'non-production' of elements, undertook a more radical apprehension of the stream of becoming.[34] The role of devoidness, *śūnyatā*, becomes especially crucial in the Prajnaparamita, and Nagarjuna makes *śūnyatā* the primary concern of the Madhyamika school. Nagarjuna's greatest work, *Stanzas on the Middle Way (Madhyamakakārikās)*, will be our major access to his thought, and significantly it exhibits both an Abhidharmic interest in analysis and Prajnaparamitan interest in the 'realization' of *śūnyatā*. Frederick J. Streng maintains that the formulative or discursive elements in Nagarjuna's work reflect the Abhidharmic influence, and the dialectical elements, which are the stronger, reflect the Prajnaparamitan tradition. And Streng argues that the two sub-schools of Madhyamika which develop over the next few centuries from Nagarjuna's work reflect these two interests: the Prasangika, represented by Aryadeva, Dharmapala, Buddhapalita, Candrakirti, and Santideva, is 'dialectical' (and shall prove very useful to us in terms of Derridean logic); and the Svatantrika, represented by Bhavaviveka, which is more discursive and more moderate in its treatment of the Two Truths controversy.

Nagarjuna's understanding of *śūnyatā* is not logocentric, not 'absolute' in such a sense (i.e., in the Derridean sense of being 'closed' within a signifier and signified of any kind, see *ab-solvo*—"cut off from," "segregated").[35] The consensus of contemporary opinion seems to be that most of Nagarjuna's disciples, over a period of several generations, 'absolutize' his *śūnyatā;* and the slow but persistent absorption of Madhyamika by the Buddhist Yogacara school (which is idealist and, most would agree, patently logocentric[36]) and other Mahayanist[37] movements contributes even more to this 'hypostatization'. The Madhyamika reaches China by the fourth century through the efforts of the great translator and missionary Kumarajiva,[38] blossoms in the "old" Three Treatise school (fourth century–) and "new" Three Treatise school (sixth century–), but also undergoes assimilation (the pressures on Madhyamika are, among others, from Taoism, and from Buddhist syncretism—especially T'ien-T'ai) and disappears shortly after the ninth century. Throughout the period of growth and assimilation, the number of works attributed to Nagarjuna[39] (some extant only in Chinese) increases remarkably, and their content often alters the teaching of the *Middle Stanzas* and the rest of the earliest Nagarjunist literature. Legends of his life likewise proliferate and his role in the history of Buddhism is repeatedly reassessed as the Mahayanist tradition tries to provide historical continuity to a very diverse past: Nagarjuna is portrayed as one of the official patriarchs in the 'unfolding' of Buddhism, for example, and his teaching on *śūnyatā* brought into line with later doctrinal developments. In the face of such complication, Buddhologists for the last several years have been attempting to 'demythologize' Nagarjuna. The process has involved not only scientific and other research into historical origins of Indian Madhyamika, but also a refined attempt at separating out inappropriate Occidental perspectives from the interpretative process. Ideological bias, it seems, affected with quite damaging results even such pioneering Buddhologists as Louis de la Vallée Poussin and Theodor Stcherbatsky, who engaged in a famous controversy over the nature of Nagarjuna's *śūnyatā*: whether indeed it was the negativism Poussin felt it to be or the mystical absolutism Stcherbatsky claimed to see in it. Though contemporary norms have been improved by new data and by more developed appreciations of the Buddhist mind, past and present, debate over Nagarjuna's Madhyamika continues.[40]

Throughout this chapter, I identify myself with a body of Nagarjunist scholarship which is very substantial (perhaps dominant) and which is most current.[41] It shall become clear to the reader, I believe, that Nagarjuna's middle path is Derrida's "and/or" between "and/or," though Nagarjuna attains a *supplémentation* (permit me, please, the earnest jest) that Derrida never quite does. At the same time, it shall become clear to the reader why Nagarjuna remains unduly abstruse for some researchers. For it eventuates that without Derrida it is difficult for a 'moderner' to understand Nagarjuna! Before we undertake a detailed comparison of Nagarjuna and Derrida, perhaps an adumbration of what is in store will in a general way dispose us. Streng, in his well-received book on *śūnyatā*,[42] first explains the "mythical structure" characterizing currents of Indian thought which accept a "correspondence theory" of truth (i.e., language and reality, here the "ultimate reality," can "match" each other; and the "logic of mutual exclusion" holds). Then Streng explains the "intuitive structure" characterizing some other Indian systems, wherein "the whole point of inner control is to realize one Reality pervading each particular manifestation of this Reality."[43] In such systems "there is a recognition of a mutually interdependent duality pervading existence; both parts, however, are derived from the unity of all things, yet not identified with it"[44] (ultimate reality transcends words and transcends the dichotomies marking language; the reality, in one way or another, "grounds" existential duality, and the "logic of convergence" holds). Finally, Streng introduces the Nagarjunist "dialectical structure,"[45] which escapes the principle of identity and does not impute identity of any kind to *śūnyatā* (and identity, in Streng and our other scholars, means what it does in Derrida—"whatever is, is," and logical variants thereof, all understood, over the short or long haul, in terms that are either [1] functionally equivalent to what our Part 1 called the 'dyad of factor and mirror', or [2] convertible into such a dyad).

Streng asserts: "A major difference between Nagarjuna's negative dialectic and the Upanishadic analogic use of words, however, is that unlike the 'Neti, Neti' (not [this], not [that]) expression in the *Upanisads* there is *no inexpressible essential substratum which the negations attempt to describe.* For Nagarjuna, in place of the Brahman-Atman is

anātman (no individual identity). The purpose of Nagarjuna's negations is not to describe *via negativa* an absolute which cannot be expressed, but to deny the illusion that such a self-existent reality
exists."[46] Nagarjuna "is not saying that the true eternal state of reality is a blank; the calmness of *nirvāṇa* does not refer to an ontological
stratum beneath or behind the flux of experienced existence."[47] And
Streng quickly scotches the notion that perhaps Nagarjuna is reify-
ing the "dialectic" itself: "No, the dialectic is never an independent
force or first cause, but is operative only in relation to phenomenal
or ideal entities [both of which it deconstructs]. It is the spiritual
answer to the problem of grasping after self-existent entities. It is the
means of quelling the pain found in existential 'becoming' which results from longing after an eternal undisturbed entity."[48] In such a
context, resort to words such as "ultimate" and "reality" can become
very misleading.[49] Mervyn Sprung gives the ensuing account:

> It follows that the middle way is not a means to some final truth; it is
> not a path leading to knowledge. Whatever it is, it is the end of soc-
> ratizing, of theory, and of [logocentric] knowing. It is the practice of
> wisdom, not a means to it. . . .
>   Again, the middle way is not a means to some goal or end beyond
> itself. It is not a course of conduct undertaken with a view to attain-
> ing some result—perhaps enlightenment. It has often been so un-
> derstood, but my interpretation of Madhyamika turns on what I am
> saying about the middle way. . . .
>   The middle way is not [logocentric] knowledge but it is not a prac-
> tical [i.e., instrumental] undertaking either. It renders the dichotomy
> of theory and practice inapposite. There is no inner or outer here.
> There are no subjects, no doers, set against a world of objects to be
> manipulated in doing. The 'way' invalidates such opposition. . . .
> There are no things on the middle way; they disappear into the way
> itself. The 'way *things* really are' (*tattvam*) is the way of the *wise man.*[50]

Sprung, to our astonishment, concludes with words that resonate
with Derrida's own phrase, Derrida's 'beyond thinking', but invoke a
Nagarjunist "way":

> Is he [Nagarjuna] telling us that the end of philosophical thought is
> not the answer to a question with which it began nor even the end of
> a quest, but the transmutation of 'thought' into what is more than
> thought: into a 'way'. . . ?
>   . . . Does the middle way not supervene at precisely the point
> where thought is driven beyond itself, having failed to achieve its
> aim—that of making sense out of all matters brought before it? Is
> the end of philosophy to discover that philosophical questions all
> along, were not in the service of philosophical answers?[51]

R. S. Misra,[52] in an interview with Dom Aelred Graham, limns the
following useful sketch of what is involved:

> To me it seems that *śūnyatā*, as expounded by Nagarjuna, the great
> exponent of the Madhyamika philosophy, does not posit any Abso-

lute as such; it does not propound any transcendent reality which
may be said to be the essence of this world, or the ground of this
world. *Śūnyatā* is what may be called *prajñā* (wisdom). This is, as I
said, awareness of the essencelessness of things, which is another way
of expressing *nirvāṇa* itself. . . . Now, if we say that *śūnyatā* is absolute,
we are forced to conceive some reality which is there, even though it
can't be described. The way some contemporary scholars try to interpret *śūnyatā* is, as you say, in the sense that *śūnyatā* comes very close to
the *Advaita* (non-dualist) view of *Brahman* (God). These scholars
imply that *śūnyatā* posits some sort of Absolute, which is very much
analogous to *Brahman*. Here I find difficulty, because Nagarjuna does
not convey any idea of such an Absolute.

Dom Aelred pursues with a question which in effect asks whether
there is an inexpressible absolute over and beyond the term "Absolute": "But when one uses a word like 'Absolute,' the term and the
concept, aren't we still in the realm of name and form? And you
have to go beyond that." "Yes," answers Misra. "But then, even our
highest imagination of the Absolute does not free us from some sort
of concept of *being*." And Misra continues, carefully avoiding the
"inexpressible Absolute" which (in Derridean terms) would also
function as an affective 'center' of some kind:

> That is, the Absolute has to be posited. It may not, if you like, be
> characterized as being, because it transcends being. But "tran-
> scendence of being"—what can it mean? If you say that *śūnyatā* is
> absolute and analogous to Brahman, then you are obliged to call this
> Absolute *sat* (being) or else you must call it "consciousness," pure con-
> sciousness. The Vijnanavadins do say that the Absolute is pure con-
> sciousness; they say it, but the Madhyamika school do not say that.
> They say that we can't describe it in any way, which does not neces-
> sarily mean that there is some 'It' that can't be described. Both are
> negated; both knowing subject and known object are utterly negated.
> But I don't say that this is nihilism-*śūnyatā*. It is just realization of
> freedom. I will put it in two ways: *śūnyatā* is the realization of the
> essencelessness of things, and it is the realization of freedom, utter
> freedom. . . . As for Enlightenment, or Buddhahood, enlightenment
> *itself* is reality, in my view, not anything about which one is
> enlightened. And this is, according to me, the basic distinction
> between the Vedanta and the Madhyamika: that in Vedanta
> enlightenment is enlightenment of *Brahman*, the awareness of
> *Brahman* as the Absolute, and in Madhyamika enlightenment, or *pra-
> jñā*, does not mean the awareness of any reality. It means the aware-
> ness that things are essenceless or *śūnya* (empty of essence), or the
> awareness of the relativity of things, and this is freedom.[53]

The above excerpts are enough of a rehearsal. Even upon first
perusal they convince the reader, I think, that to impute absolutism
to Nagarjuna's Madhyamika, out of hand as it were, and categorically, is critically unsound. The excerpts have also represented what
are still for us vague and tentative norms, but nonetheless helpful
ones in that they enable me to sketch, at least, another historical

linkage. Two of the norms for recognition of Madhyamika are that (1) *śūnyatā* escapes the identity principle and that (2) the "way" involves "the flux of experienced existence," the " 'becoming,' " the "relativity of things," but does not involve an "eternal undisturbed entity," a "final [teleologically conceived] truth"; nonetheless, wisdom or *prajñā*, the "calmness of *nirvāṇa*," is a "spiritual answer." All these terms, especially in English translation where they evoke historically accreted semantic which is in our context irrelevant (for example, the terms "relativity" and "becoming," which evoke Western metaphysical baggage) beg for an accounting. I will offer an accounting, but suffice it now to say that together they indicate our second norm: the mundane is involved with bliss, but not ordained towards "supreme identity." Not so astounding an assertion, as it stands, but the "doctrine of Two Truths" in Buddhism (the truths of *saṃvṛti* and *paramārtha*) is very sophisticated, and Nagarjuna's interpretation very distinctive (as we shall soon see). Our keynote now is that Nagarjuna enstates the mundane, the concrete, as privileged over metaphysical speculation and indicates the mundane can entail bliss. That the mundane involves bliss permits us a "link up" with some forms of the Ch'an/Zen Buddhist current, significant in terms of our study because this current provides history with many cases of authentic Nagarjunist discipleship. (This is not to deny that much Ch'an/Zen Buddhism is logocentric; rather it is to assert that recurrent in Ch'an/Zen are instances of Nagarjunism, or what we are about to call 'differential Ch'an/Zen'.) Buddhism of all kinds was to wither away in India proper after the eleventh century, largely because of a Hindu revival and the Moslem invasions. But in China, alongside the "new Three Treatise school," another Indian Buddhist importation—the Yogacara or "school of Consciousness Only,"[54] a school of pure idealism (absolute mind)—was prospering. In between the Madhyamikan "Three Treatise school" and Yogacaric "school of Consciousness Only," still a third school was expanding rapidly,[55] the "Meditation School," or Ch'an, probably introduced into China by Bodhidharma in the fifth or sixth century.[56] Kalupahana and others maintain that possibly in its Indian origins and quite certainly in its relation to the two contemporary Chinese schools mentioned above, Ch'an was syncretistic. It combined motifs of the Madhyamika and Yogacara.[57] In the seventh century, Ch'an divided into the northern school of Gradual Enlightenment and the southern school of Sudden Enlightenment. Only the southern school was destined to survive formally (though some "northern" tenets were to resurface later), proliferating into many sects and then reducing to two, the Lin-chi and Ts'ao-tung. During the eleventh and twelfth centuries, the Japanese formed their own institutions specializing in meditation. In the lineages they derive from China, the two Ch'an (in Japanese, Zen) sects, Lin-chi and Ts'ao-tung, take on the Japanese names Rinzai and Soto respectively. The involvement of the 'concrete world', of mundane matter, that is to say, and the bliss of the *nirvāṇa* which is *saṃsāra,* is very characteristic of Ch'an/ Zen. The exquisite Japanese tea ceremony, for example, is performed by Zen as the *saṃvṛti* which is *paramārtha*—whence the overall importance of the historical link between Madhyamika and Ch'an/Zen. The Zen tea ceremony and esthetic activities like it function in the history of Oriental thought as reinstatements of the mundane in the face of nihilist and "other worldly" depradations.

As for "abrogation of the identity principle," an abrogation which is the first norm of genuine Madhyamika (that is to say, Nagar-junism, or Madhyamika which has remained faithful to Nagarjuna's original attitude towards *śūnyatā*), the historical linkage between Ch'an/Zen and the origins is more complex. The nature and history of the *kung-an* (literally, "public case": in Ch'an it comes to mean a very brief anecdote, operating in a "question and answer" format; in Japanese, *koan*), for example, is subject to great academic con-troversy, with some researchers claiming it operates quite purely in Nagarjuna's mode, viz., a rigorous rationalism whereby logic cancels itself out—leaving devoidness to lapse (slide) by, interminably; and others seeing it as operative in a Yogacaric mode, as an intuitionism, so the monk does *not* through the assiduous use of reason *deduce* self-contradiction, but rather *transcends* reason "in a flash."[58] When W. T. de Bary speaks of Zen's interest in Indian Hinayanist sources[59] and when Ninian Smart calls Zen "Japan's substitute for Lesser Vehicle Buddhism,"[60] they are indicating a movement in Zen away from what was the increasing absolutization of *śūnyatā* occurring in most of the later Buddhist schools. But Westerners, through the good offices of Zen's great missionary to the West, D. T. Suzuki, know only of logocentric (and thus absolutist) Zen, and indeed there is no question that logocentric Zen has been for quite some time now Zen's most popular form.[61] Or, to avoid needless confusion, let us call it "centric Zen," since its whole effort is to transcend *logos* un-derstood as the language of *is* and *is not* and to achieve the 'undiffer-entiated center' (of course, 'undifferentiated center' is just a permu-tation of *logos,* in the specialized Derridean terms we have already worked through at such length). Thus Suzuki declares that "The meaning of the proposition 'A is A' is realized only when 'A is not-A,' "[62] that Buddhist philosophy is the "philosophy of self-identity," and that in this self-identity "there are no contradictions whatsoever."[63] The supreme self-identity,[64] indeed the only self-identity in the ultimate sense, is centric Zen's *śūnyatā*: "Emptiness is not a vacancy—it holds in it infinite rays of light and swallows all the multiplicities there are in this world."[65] Centric Zen relies heavily on the Yogacaric *Laṅkāvatāra-sūtra* and on passages such as the follow-ing from the third Ch'an patriarch, Seng-Ts'an:

> Objects are objects through subjects;
> Subjects are subjects through objects.
> If you wish to know the two parts,
> At the source they are the one void.[66]

Notice how the following aphorisms fron Seng-Ts'an likewise strike dramatic contrast with the Derridean attitude: "Give a hair's breadth of difference / Heaven and earth stand far apart," and "Perfection resembles great space— / Nothing short and nothing extra."[67] Of course Derrida's strategy is precisely to wedge open interminable hairbreadths of difference, so he can expose alterity, the slide of differentiation; and Derrida's strategy is to show "things" are recurrently "falling short," or, if you will, running over into "extra."

The differential movement in Zen of course opposes the centric Zen just instanced and can be demonstrated by way of the following primary sources in Zennist literature and their appended commentaries. These old Buddhist narratives are well worth our while.

From *The Wisdom of the Patriarchs*[68]

The Fourth Ancestor, Ubakikuta Sonja[69]

. . . Ubakikuta hailed from the country of Dali and belonged to the Suda race. He was taught from the age of fifteen, became a monk at seventeen and was enlightened at twenty-two. He then went to Matsala to teach others. Because there were many people who were ordained by him, devils were afraid of him. Every time he ordained someone he put a numbered piece of bamboo, the length of four fingers, into a stone room. The size of this room was eighteen *chu* in length and twenty *chu* in width [a *chu* is roughly equivalent to a foot], and the room was filled with them. He was cremated with these bamboo sticks because there were so many people ordained during [his] the Lord's lifetime. . . . When Ubakikuta shaved his head at the age of seventeen, Shonawashyu asked him, "Are you a monk of body or a monk of mind?"

There are two kinds of monks: monks of body and monks of mind. The so-called monk of body severs family ties, lives away from home, shaves his head, changes the colour of his clothes, has no servants, becomes a trainee and seeks for the Truth throughout his life. . . . [The monk of body cloisters himself bodily from the secular world. And he understands Buddha to mean by Truth a psycho-philosophical idealism: the so-called phenomenal world is a mental construct.]

[The monk of body ironically makes the mistake of seeking an *idealist* Truth:—] He does not look for the real self but seeks only the Truth. Because of this he stays neither in delusion nor enlightenment, and so he is a *real* man. This is a monk of body [in other words, the *real* is paradoxically the *ideal* man].

The so-called monk of mind does not shave his head and change the colour of his clothes. . . . [Ironically, he seems to seek out 'pure' matter:—] He knows that Nirvana, birth and death are illusions in the sky and has no concern with the Truth and delusion. This is a monk of mind [the monk of mind, while not cloistering himself bodily from the world, affirms the singular materiality of all things; he does not trouble himself with mentalist problems such as Truth and delusion].

Therefore Shonawashyu asked his question. If Ubakikuta is a monk outside these two kinds, he is not a real monk; because of this the question was framed. Ubakikuta answered, "I am a monk of body." It was obvious that he was not a monk of mind, nature or anything else but a monk of body. He could reach this understanding and knew it, and with this he was completely satisfied. He got this far without looking and so understood that everything he could not understand was what it was. Therefore he said he was a monk of body. [At this point the still unenlightened Ubakikuta cannot even distinguish between the respective meditational modes of the monk of body and the monk of mind. A favorable side of this ignorance, however, is that Ubakikuta at least knows how to let matters be—the important Zen quality. In any case, he takes his Master's question literally, and since he is a cloistered monk, simply affirms that he is indeed a monk of body.]

But the excellent Truth of Buddha should not be understood as above, as Shonawashyu pointed out. Buddha should not be a monk of body or a monk of mind and be seen as a material or mental existence. [In the Buddhist tradition the debate between monk of body and monk of mind represented a controversy over the nature of the Two Truths (loosely put, the truth of worldly existence and the truth of enlightenment), and how to define and relate them. The Zen approach is to discard so metaphysical a discussion, since—for Zen, as for the Madhyamika—*śūnyatā* is not accommodated by the metaphysical categories of materialism and mentalism.]

He was beyond both the holy and the unholy and conquered both mind and body. He was like the sky, with neither inside nor outside, and like the sea-water, with neither an obverse nor a reverse. Although he taught many doctrines, he only pointed out this one true fact. We should not say that he was a Buddha because he was the most excellent person in the world. Buddha should not be spoken of as non-coming and non-going. [Actually, the Buddha has been sometimes so described, but *Tathāgata*, the title of the Buddha, means "he who comes/goes *thus*." Differential Buddhism in particular can emphasize that the Buddha-nature (i.e., the way "all matters go on") is differential and *not* centric, *not* a focus or stasis.]

Nor should we speak of existence before parents were born and before the world existed. The Truth of Buddha is beyond both birth and no-birth and is outside the argument of mind and no-mind. It is like the water within vessels and the emptiness of the sky. . . . ["Water" and "empty sky" are common poetic symbols for *śūnyatā*, which eludes the categories of mind and no-mind. As symbols they can lend themselves to either a centric or differential reading of *śūnyatā*. Thus far, nothing in this text seems to compel a differential interpretation. The narrative, as we are about to see, saves its remarkable display of differentialism for the last few lines.]

Although there are neither "he" and "I" nor "good" and "bad" between them [that is, between the Master Shonawashyu and Ubakikuta; the designations "he" and "I," and the attributes "good" and "bad," and so on, imply entitative assumptions and as such are repudiated], they sound like an echo and seem like the endless sky. If one does not experience the Truth with his own body, the Truth may become delusion. When this was pointed out Ubakikuta was enlightened. It was like thunder in a clear sky or a great fire on the ground.

When the thunder beat on Ubakikuta's ears, he lost his previous

life. Fire burned the Law of Buddha and the teachings of the ancestors to ashes. These ashes became Ubakikuta, and they were hard as
stones and black as lacquer. [In the rush of fire and the roll of the
thunder (fine symbols for differential emptiness, really), Ubakikuta
assimilates the import of the Buddha's Teaching, which becomes in
him "hard as stones" (a Buddhist truism: all adversaries break their
teeth on the impermeable gem of the Teaching) and "black as lacquer" ("a jet black iron ball speeds through the dark night," Keizan
himself had said when enlightened).]

Ubakikuta threw away the dirty surface of others and took many
disciples. [Ubakikuta converts many to the Pure Teaching.] In vain he
threw bamboos into a room and counted emptiness, then burned
emptiness and left the mark in emptiness. [And here it finally has
come: the overwhelming display of differential Zen. The logocentric
"counting" of emptiness, now in vain, cedes to undifferentiated emptiness; then undifferentiated emptiness yields in turn to the rushing
fire; and then—precisely where centric Zen expects to void everything into the Absolute (the "mirror without speck" of centric
Buddhism)—a "mark," a speck, continues on in the emptiness. Triple
negative evocation, with the 'end' still open. Ubakikuta is frequenting
Derridean trace.]

Now I [that is, Keizan Zenji], a disciple in Daijo Temple, want to
look for the mark beyond the clouds and to write my words in emptiness. Do you want to hear?

The house is broken; the man has disappeared.
There is neither inside nor outside,
So where can body and mind hide themselves?

[Keizan too must follow in the tracks of Ubakikuta, and trace the
mark, write in emptiness. Logocentrism disseminates in *différance*.]

Apropos the next source, a little Buddhist story, permit me to
offer a short introduction. Mahayana Buddhism regards the universe as composed of infinite numbers of spheres and proceeding
through an infinite sequence of cosmic periods. The Pure Land is
the sphere, or Buddha-heaven, established by the bodhisattva
Dharmakara when he earned Buddahood and became Amitabha. All
on earth who call upon Amitabha's name in good faith are promised,
upon death, a blissful stay in the Pure Land. Though this stay is not
eternal, most Buddhists had come to regard the Pure Land teleolog-
ically, as a kind of lasting haven. What is so adroit about the following story, an anecdote about grandmother and granddaughter, is
that the crane and tortoise are candles and are melting away; they
are candles in their own right and also emblems of humankind and
all things, for all are melting, melting.

From Buddhist Folklore[70]

A little girl sat close to her grandmother before the Buddhist altar,
and pressing her little hands together in prayer, she inquisitively
asked one morning: "Why are the crane and the tortoise [candlesticks

in the shapes of a crane and a tortoise] up there in the altar, Grandma?" [The crane and tortoise are traditional emblems for a "blessed" life, and they live, according to symbolic numerology, a "full" number of years.] "My dear," the grandmother replied, "A crane lives for one thousand years, and a tortoise for ten thousand years. Because they are such blessed creatures, they can be there in the altar where it is as beautiful as the Pure Land." The granddaughter looked all the more inquisitively and asked, "What would the crane do after one thousand years, and the tortoise after ten thousand years?"

The grandmother answered: "They die naturally. You should know that, my dear." [There are at least two points to notice at this juncture. First, the grandmother had, just prior, emphasized the crane and tortoise are *already* blissful. Second, the granddaughter has just asked what is really a very cogent question: What will the crane and tortoise *do* after their sojourn on earth? If they, *as* candlesticks which are slowly dissolving, are blissful, how can they retain their bliss afterwards? It is in the nature of all things that they expire, the grandmother answers.]

The granddaughter continued: "What will happen to the crane and tortoise after they are dead?" [The granddaughter, with that relentless logic which—because they can see matters truly—characterizes the innocent, continues her questioning: What will *happen* to the crane and tortoise after they are dead? That is, if they are already happy and if they are to undergo change, can they go on being happy?].

The grandmother said: "Because the crane and the tortoise are blessed creatures, they will go direct to the Pure Land when they are dead." [The grandmother's answer, in effect, is to say the crane and tortoise will indeed continue to be happy]. The granddaughter persisted: "What would they do in the Pure Land, Grandma?" [That is, the granddaughter persists: If the crane and tortoise are candles-which-melt, and are blissful in so doing, what would the crane and tortoise *do* in the blissful Pure Land?].

"What a dull child you are! They would be candlesticks in the Pure Land." The grandmother's answer sounded laboured, but the innocent child nodded her little head contentedly. [The granddaughter intuitively grasps and accepts the response. The grandmother's response sounds "laboured" because—as part of the narrative—it is necessarily cast in discursive terms.]

What is so extraordinary about the grandmother's response above, even when expressed conceptually as it is, is that it defies all the 'solutions' a centric Buddhist would be by this time expecting. Centrism would expect the candlesticks to become, perhaps, *real* cranes and tortoises (that is, empirical ego and its garment of craving dissolve, and crane and tortoise each find their True Self, the Buddha-nature). Or perhaps they would cease to be crane and tortoise of any kind and simply cede to the One. Whatever the formulaic solution, centrism expects an attained *telos*, an 'end' in the philosophical sense. And imagistically this should work out in the narrative as a cessation of the 'candleness' of crane and tortoise. Candles *melt away;* candle-cranes and candle-tortoises by nature seem to *evoke* real (or ideal) cranes and tortoises. In other words, candle-cranes and candle-tortoises are by definition "on the move"—their way of 'going on' is precisely to be *passage,* a passing, a being FOR. What kind of Pure Land, after all, allows its clients to be candles again, evoking Pure Land again, and dissolving again! Only Pure Lands working as Derrida's 'bottomless chess set.' Yet this is precisely the revelation: the blissful candlesticks are blissful and remain forever blissful by way of their alterity. The grandmother is teaching differential Zen.

Our next text belongs to the genre called *mondo,* short exchanges between Master and monk disciple.

From a collection of venerable Zen *Mondo*[71]

Bowing and Rising

A monk came to be taught, and Isan, seeing him, made as if to rise. The monk said, "Please don't get up!" Isan said, "I haven't sat down yet!" The monk said, "I haven't bowed yet." Isan said, "You rude creature!" (Reginald H. Blyth's commentary: We may suppose that the monk had already bowed, at least at the entrance of the room, and that when he said, "I haven't bowed yet," he was playing Isan's game of the absolute, but Isan suddenly jumps to the relative, and scolds the monk. As said before, we must always be in the absolute-relative [or relative-absolute] and then we cannot be attacked from either relative or the absolute.)

The 'plot' of the *mondo* is simple enough. The Master, playing his instructive game, has arranged matters so the entering monk catches him half-way between sitting and standing. The monk, operating on the mundane (relative, here) level, of course pleads that the Master not stand on his account. The Master retorts, "I haven't sat down yet," that is (1) How do you know I'm not on the way down (about to sit) rather than on the way up (about to stand)? And further, (2) Why do you associate my words with my bodily posture? . . . I may be talking on the absolute level ("I haven't sat down yet" meaning "I haven't guided you to enlightenment yet," and so on). The monk catches the clue, and signals this to the Master by likewise adjusting, and shifting viewpoint: "I haven't bowed yet!" Instead of congratulating the monk, which would be the more likely centric dénouement (i.e., congratulations for transcending the mundane!), the Master pulls the monk right back to the relative again! "You rude creature!": How dare you refuse me the courtesy of a bow! Such is Buddhist differentialism: the authentic Buddhist is not centered on the logocentric (the mundane, the relative) nor the transcendent (the absolute). The Master wrenches the viewpoint of the monk this way and that, so he might learn to live the going-on of alterity. And so he might learn that alleged centers are not to be foisted onto the differential flow; rather, alleged centers are really a matter of shifting perspectives, and the adept is one who can control these shifts at will.[72]

Buddhist *différance*, in other words, belongs to no viewpoints, but can be regarded from all viewpoints. Yet these viewpoints properly understood are not points, nor is *différance* a focus.

Our last demonstration is drawn from the *Mumonkon* (Chinese: *Wu-men-kuan*), published in 1229 A.D. The *Mumonkon* is a famous collection of Ch'an/Zen 'cases', or anecdotes used for meditation. The cases are drawn from the great Masters, and are annotated with the commentaries of Mumon (Chinese: Wu-men Hui-k'ai), a great Chinese Master in his own right (1183–1260). The case quoted here is from Nansen (Nan-ch'uan P'u-yuan), who lived in the eighth century and beginning of the ninth. Nansen's case, as we are about to see, is intended to check the natural tendency of humankind to reify the 'sayings of the Masters', for the idolatry of words or concepts is a disguised lapse into logocentrism.

From the *Mumonkon*, Case XXVII[73]

Nansen's "No Mind, No Buddha"

A monk asked Nansen, "Is there a truth which no one has taught?" Nansen replied, "There is." "What is this truth," said the monk, "which no one has so far taught?" Nansen answered, "It is not mind; it is not Buddha; it is not things." [The original Chinese omits here the pronoun represented by our "It." The translation from Chinese should read, "Is not mind; is not Buddha; is not things." In the context of Nansen's assertion the omission takes on significance, because the Chinese reader is not as tempted to reify and identify a grammatical subject here.] (Blyth's commentary: . . . The word "mind" may be written also Mind, but this makes it equal to Buddha, so it is better to take it as human nature. Nansen is denying both idealism and materialism. In Case XXX Baso declares that mind is Buddha.[74] In Case XXXIII he declares it is not.[75] . . .

Nansen cuts the entangled Gordian knot by declaring that it is not the mind, nor the Mind. In doing this he contradicts 三界唯一心 , "In the Three Worlds all is simply One Mind." He also negates 一切眾生悉有佛性 , "All living things have the Buddha nature"; 唯識無境 , "All is mind and no objective thing exists"; and 識外無法 , "Nothing exists apart from mind." Nansen denies that the Eternal Buddha is the Ultimate Reality. Last, he does away with the idea that 諸法實相 , "All things in their real aspect" are reality. [The way matters "go on" is not accommodated by reduction to "mind" (all-pervasive mind is a logocentric formula), nor identification with the Buddha-nature (the Buddha-nature thus understood becomes an infinite Center—in Derridean terms, a self-enclosed or "comprehended" God), nor equation to the material ("realism" by nature *fixes* attention; in Derridean terms, it is the dialectical counterpart of idealism).] In a sense Nansen here rejects the experience of the poet that things have, in being what they are, Absolute Value. . . . [A poet who is unenlightened, in other words, sees only superficially; he, like all materialists, is guilty of 'phenomenalism'.]

Zen, like life, is fluid; the intellect solidifies it in order to grasp it, and it is Zen no longer. [Blyth's comment lodges the differentialist complaint against logocentrism.] Thus, when a Zen master makes an assertion, affirmative or negative, we are not to take it as an assertion of truth, relative or absolute. It is something moving, "something evermore about to be," so that Nansen should perhaps have said, "It is the movement of mind, of Buddha, of things." This movement is free, inevitable, and poetical. [Appropriately, the commentary ends our brief passage through Buddhist literature with an excellent indicative 'description' of *différance* — that differentialism cuts a diagonal across freedom and inevitability suggests, it seems to me, Derridean *errance*; that differentialism is "poetical" suggests its manner of accessibility, viz., evocation, verbal 'game', and so on.])

So differential Zen, like Nagarjuna's Madhyamika, disclaims "centered" experience of any kind. A question may still persist, though. Is the "middle way" an emotional focus, or any kind of supra-rational or irrational focus? Can an experience which is "beyond knowing" resist the human need (necessity?) of *focus*, and therefore, of centering? Clearly Nagarjuna considers the middle way a successful and thorough escape from centering. As Nagarjuna sees it, the Buddha is called *Tathāgata,* "he who comes/goes thus," because he is forever coming and going. The Buddha, in other words, is not one who is centered, i.e., he is not one who is coming and going at the same time, nor one who has stopped coming and going. *Śūnyatā* is BETWEEN "easy come, easy go," AND "hard to come by." Trying to give some account of *śūnyatā*, Sprung argues that in the middle way there is no question of "passion, trance, ecstasy."[76] So supra-rational and irrational centerings too are abrogated: the emotive force with which "passion" fixes on an object, and the mystical concentration with which "ecstasy" fixes on logocentric God, are excluded from consideration, as is the autonomic monism of "trance." Indeed, Nagarjuna insists that the term *śūnyatā* is "provisional" because he recognizes that such terms attract not only conceptual hypostasis, but to an even greater degree, "affective" focus.[77] To put it another way, the authentic experience of *śūnyatā* runs a sort of Maoist "continuing revolution" against focus!

The Nagarjunist "negative dialectic"[78] usually aims at the entrapment of the opponent[79] by way of dilemma, with dilemma understood in the most specialized sense: an argument which shows the opponent is limited by his premises to two conclusions, each fatal to his own case. It is most important to note that the dialectic does not use *reductio ad absurdum* in the technical sense: the invalidation of the opponent's conclusion is not taken to imply the validity of its contradictory.[80] Hence what Derrida calls "dialectical thinking" and declares fallacious (you will recall) is *reductio ad absurdum* in this technical sense. Derrida and Nagarjuna, in other words, use dilemma in precisely the same way.[81] Nagarjuna frequently places dilemma in the larger frame of the tetralemma, the famous "four-cornered logic"[82] of the Indian tradition. Tetralemma presents four assertional forms (lemmas), called the "four possibles" (*catuṣkoṭika*), which together are regarded as exhaustive of propositional possibility: (1) X is Y, (2) X is not-Y, (3) X is both Y and not-Y, and (4) X is neither Y nor not-Y.[83]

Nagarjuna sometimes runs what he considers the bankrupt argument of an opponent through all four forms and demonstrates the impossibility of its conclusion in terms of all four. For example, he does just this in chapter XXVII, verse 13, of the *Middle Stanzas:* "Consequently, the (false) views that I existed in the anterior state, I did not exist, both or neither, are all impossible."[84] At other times Nagarjuna treats the tetralemma more incrementally, so that an adversary's argument is steered through the transformations of the first, second, and third lemmas, and is dispatched as impossible at each level, but the fourth lemma "holds," in that it applies to the argument: the subject term X is neither Y nor not-Y. Witness, for example, the concluding verse of MK I: "Consequently, the effect (i.e., arisen entity) is neither with relational nor without non-relational condition. Since the effect has no existing status, wherein are the relational and non-relational conditions?" (MK I:14 IN; see also MK I:7 and XXII:11).[85]

Nagarjuna's prime attack, as we shall soon see, is on theory of *dharmas* (Abhidharmic *dharmas*, or 'elements',[86] are second-order descriptions of ordinary language/behavior, but Nagarjuna recognizes that they are in their own right logocentric or 'self-identical'[87]); and his consistent strategy is to show that all logocentric formulae, and dialectical variants thereof, contradict themselves.[88] Derrida's attack on philosophy of presence, you will recall, targets the crucial notion of signifier-signified, a notion which functions as a "clue" or *indice* for him. That is to say, when the notion of a signifier-signified dyad "cracks" under Derrida's relentless pressure, and "cracks" because it is self-contradictory, Derrida can follow the fissure—a logocentric formula, in this sense, has become a vital clue. And in this case the clue leads, you will recall, to the notion of pure signifier. In turn, the pure signifier proves to be self-contradictory, but it is placed *sous rature*. The device of *sous rature* indicates the notion in question (here the notion of pure signifier), though self-contradictory, somehow still provides a "glimmer" (what I would prefer to call a 'diascript') of *différance*. In the Nagarjunist method, the logocentric construct which is ultimately self-contradictory but functions as clue is called a *prajñapti* ("language-construct"[89]—I prefer this translation because it implies, as it should, *both* 'words' and 'ideas'). Sprung explains: "*Prajñapti* has, in Madhyamika usage, two meanings, a general and a peculiar one. In general all words which would name anything are *prajñaptis*: that is, nothing is found in the object to which they point, which corresponds uniquely to the putative name. . . . In its peculiar sense a *prajñapti* is only such a name as leads, via the Buddhist discipline, to the Buddhist truth."[90] But how does it lead to the truth? By undergoing the *prāsaṅgika,* which proves it to be self-contradictory, yet "guiding" and "conductal."[91] For example, the Nagarjunist *prāsaṅgika* compresses and cracks the theory of entitative causality (the *prajñapti,* in this case), but the theory leads to relational causality, which is put under erasure but exposes *śūnyatā.* Sprung shows how theory of *svabhāva* (self-existence) functions as a *prajñapti* for Nagarjuna and Candrakirti. Taking a retrospective glance at the *prāsaṅgika* involved, and its subsequents, he says, "a *prajñapti* is only such a name as leads, via the Buddhist discipline, to the Buddhist truth. The term *svabhāva,* for example, which was analytically nonsense, yet led, by some hidden connection, unerringly to the truth of things. . . . How is it that a *prajñapti* can guide or conduct, without giving knowledge in the ordinary sense?" Sprung goes on to discuss *prajñapti* in more detail:

> *Prajñapti* is frequently translated as "metaphor." But this does not help here, because the primary meaning of self-existence, i.e., the self-existence of things, has been shown to be nonsensical. Nonsense can hardly be transferred, as such, to the truth; so there can be no metaphor. And in fact the Madhyamika has argued that the truth is not to be understood as self-existent *things* are understood. Such repudiation is hardly a basis for metaphor. I find the same difficulty in taking the Madhyamika's understanding of the truth as self-existent to be an analogy. How can an analogy hold between what, at the one pole (the everyday) does not exist, and what, at the other (*tattvam*[93]), rejects this misconception as inapplicable?"[94]

After contrasting Nagarjunist "clue" and Kantian "ideas of reason," Sprung continues: " . . . *prajñaptis* are, however, not arbitrary fictions but apparently indefeasible ways of orienting and understanding ourselves. . . . That is, their relation to the way things are is not a cognitive one. It is, in a sense, 'practical,' but this should not be pushed very far, for *prajñaptis* are effective at a level beyond the everyday. . . ."[95]

We now turn to Nagarjuna's employ of the arguments from *dédoublement* and *effacement.* It will be noticed that the "Derridean" methodology—(1) entrapment of the adversary in self-contradiction, (2) resort to another conclusion, (3) the placement of the conclusion *sous rature,* and (4) discernment of the *lueur* given off by *différance,* from between the marks of the erasure—all characterize the Nagarjunist trail, though in Nagarjuna the *différance* is recognized and celebrated as *śūnyatā,* and frequented with certainty. Nagarjuna's employ of *dédoublement* occurs as follows. As Sprung so succinctly puts it, "It is universally recognized that Buddhist thought from the beginning was modal, non-substantive. All things, inner and outer, are seen as kaleidoscopic complexes of simple qualities—and nothing more. But by far the full weight of the original Buddhist grasp of existence is not given in this way."[96] Several of the earlier Buddhist schools, in their very academic analysis of 'dependent co-arising' (*pratītya samutpāda*), which is the term for Buddha's modal flux,[97] still, in Nagarjuna's estimation, lapse into a theory of 'self-identity'[98] (though not of 'personal self-identity', a notion so clearly non-Buddhist that discussion of it does not even occur); this lapse, for Nagarjuna, deprives them of "the full weight" of Buddha's own teaching. In Nagarjuna's words, "No *dharma* anywhere has been taught by the Buddha of anything" (MK XXV: 24 S). The problem arises because Abhidharmic and some other Buddhist groups treat *dharmas* as self-identical (though not analogous to molecules, of course: language/behavior constructs[99] what *dharma*-language recognizes as *dharmas,* so there is no Western 'subjectivity' and 'objectivity' as such[100]). A further consequence is that these schools become entrammeled in a logocentric theory of causality. As Streng puts it, phenomena arise or "become actual through the interaction of a vast complex of factors (i.e., *dharmas*) which could be identified as having characteristic features intrinsic to themselves. Nagarjuna accepted the notion that existence was a composite of interdependent relations, but extended the dynamics of the dependent co-origination notion to the causal process itself. For him, 'radical becoming' did not allow for a self-existent causal principle—as might be inferred from the earlier [i.e., Abhidharmic] explanation."[101]

In our illustration of Nagarjuna's use of the *dédoublement* argument, we shall limit ourselves to a more detailed study of its deployment against the thesis of self-identity. *Svabhāva,* i.e., 'own-nature' (often represented too by terms such as 'self-existence' or 'self-nature'), converts to the concept of self-identity because *to have identity,* in the Indian tradition, is *to be self-caused.* Self-cause, in other words, is a reflexive activity whereby the self 'causes' itself. Rendered in Derridean terms, this encapsulating dyad comprises two moments, the self as 'cause' (generator, or signified) and the self as its own 'effect' (mirror, or signifier). However, Nagarjuna in the *Mūlamadhyamakakārikās* attacks not only 'own-nature,' but all *svabhāvic* notions of causality, i.e., all notions of causality which would allow a unilateral entitative[102] *transfer,* or even connection, or any of the other dialectical transformations of entitative cause: "At nowhere and at no time can entities ever exist by originating out of themselves, from others, from both (self-other), or from the lack of causes" (MK I: 1 IN). And in MK I: 10, 11, he says, "Since existing things which have no self-existence are not real, / It is not possible at all that: 'This thing *becomes* upon the existence of that other one'; The product does not reside in the conditioning cause, individually or collectively, / So how can that which does not reside in the conditioning cause result from conditioning causes?"[103] As Sprung states, "In the middle way there are no [logocentric] causes or effects, actions or consequences, before and after."[104]

In chapter I of the *Middle Stanzas,* Nagarjuna first brings the argument from *dédoublement* specifically to bear on self-causality. The employ of *dédoublement* to entrap adversaries in dilemma, and then the dialectical playing out of whatever first lemma has been shown self-contradictory, until the whole tetralemma which has been "set in motion" exhausts itself, together forms a logical sequence that Nagarjuna uses throughout the twenty-seven chapters. The crucial dilemma of the first chapter is summed up in the sixth stanza:

> Neither non-Ens nor Ens
> Can have a cause.
> If non-Ens, whose the cause?
> If Ens, what for the cause?
>
> (MK I:6 STCH)

If an Ens ('entity', understood as *any* formulaic dyad, even Abhidharmic *dharmas*) exists by way of self-origination, the effect (the Ens, or entity) is its own cause, is itself the cause. So what is the cause for? Why postulate a cause, ". . . what for the cause?" We have the familiar Derridean figure of the effect (the "signifier" in Derrida) necessarily functioning as a cause, so the alleged cause is absolutely (totally) caused—and thus *dédoublé*, "split," or better, "torn inside out." Another example of the same argumentative formation appears in chapter XVII, which analyzes *karman,* the law of causal action:

> If *karman* is a fixed thing (i.e., enduring) because of its self-nature, then a maturity that is already matured will again seek maturity. (MK XVII: 25 IN)

If *karman* is self-caused, the effect is the cause, and conversely the cause is already the effect. Why should "a maturity that is already matured" have to "again reach maturity"? Indeed, after playing out the whole tetralemma, Nagarjuna reveals the conclusion, that the concepts of "action" and "effect" and their concatenated notions, are fallacious:

> Defilements, *karmans,* bodily entities, doers and effects are all similar to the nature of an imaginary city in the sky, a mirage, and a dream. (MK XVII: 33 IN)

And what about the second lemma of chapter I, verse 6: "If non-Ens, whose the cause?" The argument here, in other words, asks: "If there is no entity at all (i.e., no 'effect'), what's the use of postulating a cause of any kind? What is the cause for?" The other option, of course, is to propose an "other-caused" thing (as the contrary of "self-caused"), and such a proposal necessarily involves as well the proposal of "a thing which causes 'other-caused' things." Nagarjuna's most detailed treatment of *parabhāva* occurs in chapter XV, and Inada defines *parabhāva* as follows: "*Parabhāva*, in the sense of extended nature, means that an entity has an existential character of extending or reaching over into the nature of other entities. It also means other-nature in contrast to self-nature. However, the argument obtains regardless of the translation."[105] Nagarjuna's book XV, verse 3, reads:

> Where self-nature is non-existent, how could there be an extended
> nature [*parabhāva*]? For, indeed, a self-nature which has the nature of
> being extended will be called an extended nature. (MK XV: 3 IN)

When *parabhāva* means "a thing which causes 'other-caused' things"
(it extends and reaches "over into the nature of other entities"), the
following argument unfolds: If all things are "causes," we never get
to things that are effects. So why use the conceptual model of cause
and effect at all? When *parabhāva* means "other-nature," i.e., the "effect of another thing which is its cause," the argument unfolds: If all
things are effects, we never get to things that are causes. We are
involved in infinite retreat (like Derrida's 'slide of endless
metaphoricity') where each alleged "cause" is not a cause, but the
vehicle of a metaphor, and therefore an effect of still some other
cause which turns out to be a vehicle (effect). (Of course, Derrida
must also put the whole theory of metaphor *sous rature*, and the
"floating signifier" *sous rature*; Nagarjuna will do the same with the
conclusion of "effects only."[106]) Nagarjuna advances to a general attack on the entitative theory of existence (*bhāva*):

> Again, separated from self-nature [self-caused thing] and extended
> nature [either a thing which causes, or a thing that is other-caused],
> how could existence [*bhāva*] be? For, indeed, existence establishes it-
> self in virtue of either self-nature or extended nature. (MK XV: 4
> IN)

In several subsequent stanzas Nagarjuna performs upon entitative
theory just the logical maneuver so characteristic of Derrida. Just as
Derrida argues that nihilism dialectically "buys into" the model of
logocentrism, of presence, Nagarjuna argues that to affirm non-
existence is to affirm the model of existence:

> If existence does not come to be (i.e., does not establish itself), then
> certainly non-existence does not also. For, indeed, people speak of
> existence in its varying nature as non-existence.

> Those who see (i.e., try to understand) the concepts of self-nature,
> extended nature, existence, or non-existence do not perceive the real
> truth in the Buddha's teaching.

> According to the Instructions to Katyayana, the two views of the
> world in terms of being and non-being were criticized by the Buddha
> for similarly admitting the bifurcation of entities into existence and
> non-existence.

> Existence is the grasping of permanency (i.e., permanent char-
> acteristics) and non-existence the perception of disruption. (As these
> functions are not strictly possible), the wise man should not rely upon
> (the concepts of) existence and non-existence. (MK XV: 5– 7, 10 IN)

We return again to the specific argument in chapter I, which asks of
the first lemma, "If Ens, what for the cause?" If we struggle to retain
the binary model posited by "self-originating" thing, the factor
("originating" element, or "cause") and mirror ("self," or "effect")
must be, both of them, causes; or, both of them, effects. We have

either two causes or two effects. Either way, the consequence is infinite regression.

In this whole question of identity and its affiliation with theories of cause, we have seen how Nagarjuna negates the first and second lemmas. His treatment of causality, when causality appears in the form of the third lemma ("the entitative thing is both self-caused and not self-caused"[107]), is very intriguing and receives an expansive exegesis from Candrakirti, who writes in the seventh century. Nagarjuna had argued successfully that if an entity is self-originating, the effect of the operative causality is either the same as the cause or different from the cause. If it be the same, there is an absurd sort of duplicating, and no justification for self-origination; if it be different, there are two entities rather than one, and no justification for self-origination. But yet another formula, cast in the third lemma (with the predicate of the third lemma undistributed in this case), seemed at first glance to avoid the Nagarjunist assault. The formula asserted a "difference in sameness," analogous to some Western theories of potency and act. Just as mango seed gives rise to a mango tree (the mango-ness is the *"same"* in seed and tree, but clearly the tree is *different* from the seed), so in the "self-originating" thing the "originating factor" (cause) and the "self" (effect) are *different,* but share the *same* substance.[18] Or, in more apposite examples, the jar is different from its clay constituents, but both jar and clay share the same substance; the cloth is different from its component threads, but both share the same substance. Nagarjuna's response is to argue that theory of potency and act results in perpetual regress. If the substance of cloth is in the thread, but cloth still differs from thread, the thread is composed of "clothness" and "other-than-clothness." But what is the cause of the thread? This second cause must be composed of "clothness" and "other-than-clothness," plus "other-than-'clothness' and 'other-than-clothness.'" And so on, perpetually. At each stop along the perpetual slide, there is never an entitative thing which suits the third lemma: that is, there is never an entitative thing which is partly self-originating and partly not self-originating. The entitative thing is always totally not self-originating. Nagarjuna puts it this way in his chapter I, verse 13:

> The result a cause-possessor,
> But causes not even self-possessors.
> How can result be cause-possessor,
> If of non-self-possessors, it be a result?

> (MK I; 13 STCH)

Candrakirti's exegesis is very helpful:

> You [the adversary] maintain that there is a possessive relation between a result and its causes, i.e., that the result is simply a modification of its causes. This is wrong, because these supposed causes do not possess their own selves, i.e., they are no real causes.
> It is asserted that a piece of cloth consists of threads. The cloth

then could be a reality if the threads themselves had ultimate reality. But they consist of parts. They are themselves modifications of their own parts, they are no ultimate realities. Therefore, what is the use of maintaining that the result designated as a cloth consists of threads, when these threads themselves are no ultimate realities, they are not "self-possessors." This has been expressed in the following aphorism,

> "Cloth is existent in its threads,
> The threads again in something else.
> How can these threads, unreal themselves,
> Produce reality in something else?"[109]

Candrakirti and Nagarjuna are here demonstrating, in other words, that a theory of logocentric cause, logically pursued, leads necessarily to a notion of pure effect ("result," in the Stcherbatsky rendering). Translated into Derrida's terminology, Candrakirti and Nagarjuna are arguing for "pure signifier" (recall again that in more conventional Indian self-origination, identity is a binary combination of spontaneous cause and its effect; identity as defined by Derrida is a binary combination of signified [cause] and signifier [effect]). But then, just as Derrida is constrained by logic to put "pure signifier" under erasure, Nagarjuna must submit "pure effect" to erasure. For if there be no causes, after all, how can there be effects? Thus Nagarjuna concludes in chapter I, verse 14: "There is, therefore, no cause-possessor, / Nor is there a result without a cause [i.e., there is no 'result' since 'cause' is lacking]" (MK I: 14 STCH). As for non-causes, Nagarjuna dispatches them dialectically: "Nor causes are there, nor non-causes, / If altogether no results" (Ibid.). And Candrakirti's gloss reads:

> Therefore there is no cause-possessing result. Then perhaps there may be a result without causes? No, there is no result outside its material cause. If the reality of a piece of cloth is not sufficiently explained by the reality of its component parts the threads, this does not mean that it will be explained any better by the reality of the straw of which mats are made.[110]

The above argumentative formation, however, does not depend on *dédoublement,* so to achieve further exemplification of the latter we turn to Nagarjuna's treatment, in chapter IV, of *rūpa* (material form), the first of the five *skandhas* (*skandhas* are the five constituents of being[111]). Since each of the five *skandhas* was conventionally understood to be self-identical, or *svabhāvic,* Nagarjuna's motive here is to deconstruct precisely the notion of self-identity, and he uses his assault upon *rūpa* as paradigmatic for deconstruction of the other *skandhas.* The case in point is such that Nagarjuna's deconstructive technique can be quite simple. Inada sums up the crucial verse this way: ". . . the Four Great Elements [Earth, Water, Fire, and Wind— the four concomitant causes of material form] cannot be thought of in the absence of *rūpa.*"[112] The conventional notion of causality regarded the four elements as efficient causes of material form, so it follows that Nagarjuna says in verse 5, "Again, material form without a cause definitely is untenable." But the reversal, compression, and collapse forced by *dédoublement* occurs in verse 3:

> Granted that separated from material form an efficient cause of form exists, then there will be a cause without an effect. But a cause without an effect (in reality) does not exist. (MK IV: 3, IN)

That is, to be consistent with the model of logocentric causality, we must maintain that the effect (here, material form) is actually a cause, co-equal with the Four Elements as cause; and if we are to imagine, for pedagogical purposes, a dramatizing of this logical scenario, we see the supposed effect transformed into cause, and the self-identical dyad imploding. Nagarjuna goes on to remind us, as he so often does, that his deconstruction is intended only to dissolve entitative theory: "Therefore, any material form [since *rūpa* is an entitative formulation] which has been thought of (i.e., become a concept) should not (become the basis of) further conceptualization" (MK IV: 5 IN).

The other argument we have come to associate with Derrida, and is deployed frequently by Nagarjuna, is *effacement,* or "pure negative reference." The example out of Nagarjuna I have chosen for analysis involves his treatment of temporality (MK XIX). Let us first recall Derrida's deconstruction of Husserlian theory of time. Husserl's theory of the present, you will remember, recognized that there could be no "present" unless it were compounded of three present moments: (1) the immediately perceived present, (2) the past as present (a "modified" present), and (3) the future as present (another kind of "modified" present). Derrida deconstructs this compounded present by arguing, you will recall, that "past" and "future" can *only* be distinguished from "immediately perceived present" by purely negative reference: "past" and "future" can only relate to "present" if past and future are *not* present (i.e., *not* sharing the same "time" nor the same "space"). The mediating status of Husserl's "modified present" is treated as a ruse, in other words, and reduced to the stark alternatives of pure negation or no negation (pure difference or no difference, with "no difference" meaning the same as "identity"). Nagarjuna's attack is upon an entitative theory of time which, in its basic assumptions, is similar to the Husserlian formula. Nagarjuna's adversary recognizes that, to be consistent with the rest of the entitative system, one can only assert any one of the three "times" ("moments") in relation to the other two. Thus the "present" time is only viable in relation to the past and future (see MK XIX: 4 IN, and Inada's note, p. 118), and the "past" time only in relation to the present and future. Nagarjuna chooses to treat a deconstruction of past time as paradigmatic for the other two temporal deconstructions (of present and future respectively) and proceeds as follows. If, Nagarjuna declares, the present and future co-exist with the past (as

Husserl's modified past and future co-exist with the immediate present), present and future should be the past:

> If, indeed, the present and future are contingently related to the past, they should exist in the past moment. (MK XIX: 1 IN)

But the theory of time of course does not permit them to be identical with the past, or they could not be "present" and "future." Yet the same theory also holds that relation among past, present, and future is necessary, since without relation the three "times" lose their self-identities as "times" and instead become chaos (and the "continuity" necessary for temporal theory likewise collapses). Thus Nagarjuna reminds his logocentric adversary that "relation" is necessitated: "Again, it is not possible for both (present and future) to establish themselves without being contingent on past" (MK XIX: 3 IN). And here Nagarjuna inserts the notion of purely negative reference which is of such interest to us, and so pivotal to his whole dialectic. If there is a relation, it must be a *purely* negative relation; and concomitantly, only *pure* identity can follow from no-relation. (There is no assent on Nagarjuna's part to "mediating" status of some kind, so an entity is partly the same and partly different. Mediation, a version of the third lemma, is always reduced—as we saw in the analysis of potency and act—to a dilemma composed of the first two lemmas.) Therefore Nagarjuna can argue that if the present and future *relate* to the past, as the adversary has just granted (and present and future are not the past, as he has just granted), then it must follow that past and future are absolutely *not* the past: "If, again, the present and future do not exist (i.e., in the past), how could they be contingently related?" (MK XIX: 2 IN). And if they are absolutely *not* the past, their self-identity (as well as the self-identity of the "past") dissolves: "Therefore, there is no justification for the existence of a present and a future time" (MK XIX: 3 IN). Or, as Nagarjuna puts it in book XXI, "Consequently, the continuity of being is not possible within the three temporal moments. As it does not exist within the three temporal moments, in what manner does it exist?" (MK XXI: 21 IN).[113]

We can now turn to *śūnyatā*, or devoidness, as Nagarjuna uncovers it. In chapter XXIV Nagarjuna first offers, premise by premise, the argument of his adversary against *śūnyatā* (and it is clear that the adversary understands *śūnyatā* to mean "voidness"—the absence of dharma-entities and the absence of entitative causality, with the latter taken as the necessary process whereby "production" and "destruction" occur):

> If everything is *śūnya*, there will be neither production nor destruction. According to your assertion it will follow that the Aryan Fourfold Truths are non-existent. (MK XXIV: 1 IN)

Buddha's Fourfold Truths are (1) that everyday life, for those who do not have true-realization, is unregenerate (*Duḥkha*); (2) that unregenerate life is dependent on craving (*Taṇhā*); (3) that unregeneracy ceases when craving ceases; and (4) that craving ceases when one follows the path (*mārga*) of Buddhist discipline.[114] Nagarjuna's adversary maintains, in other words, that Buddha's theory of craving, cessation of craving, and so on, necessarily implies an entitative theory of causality. When Nagarjuna asserts *śūnyatā*, he rejects causality and thus renounces the keystone of Buddha's teaching. Like the proverbial row of dominos in full collapse, the whole length of Buddhist teaching comes tumbling down: the "eight aspirations" (these issue from Buddhist discipline), the "three treasures" (the Teaching, the Monastic Life, and the Buddha, which together found Buddhist life), and so on, are by definition preempted (see MK XXIV: 2–6). In sum, the adversary maintains that Nagarjunist *śūnyatā* forces one to be a heretic: "If the eight aspirations of men do not exist, there will be no *Saṃgha* (i.e., the Buddhist order). From the non-existence of the Aryan Truths, the true *Dharma* [here meaning the Teaching, "True Doctrine"] also does not exist" (verse 4); and "Without *Dharma* and *Saṃgha*, how could there be *Buddha*? Consequently, what you assert also destroys the Three Treasures" (verse 5, all from Inada translation). Indeed, Nagarjunist *śūnyatā*, it is charged, preempts all activity, religious or secular: "Delving in *śūnyatā*, you will destroy the reality of the fruit or attainment, the proper and improper acts, and all the everyday practices relative to the empirical world" (verse 6 IN).

Nagarjuna's immediate response is no less severe; he says his opponent is missing the point completely:

> Let us interrupt here to point out that you do not know the real purpose of *śūnyatā*, its nature and meaning. Therefore, there is only frustration and hindrance (of understanding). (MK XXIV: 7 IN)

After a very important sequence on the doctrine of Two Truths, a sequence which we shall treat in a moment, Nagarjuna presents his own case (beginning with MK XXIV: 16). His argument, when fully deployed, can be mapped out as follows. First, he affirms that what we can call 'happenings' really occur and that these happenings everywhere show forth *dependency*[115] (this is the most Buddha says about dependent co-arising, *pratītya samutpāda*, Nagarjuna would insist: Buddha does not affirm a theory of entitative causality, not even for second-order *dharma* entities[116]). Nagarjuna continues, this time posing a question. If we agree, hypothetically, to regard happenings from the "standpoint of self-nature," i.e., from what Derrida would call a logocentric standpoint, what logically follows? The only logical conclusion, Nagarjuna answers in turn, is that the theory of self-nature, of self-origination or entitativeness, itself destroys itself! For if one affirms an everywhere-manifested dependency (as both Nagarjuna and his opponent do), and if one identifies dependency and causality, then one cannot also affirm entitativeness (remember that Nagarjuna has already shown as absurd an entitative causality whereby entitativeness occurs by transfer or positive connection). And vice versa, if one affirms self-origination, or entities ("true beings," including second-order *dharma* entities) of any kind, one cannot also affirm dependency (Nagarjuna has already shown that entitativeness absolutely precludes dependency):

> If you perceive the various existences as true beings from the standpoint of self-nature, then you will perceive them as non-causal conditions. (MK XXIV: 16 IN)

Then, adds Nagarjuna, the very values the opponent hoped to preserve necessarily go "down the drain":

> You will then destroy (all notions of) cause, effect, doer, means of doing, doing, origination, extinction, and fruit (of action). (MK XXIV: 17 IN)

Nagarjuna can so argue because, as we have already seen, he has already shown that a carefully reasoned logocentrism leads to pure negative reference. One must conclude, then, that all happenings, being utterly dependent, must be empty (*śūnya*) of self-nature and empty of entitative transfer or continuance. Nagarjuna's adversary, in displaying dependent co-arising as a keystone of Buddhist thought, has thereby vitiated rather than proven entitative existence.

Nagarjuna continues, and does so in a way which permits us a restatement of the question. The very logic of the logocentric standpoint, provisionally adopted, has brought forth as one of its conclusions that happenings are purely *not* self-caused. Within this logocentric frame, then, they are *totally* other-caused, or "pure effects"; or they are "not-caused," and thus *not* "effects" at all. But these "second lemma" options (remember again that the third lemma option reduces here to the first two lemmas[117]) logic compels us in turn to put "under erasure" (as we saw earlier). In any case, among the most interesting parallels with Derridean practice here is that Nagarjuna declares 'happenings' *empty* (as Derrida declares so-called 'things' *empty*) exactly because of pure negative reference: happenings are empty (*śūnya*), for Nagarjuna, because they are just signifiers (as entirely "dependent," they point entirely to what they are not—they are entirely *not* self-caused).

Nagarjuna goes on, however, to prefigure Derrida still more. For the erased contraries of "self-caused (*viz.*, totally other-caused and totally non-caused)," and the basal formulation itself, namely, "happenings are not self-caused," Nagarjuna regards as *approximations* which let the "glimmer" shine (the approximations are, in other words, what I call Derridean diascript). Happenings are not caused but are still dependent because "dependent co-arising" (*pratītya samutpāda*) *acts* in such wise that the question of entitative causality is irrelevant. (See pp. 16–18 of Inada, where he at length explains "dependent co-arising" is neither entitative causality nor relativity, neither presence nor void.) The *action* which is dependent co-arising, and which comes within the range of pure negative reference *sous rature*, Nagarjuna calls *śūnyatā:*

> We declare that whatever is relational origination [dependent co-arising] is *śūnyatā*. It [*śūnyatā*] is a provisional name (i.e., thought construction) for the mutuality (of being) [dependent co-arising] and, indeed, it is the middle path. (MK XXIV: 18 IN)

Notice that even the name and concept of *śūnyatā* are "provisional," i.e., "crossed-out." *Śūnyatā*, like Derridean *différance*, should not be hypostatized and cannot be framed by ratiocination. Remark as well that *śūnyatā* is the "middle path." Clearly, Nagarjuna means *middle* in the sense of the Derridean *between*, tracking its 'and/or' [absolute constitution and absolute negation] *between* the conventional 'and/or' proposed by entitative theory. *Śūnyatā* is not voidness but devoidness:

> Whatever is in correspondence with *śūnyatā*, all is in correspondence (i.e., possible). Again, whatever is not in correspondence with *śūnyatā*, all is not in correspondence. (MK XXIV: 14 IN) [Inada adds the note: "The meaning conveyed here is that *śūnyatā* is the basis of all existence. Thus, without it, nothing is possible" p. 147.]

As long as one understands that *śūnyatā* always "works," i.e., always is the process of happenings (always is "in correspondence with" happenings), Streng's translation of the same stanza is perhaps more helpful:

> When emptiness (*śūnyatā*) "works," then everything in existence "works." If emptiness does *not* "work," then all existence does *not* "work." (XXIV: 14 S)

Nagarjuna's language, and more so that of his translators, strain to represent a process of ongoing, ever-altering dependency. And this slide of pure dependency which is forever without originating cause is *śūnyatā*. Nagarjuna gives us the wherewithal to supplement our off/cognition of "slide" in chapter XXII, where he tells us:

> The *Tathāgata* is not the (aggregation of the) *skandhas* nor is he different from the *skandhas*. He is not in the *skandhas* nor are the *skandhas* in him. As he cannot possess the *skandhas*, what actually is he? (MK XXII: 1 IN)

The Tathagata, as Inada explains, is the Buddha, the Buddha as "the foremost enlightened state,"[118] that is to say, the Buddha as "this worldly existence" (the "enlightened state" *is* "this worldly existence," *is* the 'slide of pure dependency'):

> The *Tathāgata*'s nature of self-existence is also the nature of this worldly existence. The *Tathāgata* (strictly speaking) is without the nature of self-existence and this worldly existence is likewise so. (MK: XXII: 16 IN)

Any attempt to distribute the above 'description' in terms of an 'enlightened' individual on the one hand, knowing a "this worldly existence" on the other, misses the point. True-realization, for

Nagarjuna, is the art of dissolving the *Gestalt* of self-origination, so self-identity melts into the 'slide'.

Nagarjuna's further attempts in chapter XXV to evoke for his interlocutor a surmise of realization give us the chance to display again the trail of erasure and of diascript. What is more, having already shown typical Nagarjunist use of the first three lemmas, we can now exemplify his appointment of the fourth lemma. In what is perhaps his most dazzling technical maneuver, Nagarjuna—at choice moments—climbs the ladder of the three forms, and then affirms the fourth form as provisionally true, only to cross it out but still regard it as precious palimpsest. Chapter XXV treats *nirvāṇa*, i.e., the "mode of bliss," and the relation of *nirvāṇa* to logocentric formulae. In stanzas 4, 5, and 6, Nagarjuna examines the pertinent first lemma, that *nirvāṇa* is accommodated by the concept of self-existence, and he disproves this assertion (see Inada, p. 158). In stanzas 7 and 8, he examines the second lemma, that *nirvāṇa* is accommodated by the concept of non-existence, and he dispels this assertion too (see Inada, p. 155). Verses 11 through 13 argue against the third lemma, that *nirvāṇa* is suited by the mediating concept of "both existence and nonexistence"; and stanza 14 proffers the conclusion here:

> How could *nirvāṇa* be (in the realm of) both existence and non-existence? Both cannot be together in one place just as the situation is with light and darkness. (MK XXV: 14 IN)[119]

As is his wont, Nagarjuna places the fourth lemma (which formally follows the third lemma) in the rhetorically most effective position: since, according to this usage, it is provisionally true, it appears in stanza 10 and is provisionally affirmed:

> The teacher (Buddha) has taught the abandonment of the concepts of being and non-being. Therefore, *nirvāṇa* is properly neither (in the realm of) existence nor non-existence. (MK XXV: 10 IN)

Indeed, the incremental force of the arguments has driven towards this conclusion, the fourth lemma assertion par excellence. Then, (just as Derrida puts a strike through the fourth lemma rejection of matter and form, so even the formula "neither matter nor non-matter" is crossed-out), Nagarjuna crosses-out the fourth lemma rejection of existence/non-existence:

> The proposition that *nirvāṇa* is neither existence nor non-existence could only be valid if and when the realms of existence and non-existence are established.

> If indeed *nirvāṇa* is asserted to be neither existence nor non-existence, then by what means are the assertions to be known? (MK XXV: 15, 16 IN)

Nagarjuna has come the length / through the length of the incremental ladder: true *nirvāṇa* 'glimmers' from beneath the fourth lemma *sous rature*.

When relating *śūnyatā* to logocentric formulae, Nagarjuna wields the same tactic again: he climbs the tetralemmatic ladder through several chapters so as to build momentum towards the conclusion, *śūnyatā* neither exists nor non-exists. Though the fourth lemma statement permits diascript, it has to come under erasure:

> One may not say there is "emptiness" (*śūnya*) nor that there is "non-emptiness." Nor that both (exist simultaneously), nor that neither exists; the purpose for saying ("emptiness") is for the purpose of conveying knowledge. [In Inada's translation, the last phrase reads, "for the purpose of provisional understanding."] (MK XXII: 11 S)

Borrowing from the linguists and language philosophers, perhaps if we redeploy the above problematic in terms of 'orders of discourse' (and of abstraction), the role of Nagarjunist diascript can become clearer. Douglas Daye provides the following description of the metalanguages involved:

> There are at least four orders of description and abstraction operative in the *Mūla-Mādhyamika Kārikās*. First, there is the ordinary language abstraction level of 'things' in the world., e.g., trees, stones, and properties of relationships such as hate, anger, and love. Second, there are rival metaphysical and epistemological theories which utilize such generic terms as Abhidharmic *dharmas, prakṛti*, etc., which the *Mūla-Mādhyamika Kārikās* holds are incorrect and inherently contradictory. The general word (in the text) for such generic terms is own-being (*svabhāva*). These rival metaphysical and epistemological theories are the objects of the polemics in the *Mūla-Mādhyamika Kārikās*. Third, there is the third-order capstone *reflexive* concept of emptiness (*śūnyatā*). Everything is empty, including 'emptiness' itself. Fourth, there are certain implicit prescriptive relationships which involve a fourth order abstraction level, the concept of language-constructs (*prajñapti*).[120]

This is to say, in Nagarjuna there is a first-order language, and three meta-orders each of which deconstructs the preceding order. First, there are descriptors which are keyed to the entitative way in which life is "ordinarily" experienced. Second, there are descriptors which operate in terms of *dharmas* (i.e., epistemic[121] and descriptive components of an alternative map of experience: they are designed to preclude "naming" in terms of "things"[122]). Third, upon the logical demonstration that even *dharma*-theory contradicts itself and falls into "own-nature," there is the third-order meta-concept that all is *śūnyatā*; and that even *śūnyatā* is *śūnya*, or "empty." And fourth (the meta-meta-meta-concept, if I may be permitted this prefixal flourish), there is the (a) erasure and (b) diascript which characterize the working of fourth-order *prajñapti*. Erasure is involved because even third-order emptiness should be regarded as a clue which must be crossed-out. But diascript is also involved because third-order emptiness, as *prajñapti*, is "for the purpose of *conveying knowledge*" (is "for the purpose of provisional *understanding*" [see MK XXII: 11, above[123]].) To rephrase more succinctly still, third-order emptiness is "provisional" (and thus must be crossed-out) but "conveys [differential] knowledge," "understanding" (and thus comports enlightenment from beneath the erasure).

To the extent that several of the stanzas cited above involve non-originative "this worldly existence" and the mode of the Tathagata *as* "this worldly existence," they naturally lead us to the Buddhist Two Truths, and the Nagarjunist treatment thereof. Before undertaking comment on this critical topic, though, I wish to show how Nagarjuna "winds down" his defense in chapter XXIV. Recall that the opponent has charged *śūnyatā* nullifies the Buddha's teaching. And Nagarjuna responds by arguing that only *śūnyatā* can account for "dependent co-arising," the doctrinal core of the Buddha's teaching. Nagarjuna winds down his rebuttal in chapter XXIV by turning the tables on the opponent:

> Any factor of existence which does not participate in relational origination [dependent co-arising] cannot exist. Therefore, any factor of experience not in the nature of *śūnya* cannot exist.
>
> If everything were of the nature of non-*śūnya*, then there would be neither production nor destruction. Then also the non-existence of the Aryan Fourfold Truths would accordingly follow. (19, 20 IN)

In short, it is the opponent's standpoint which preempts the Buddha's values! Stanzas 20 through 39 apply the key argument, that entitative causality contradicts *pratītya samutpāda*, to the whole sequence of Buddhist teaching: without Nagarjunist *śūnyatā*, there can be no craving, no cessation of craving, no disciplined path, no Three Treasures. Perhaps stanza 36 phrases the problem best:

> You will thus destroy all the everyday practices relevant to the empirical world because you will have destroyed the *śūnyatā* of relational origination [dependent co-arising]. (36 IN).

Nagarjuna does not want to destroy the "everyday practices relevant to the empirical world" (just as Derrida does not want to stop the knock at the door, the decision, the opening of the door, and so on). Nagarjuna and Derrida are not absurdists. So on, now, to the problematic of the Two Truths.

The Buddhist doctrine of the Two Truths, simply phrased, is this: "Happenings" can be regarded in a "gathered" (*samvṛti*) and "ungathered" (*paramārtha*) way. *Samvṛti* is variously understood to mean "conventional," "empirical," "worldly," "expressional"; *paramārtha* variously understood to mean "transcendental," "ultimate," "absolute."[124] Nagarjuna shatters previous Buddhist interpretations of the Two Truths, interpretations he considers dualistic, or monist in a self-identical way, by proclaiming:

> The limits (i.e., realm) of *nirvāṇa* are the limits of *samsāra*. Between the two, also, there is not the slightest difference whatsoever. (MK XXV: 20 IN)

And this stanza should be glossed by the following sequence, from the "Examination of the Four-fold Noble Truth" (chapter XXIV), which we promised earlier to treat here:

> The teaching of the *Dharma* [here meaning Buddhist Truth] by the various Buddhas is based on the two truths; namely, the world-ensconced truth and the truth which is the highest sense.
>
> Those who do not know the distribution of the two kinds of truth do not know the profound point in the teaching of the Buddha.
>
> The highest sense (of the truth) is not taught apart from practical behavior, and without having understood the highest sense one cannot understand *nirvāṇa*.
>
> Emptiness, having been dimly perceived, utterly destroys the slow-witted person. It is like a snake wrongly grasped or knowledge incorrectly applied. (MK XXIV: 8–11 S)

Streng explains the above sequence:

> What then does Nagarjuna mean when he says there are two kinds of truth: the world-ensconced [I prefer the Sanscrit term to be rendered "gathered"] and the Ultimate ["ungathered"] Truth? It appears clear from MK XXIV and elsewhere that the world-ensconced truth refers to the practical understanding which is required to live. There is a practical value in regarding tables and chairs as 'things' (which do not disintegrate because from an ultimate viewpoint they are considered to be empty of self-existence). It also means affirming general and broad distinctions between good and bad, real and illusory, and full and empty as practical distinctions. To say 'Gold is the same as dirt' is false in the context of practical truth. *Each of the two kinds of truth are valid when correctly applied;* and wisdom is insight into the nature of things [happenings] whereby the proper means for knowing the truth is used in a given situation.[125]

Streng's remarks on the Nagarjunist version of the two truths can be augmented by those of Bimal Krishna Matilal,[126] who involves in his discussion the arguments ranged against Nagarjunism by adversaries we can call 'realists', and other adversaries who can be identified as 'pluralists' (indeed, almost as 'pluralists' in the 'Taoist' sense of the late-phase Heidegger, as our study uses this term). Matilal begins by developing the third of Candrakirti's three interpretations of Nagarjunist *samvṛti*, namely, the 'gathered' understood as "worldly behavior or speech behavior involving designation and designatum, cognition and cognitum" (in other words, Matilal and Candrakirti begin with signifier and signified, just as Derrida does). After an account of *paramārtha* and *samvṛti* in onto-psychological terms (so that *samvṛti* is the logocentric 'objectification' or gathering of the co-arising which, as ungathered, is *paramārtha*[127]), Matilal refers to Nagarjunism's Hindu opponent, Kumarila:

> This doctrine of 'two truths' can, however, be criticized on obvious grounds. One may be rather suspicious of this bifurcation of truths

into two levels. Kumarila, for example, has argued that it is difficult
to see how truth can be of one kind at the conventional level ('empirical' plane) and totally different in the ultimate ('metempirical')
plane. . . . [Kumarila argues] that Truth cannot be of two types. If
something, say the causal law, is held to be true at the 'concealing'
level, it can mean *either* (i) that the causal law is actually unreal, *or* (ii)
that the causal law *conceals* the actual state of affairs, i.e., the ultimate
truth. The Madhyamika [Nagarjunist, here] position is not equal to
that of the Lokayata Carvaka who should probably categorically
assert that the causal law is *unreal*. The Madhyamika would rather
accept the second alternative and maintain the *reality*[128] of the causal
law at the conventional level only. Kumarila claims that this is a kind
of philosophical 'double-talk'. He argues that reality at the 'concealing' level is, in fact, indistinguishable from unreality. Unreality of
everything at the 'concealing' level can be maintained only if we are
clear about what truth is like at the ultimate level, which is supposed
to be concealed by the 'concealing' level. But, as we have already
noted, short of some mystical intuition (cf. *aparapratyaya* [differential
mysticism, in our terms]), this ultimate truth or *tattva* cannot be
comprehended.

Matilal goes on to present the Nagarjunist response, which begins
not by recourse to differential realization but by a deconstruction of
'realism' itself:

The Madhyamika may reply that this [Kumarila's attack] is not a fair
criticism of his philosophic motivation. He [the Madhyamikan] con-
tends that cause and effect are only concepts which are hypostatized
by the objectificatory bias ["bent"] of human understanding. But if
we assume these concepts to be metaphysically (ultimately) real [as
the 'realists' do], we face logical antinomies or other absurdities. It is
just because of this difficulty, i.e., just because of the predicament
that we get into when we take our working hypotheses to be true and
final, that the Madhyamika wants to leap to the ultimate level and
rules that from the ultimate point of view cause and effect are *empty*
concepts.

For the Madhyamika, all phenomena (i.e., all 'entities', since entities
'gather' by way of 'objectification') are "indeterminable"—they cannot exist in their own right. Matilal thus develops next the notion of
Madhyamikan "indeterminacy":

A phenomenon is, in some sense, a perceived fact and thus it cannot
be regarded as a *mere* fiction in the sense that the son of a barren
woman would be regarded as fiction. It is, therefore, conceded that
the phenomenal world has a provisional existence. In fact, if the
phenomenal world were a non-entity [i.e., if it did not function in an
'entitative' way when 'gathered'], all practical activities would have
been impossible, and even ethical and spiritual disciplines would lose
their significance. Thus, it is asserted that this world of phenomena
[when regarded from the differential attitude] is neither real nor unreal, but logically indeterminable and unjustifiable. This indeterminacy of the phenomenal world is called, in the language of Nagar-

juna, 'the character of dependent origination of everything' or 'the *śūnyatā* (emptiness) of everything'. Here we are actually faced with an apparent contradiction that is very interesting. Each phenomenon is logically indeterminable; it can neither be said to exist, nor not to exist, nor both, nor neither. When these four alternatives are thus denied, the phenomenon becomes indeterminate, or *śūnya* ('empty') . . . i.e., devoid of any absolute value (cf. 'zero'). . . . In fact, the ultimate [the 'ungathered'] is the *śūnyatā* (emptiness, indeterminableness) of everything, every phenomenon. . . . The Absolute ['ungathered'] and the Phenomenal ['gathered'] are not different. This world, when it is understood with reference to causal conditions and plurality, is called the Phenomenal or the 'concealing' [*saṃvṛti,* our 'logocentric'] one. But, when it is understood without reference to such causal conditions and plurality, it is called *Nirvāna,* the Ultimate [the 'differential']. . . . Thus, we see that there is a sense in which it will be unfair to criticize the Madhyamika on the ground that he bifurcates truth into two levels. Phenomenon is the 'concealing' form of the ultimate, but it is not actually different from the ultimate. It thus needs to be emphasized, even at the risk of repetition, that the doctrine of emptiness does not actually consist in the rejection of the phenomenal world, but in the maintenance of a non-commital attitude toward the phenomena and in the nonacceptance of any theory of the phenomenal world as *finally* valid [i.e., as 'resting in itself'].

Matlal concludes his study of the Madhyamika's Two Truths by representing the Madhyamika in contrast with the Jainist position (which is loosely analogous to pluralism and to our part 2's redaction of late-phase Heideggerianism), and in contrast with the position of the Nyaya (which is analogous, broadly, to rationalism/realism/empiricism). Matlal's comparisons are deployed in terms of truth-functional logic:

In modern logic, we frequently talk about validity, consistency and inconsistency of schemata. If we talk in terms of truth-functional logic, we can define a truth-functional schema to be *valid* if it comes out true under every interpretation of its letters. And, a truth-functional schema is *consistent* if it comes out true under some interpretation of its letters; it is *inconsistent* if it comes out true under no interpretation of its letters. These three well-defined terms may somewhat loosely be used to explicate the differentiating marks of the Madhyamika doctrine of 'emptiness' (*śūnyatā*), the Jain doctrine of non-onesidedness (*anekāntatā*), and any other classical theory of the phenomenal world, such as that of the Nyaya-Vaisesika. A philosophical system like the Nyaya-Vaisesika puts forward a theory of the phenomenal world and asserts that it is a valid theory of reality. To be more specific, the Nyaya-Vaisesika expounds the notion of causality and believes that there are causes and their effects and hence the theory of causality is valid. The Madhyamika claims that each theory of the phenomenal world can be shown to be internally inconsistent or absurd. The Jaina claims, on the other hand, that each theory of the phenomenal world is consistent only with some particular point of view, although it is not absolutely valid. . . . For the sake of showing the contrasts in general terms, we may use the following tabulations. Suppose 'X' represents a particular theory of reality:

The Madhyamika: X is inconsistent because if we can assert 'p' under X we can also assert 'not p' under it.

The Jaina: X is consistent in the sense that given certain presuppositions for a particular point of view, X will follow it. In other words, an interpretation can be given to X to make it true.

The Nyaya: X is valid because it is based upon self-evident truths.

My own argument for the integrity of logocentrism, advanced in my part 4 and crucial for my reinstatement of logocentric thought, develops out of the above very succinct 'tabulation' of the Madhyamika. For I argue that the Madhyamikan 'tabulation', when leveled against the principle of identity itself, so that 'X' becomes 'whatever is, is' and the Madhyamikan schema of indeterminacy then deconstructs it, is a *differential, not a purely logical moment.* In other words, the instant one alters his provisional acceptance of the principle which *founds* logic, he is 'stepping outside' the logocentric frame (and because, in the process, logic has been used against itself, the departure from the frame is off/logical, not non-logical). The logocentric and differential become, then, two 'frequentings'. And the two frequentings are at the command of the 'enlightened person' (or, more accurately, at the command of 'enlightenment').

One way of reading Nagarjuna's famous verse 70, in his *Vigrahavyā vartanī* (*Averting the Arguments*)[129] is to see it as a celebration of the Two Truths: "All things prevail [keep going on logocentrically] for him for whom emptiness [*śūnyatā*] prevails; / Nothing whatever prevails [nothing keeps going on logocentrically] for him for whom emptiness [*śūnyatā*] prevails."[130] Perhaps the beauty of the Buddhist Two Truths is best captured by *mondo* of the following sort, and their unexpected *dénouements:*

> Hogen of Seiryo went to the hall to speak to the monks before the midday meal. He pointed at the bamboo blinds. At this moment, two monks went and rolled them up. Hogen said, "One [has] profit; the other [has] loss."[131]

Blyth's differentialist commentary does not deliver the expected distinction between enlightenment and unenlightenment, but rather a lesson in the Two Truths:[132]

> Forms without things, things without forms, loss without gain, gain without loss, loss which is loss only, gain which is gain only,—how can we see the two monks rolling up the blinds, not two but one, not one but two, *one perfunctorily, trivially, the other cosmically, but both perfectly, both Buddhistically,* loss here, gain there [i.e., the binary exchange of logocentrism], but loss in every thing [the Buddhist ver-

sion of Derridean 'inside the inside'], gain in everything [the Buddhist version of Derridean 'outside the outside']—how shall we see
this?

And a *mondo* from the *Hekiganroku:*[133]

A monk asked Haryo, "What is the Daiba (Deva) Sect?" Haryo answered, "Snow piled up in a silver bowl."

The monk's question asks which is the true Daiba (or Teaching) sect.
Blyth says of this 'case', that "The monk expected Haryo to say
something about the Daiba sect. In Buddhism there are two sects,
the Buddha Heart sect [which is 'silent'] and the Buddha Word sect
[which 'talks']. But if there were no talking sects there would be no
silent one." That is, the Master Haryo refuses to involve himself in
the binary thinking which characterizes logocentrism. He wants,
rather, to make another point. He deploys the image of snow and
silver bowl to represent the Buddhist Two Truths, the Truth of
logocentrism (white snow) and the Truth of differentialism (silver)
respectively. Most importantly, what is to be noticed is that white and
silver are not binary opposites: they are, instead, off/colors of each
other.[134]

At this juncture in part 3, it behooves us to examine in a more
general sense what I call the 'onto-psychological', a Buddhist approach to epistemology which has great potential for 'healing' Derridean anxiety. You will recall that Derrida's quandary, as I see it,
stems from a latent Cartesianism, an irremediable split between
'mind' and the 'outside'. Human mind, be it regarded individually or
collectively, cannot reach the 'outside' as it 'really' is. For humans,
the 'outside' is 'always already' structured in terms of human ideas
and other human patterns. When Derrida deconstructs logic, his
very surmise that human kind is 'on the verge' of another way of
knowing (realizing) which is somehow differential is a surmise *fed* by
experience. Otherwise, how could he affirm the 'glimmer', the diascript, as he does? And his unacknowledged trust in 'experience' is a
kind of unacknowledged 'phenomenology'. But as a Cartesian "rationalist to a fault" (should you forgive the pun?), he cannot concede
a 'knowing' which is not consciousness-bound and logical.

I suggest here that if Derrida were to dissolve this epistemological
model which so surreptitiously engineers his quandary, perhaps the
off/way would be clear to serene joy—a differential joy. I suggest
that Derrida regard the 'going-on' (*yathābhūtam*, or the 'real' in this
and only this non-Cartesian and also non-dialectical sense) as a co-
arising[135] which is forever constituting/negating. Human ego— indeed, Derrida's ego—is a phase 'on the swing' towards greater and
greater objectification. That is, the goings-on 'constitute' along a
range of possibilities, from devoidness (where there is no objectifying) through a gradually crystallizing entitativeness and on to the
most elaborate of logocentric formulae. What I have heretofore
called language/behavior is, then, a constituting which moves

towards greater and greater objectification (or 'making of objects', including one's 'self'). The Buddhist 'wise man' dissolves objectification, at will, when 'he' becomes the going-on at work in a devoid (off/entitative) way. Streng puts all this very well:

> The *anātma*-teaching of pre-Mahayana Buddhism had denied any essence of man which could be considered unchanging. . . . This doctrine also denied the existence of an absolute universal essence and suggested that the proper place to gain an understanding of reality was with phenomenal existence, which is seen as a succession of constructions. This is unlike most Western philosophies which think of the 'uncombined' as equivalent to 'simple' and which begin with the simple absolute as a fundamental category for interpreting the nature of reality. Nagarjuna extended this *anātma*-teaching to show how 'the uncombined' is logically and linguistically dependent on the 'combined' (*saṃskṛta*). Thus the notion 'uncombined' functions in Madhyamika philosophical thought, (1) without necessary substantial connotations, (2) as a term dependent on conceptual fabrication.[136]

The key for at least a rational (and thus, 'mere') cognition of Buddhism here is the notion, as Streng puts it, that " 'becoming' and knowledge are coextensive."[137] For example, in proportion to the lessening of objectifying activity, 'perception' disappears because the Cartesian dichotomy of subject and object disappears. Would that Derrida meant all this by his famous remark, "There is no perception!" Becoming and knowledge are coextensive, says Streng, and he continues:

> The English word 'realize' captures the two elements [of the above Buddhist idea] in the sense that man can be said to 'realize' certain possibilities. He both 'knows' and 'becomes' the possibilities. In Buddhism as in other yogic forms of 'realization', the character of knowledge and the character of 'becoming' change along the scale from illusion [i.e., the mistaken belief logocentrism 'rests in itself'] to ultimate knowledge (*prajñā*-wisdom). Unenlightened man constructs his existence through his discrimination and produces emotional attachments in the process. As long as his knowledge is discriminatory, i.e., [only] about 'things', man is simply producing the energies (*karma*) to continue this fabrication.[138]

Streng, in the following passage, further clarifies the meaning of 'detachment', and then introduces the 'charism' of 'exercising the capacity', our very next topic:

> Here we see that one way to give value to human life—and thereby determine the manner in which a person actualizes the fullest context of experience—is to cultivate an awareness that is free from attachment to the psychological, social, and linguistic patterns that, indeed, give order and meaning to conventional experiences. To perceive this as an ontological act is to take it out of the interpretation sometimes given to 'mystical traditions' which present them as escapes from the real world. Such an interpretation uses a different norm for identifying reality than the one found in this structural process. Here every perception, every thought, every conscious

moment is already within some mental-emotional process of consciousness; and every act of consciousness is participating in tenden-
cies that make a person less or more dependent on conventional psychological, social, and linguistic ordering forces. To become aware of
the spectrum of consciousness is the first step to be free from the
reinforcement patterns, or 'karmic residue', that keep one bound to
one's own fabrications [objectifications]. Then, according to this perspective, one needs to 'exercise' the capacities of 'mind' (or consciousness or 'heart') [all understood, themselves, as phases along the
spectrum of constitution] so that one can experience the variety of
consciousness-states and gain the insight to recognize one's freedom.
Ultimately, one should manifest the freedom gained through insight
in daily life—a life of serenity, compassion, and awareness.[139]

The distinctions to be made between Derrida's own differential
activity and the differential frequenting identified with Nagarjunism
are two: (1) while the Derridean alternately celebrates and
anguishes, hopes and waxes nostalgic, the Nagarjunist is aware and
serene, and has the security which comes with liberation; (2) while
the Derridean performs the logocentric and differential self-
consciously and piecemeal, the Nagarjunist performs them by means
of a grace which is spontaneous but 'at will', a kind of off/self that
moves freely between the objectivism of ego and pure devoidness.
The Nagarjunist freely, fully, and gracefully 'moves' because he has
prajñā-knowing, or realization; and because he has that enabling
power which smoothly exercises the shift to and fro between the
logocentric and differential—that is, he has *tathatā* ('thusness/
suchness').[140] But how does one Realize, how does one 'attain'? The
Nagarjunist works long and hard at the Path of Buddhist Discipline.
As Inada puts it, "The truth cannot be arrived at without first going
through or experiencing the mundane, relative truths of everyday
living."[141] One must *work through* them, not only by the intellective
process of the four lemmas and placement *sous rature,* but by asceti-
cal rigor: fasting, abnegation, love for others, service to others.[142]
Then, through the way-*rending* way, realization can come:

大道無門 ：
千差有路 .
透得此關 ，
乾坤獨步 .

The Great Way is gateless[143];
There are a thousand alleys.[144]
If once you pass the barrier,[145]
You walk alone [but not lonely] through the universe.[146]

Intellective effort, unaccompanied by both asceticism and selfless
love, cannot 'attain'. The transition, be it 'gradual' or 'sudden', from
surmise of glimmer to pure 'frequenting' is (differentially) mystical:

Beware of gnawing the ideogram of nothingness [devoidness]:
Your teeth will crack. Swallow it whole, and you've a treasure
Beyond the hope of Buddha and the Mind.
The east breeze fondles the horse's ears:
How sweet the smell of plum.[147]

Sprung, while discussing how Candrakirti justifies the use of ordinary language "to speak of the way things are really," provides as well an inkling (Zounds!—another Derridean pun) into Realization:

> . . . Candrakirti, apparently not knowing how else to proceed—having denied himself the right to define self-existence [= 'devoidness', here]— has recourse to the Buddhist wise man—the yogi. Candrakirti does not have the yogi say anything: the wise man does not inform us how things are, really. Candrakirti adopts what may be called a functional approach; he refers to a certain context—the yogi's world—and says that what is present there is self-existent ['devoid']; the way things are for the yogi is the way they truly are.[148]

And a few paragraphs later, Sprung further clarifies:

> It must be understood at once that this is not the philosphy of the 'als ob', of the 'as if'. The yogi does not orient to things 'as if' they neither were nor were not. He orients, understanding that it is the nature of things neither to be nor not to be. He takes things in their truth. *We* may describe his way of taking things as 'as if', but that is for our purposes, not his; the everyday for the yogi could not be 'as if', because there is nothing outside the middle way for it to be as, for it, that is, to be compared with.[149]

Realization brings with it the enabling power of *tathatā* (thusness/suchness), the capability which is differentially *between*.[150] This 'enabling' frees the differential mystic to shift to and fro between the logocentric and differential, according to what the situation-at-hand requires. It releases the differential mystic to be always, in the deep sense, happy. Our rejoinder might be—Happy, but deluded! But the lie is given to this last charge, it would seem, by the successful performance of a differential mystic in the 'ordinary' world. Such an individual is not only happy, but by worldly standards often an eminent success. He is the artist, the scientist, the diplomat, the clergyman, or the tailor, the doorkeeper, but he serves the community well (and indeed, he serves more intensely than others).[151] By the accepted definitions of sanity, he is sane.[152]

Tathatā, I argue, is Derrida's longed-for *exergue*.[153] *Tathatā* is neither finite nor infinite, neither limited nor unlimited, neither conventionally between the former, nor conventionally between the latter: *tathatā* is, somehow, off/finite and off/limit. The Chinese names for this 'thusness/suchness' evoke this situation remarkably. There are really two names for *tathatā* in Chinese—

與 麼　and　只 麼

—rendered in our own alphabet as *yu-mo* and *shi-mo* respectively.[154]
The first name is the character for 'and' (in the sense of 'addition')
followed by the character for 'question mark' (i.e., 'interrogation').
The English translation reads literally, 'and/?. . . . ' In other words,
the logocentric 'and' is 'put in question' by the interrogative character which follows it; the 'and' is not canceled, as it would be by a
Chinese character representing the opposite of 'and'—a disjunctive
'or', for example (i.e., 'and/or'). As I have pointed out before, to
cancel out the 'and' would be a lapse into a mystical centrism of some
kind. Here, instead, we have the differential 'and/*put in question*'. The
second name for *tathatā* is no less intriguing. Composed of characters
for 'limit' and 'question', the name rendered in English becomes
'limit/?. . . . ' The first character poses the concept of 'limit'; then this
concept is *put in question* by the second character, again the ideo-
graph for 'interrogative'. From these calligraphic versions of *sous
rature,* the 'thusness/suchness' or authentic going-on of happening,
glimmers. Or, since they are really calligraphs-under-erasure, they
present us remarkable examples of Derridean 'writing'—palimpsest
so *différance* can be off/read.

As will become clearer towards the end of part 4, the diagonal
'cross-cut'[155] which in the Madhyamika is called *tathatā*, but which
operates in other differentialist approaches also, *always* enables
differentialist 'practice' *while* enabling the free practice of logocentrism as well (just as[156] what we designate as 'devoidness' is the perpetual going-on which is *différance,* but which *reinstates* logocentrism).
The propriety (though no longer an *absolute* propriety) of
logocentrisms[157]—of conventional language, of ratiocination, of
organicism in literature and literary theory, of centric non-
rationalisms and mysticisms, and so on—is vindicated *thus.*

To say the preceding is not to say, of course, that for us the problematic is so simply 'solved', once and for all. In terms of our project
and its norms,[158] some vexatious questions remain, e.g., How is
tathatā, which sounds so much like the old 'faculty-psychology', not a
lapse back into logocentrism? We begin next our inquiry into Christian differentialism, theological and mystical. And towards the end
of this fourth inquiry, lingering 'vexatious questions' will receive, I
hope, their measure. But let us end the present part 3 with due
grace. I cite another famous and venerable passage evoking *śūnyatā:*

行く川の流は絶えずして、
而も本の水にあらず

（方丈記）

The moving water flows ceaselessly,
Yet the water is never the same.[159]

And I summon the reader to the Disciplinary Path:

> If you do not believe,
> Look at September!
> Look at October!
> The yellow leaves, falling, falling,
> To fill both mountain and river.[160]

Part 4

Across the *Tao*: Christian Differentialism (Athwart the a/Mid and Between, II)

Derrida, as we have seen, views the metaphysics of Western theism, first in its Hebraic formulation, but most elaborately in its Christian trinitarian formulation, as the epitome of logocentric thought. Taking the Hebraic 'name' for God, "I am who/what I am," as the formula for Supreme Identity (Factor perfectly expressing Itself, "I am" finding, or better, showing expression as "I am"), Derrida brings the arguments of *dédoublement* and *effacement* to bear and proceeds to deconstruct the theistic formula.[1] Modern biblical scholarship, of course, in its effort to recoup the original sentiment meant by *Ehyeh asher ehyeh*, "I am who/what I am," tends to devalue the metaphysical import of these words. Though Derrida does not allude to the historical development from a more primitive Semitism to the intricate metaphysical gloss of these words supplied by the later rabbinical tradition, it is evident that he regards the original meaning as a clear even if primitive proclamation of self-identity and, therefore, as a logocentrism. And that the later, very refined readings of the formula are for Derrida logocentric is of course obvious.

As for the Christian trinitarian format, declared the most conspicuous of logocentrisms, Derrida's treatment, it must be said, is really quite simplistic: the Trinity is the Holy Triangle and as such is just a more finessed version of 'self-enclosed identity', triadic this time instead of dyadic, and with the Holy Spirit acting as the reified movement of the Father's reflexivity (i.e., the reified movement of the Father knowing His Image, the Son). Specialists in theology will recognize at once that Derrida's grasp of the trinitarian problematic is very unsteady, and quite uninformed (that this is the case shall clarify momentarily). But what will be most fruitful for us is Derrida's notion of "protowriting, prototrace [*archi-écriture, archi-trace*]," which he also calls "primary writing [*écriture primaire*]," and "differance originating from . . . [*différance originaire*]."[2] I have deliberately opted for so cumbersome an English translation of this last because the rendering at least conveys the French, and part of Derrida's motive: *originaire*, as opposed to *originel*, say, or *original*, is an adjective which means "deriving origin from," with the origin 'elsewhere' and the question of its identity left open. A "differance originating from . . . ," then, if regarded as prior to origin, subverts

133

the whole concept of Origin. Since Derrida equates God exclusively with the logocentric theory of Origin, he considers his own notion of "prototrace,"[3] or "differance originating . . . ," to be an atheistic (more properly, a non-theistic) proposal. Alterity, a forever regressing mitosis, *precedes* the fabrication by the human race of a God, i.e., the fabrication of a logocentric theory of Origin. For Derrida, a self-identical God is historically second to alterity.

However, the Gospel according to Matthew tells us "the veil of the Temple was torn in two from top to bottom"[4] when Christ's sacrifice was completed, and if I may be permitted an unconventional anagogic reading (so I can accomplish this transition with some rhetorical grace), I say that Christ's revelation did precisely this: the One God of the Jewish religion, of which the Temple is the allegorical type, was revealed to be in reality a God rent down the middle (rent 'between'). That is, Christ's revelation of the Blessed Trinity, when taken in its several scriptural formulations, sends incongruent (better, 'decongruent') messages proclaiming a Trinity which is sacred differance.[5] This chapter, while acceding to Christian orthodoxy on all counts, will apply Derridean method to the theology of the Trinity. It shall be my purpose to show that such an application can clarify the roles of ecclesial definition and of rational theology, respectively, and that such an application can elucidate the nature of what is called nowadays 'God talk'—magisterial discourse, theological discourse, and mystical discourse, and the distinct functions of each. Christ said, of course, "you will learn the truth and the truth will make you free,"[6] and "I have come to bring fire to the earth. . . ."[7] If the way of Nagarjuna solves the quandary of Derrida, these are both superseded by the *mysterium*[8] of the Blessed Trinity—and my most important claim shall be that the mystery of the triune God can be *apprehended anew* in terms of 'deconstruction', 'erasure', and 'alterity'; and that furthermore, when "frequented" by heart as well as mind, the liberating power, like quickfire, can sweep all in invigorating dispersal.

How, then, does what we learn from Derrida apply to trinitarian theory? *Of Grammatology* offers a most useful passage in this regard, though no doubt Derrida himself does not recognize the pertinence:

> Representation mingles with what it represents, to the point where one speaks as one writes, one thinks as if the represented were nothing more than the shadow or reflection of the representer. A dangerous promiscuity and a nefarious complicity between the reflection and the reflected which lets itself be seduced narcissistically. In this play of representation, the point of origin becomes ungraspable. There are things like reflecting pools, and images, an infinite reference from one to the other, but no longer a source, a spring [*source*]. There is no longer simple origin. For what is reflected is split *in itself* and not only as an addition to itself of its image. The reflection, the image, the double, splits what it doubles. The origin of the speculation becomes a difference. What can look at itself is not

one; and the law of addition of the origin to its representation, of the
thing to its image, is that one plus one make at least three.[9]

Stripped of the bigoted tone imported by such words as "promiscuity" and "nefarious complicity" (these phrases seem no more than
Derrida's truckling to the trendiness of Freudianism and the 'hermeneutics of suspicion'), the argument stands as a very straightforward account of *dédoublement* (indeed, for this purpose we have used
once already the catchphrase, "The reflection [the image, the dou-
ble] splits what it doubles"). Since the alleged "image" in reality totally causes the alleged "origin" (and the vice versa, of course, holds
equally true), the "image" perpetually[10] doubles back on the "origin,"
as it were, and prevents a dyadic relation of signifier and signified
(there is perpetual split of the dyad, in other words). The 'split' of
the dyadic relation is a perpetual release (indeed, *dissémination!*) of a
third force—"one plus one make at least three." That is to say, there
is (1) "origin" as totally cause; there is (2) "image" as totally effect;
and, perpetually issuing from the perpetual 'doubling back', there is
(3) the third force, 'origin as totally effect and effect as totally
cause'.[11] That the deconstruction of the dyad does not leave room
for a Taoism, we have already shown (we argued that an "origin"
which is totally, i.e., all and only cause, and which is totally, i.e., all
and only effect, precludes the mutual and closed implication associated with the Tao[12]). But here we must note that neither does the
Derridean deconstruction permit a closed triad of some kind: rather,
the notion that both "origin" and "image" can be—each of them—
all and only cause and all and only effect collapses logic, and collapses triadic models based on conventional space and time. The
"origin" and "image" of the Derridean dyad are perpetually canceling each other, as it were, and releasing a perpetual "third" which is
'energy', dispersal. If we are to look at all for a more developed
physical analogy (and indeed, Derrida says that to an extent it is our
fate to think in such wise), perhaps the more apposite analogon is of
imploded nucleus and explosion.

I hold that Derrida's account of the "one and one which make
three" provides us with a more accurate understanding of the Holy
Trinity than metaphysical theology can. Crucial to my discussion is
an adequate grasp of the distinction between metaphysical (i.e.,
logocentric) theology and magisterial declaration in the Catholic
Church (a matter we shall address promptly). The argument shall be
that Christ's revelations about the nature of the Trinity, as communicated in scripture and clarified by the magisterium, persistently serve
to *deconstruct* trinitarian theories which propose a self-enclosed,
entitative triadic model. The argument shall be, furthermore, that
the glimpse of trinitarian mystery delivered by Christ (and on the
intellectual level, the glimpse Christ provides is an ensemble of descriptive phenomenology and abbreviated logic) is a glimpse of
differential Trinity. The Father and Son (the Son is the "Image of the

Father"), through the perpetual 'doubling back' of the Son in knowledge and love, release the third force—the Holy Spirit ("proceeding
from the Father and the Son," in infinite dispersal). But if Derridean
differentialism helps us to better understand the Christian Trinity, it
is also true that the Christian Trinity, as communicated by scripture
and magisterium and now glossed by Derridean comment, brings
liberation to the 'quandaried' world of Derrida. Trinitarian doctrine,
for example, emits clear signals on the nature of the differential universe, and trinitarian doctrine justifies the wherewithal of non-
rational knowing.

What knowledge we have of the Trinity—we may call the
ensemble of this knowledge a 'theology' as long as we recognize it is
not in itself a 'metaphysical theology'—is provided by the New Testament.[13] Given the rational drive of the human mind and the respect which Catholic Christianity[14] has always conferred on the intellect, metaphysical (i.e., logocentric) theologians from the beginning
tried to rationally 'harmonize' the scriptural assertions (the 'scriptural theology', if you will) about the Trinity. In this context, the
magisterium, or teaching authority of the Church (i.e., the college of
bishops, and—as the precise nature of his office became clarified—
the bishop of Rome as president of the college, or Pope) functioned
as the protector of the Church from error. That is, the history of
trinitarian theology for the first several centuries[15] can be regarded
as the proposal (by theologians) of one logocentric theory of Trinity
after another, and what accounts for this very diversity is the ambiguity of the scriptural assertions themselves. Because of this ambiguity, it became increasingly clear that God—Who had promised
through the Son that He would dwell with the Church to the end of
time[16] and shield her from error[17]—intended to use the magisterium precisely as that shield. In other words, as metaphysical theology proposed its various grand trinitarian rationales, the
magisterium—infallibly interpreting the ambiguous[18] scriptures—
uttered its own *neti, neti*[19] ("not this, not that": this theory cannot be
right because it contradicts such and such a scriptural passage; that
theory cannot be right because it contradicts yet another scriptural
passage; and so on). Nowhere does the magisterium propose a grand
trinitarian rationale of its own, and this refusal is of course crucial to
an understanding of how the teaching authority operates: essentially, it makes carefully circumscribed declarations which preserve
fidelity to each assertion made by scripture, and it makes declaration
on the grounds of its own special charism (the guidance of the Holy
Spirit) rather than some prior commitment to a grand trinitarian
scheme which harmonizes all the scriptural assertions (this is not to
say, of course, that the magisterium does not use logic in its investigation of whatever proposal is at hand: much like Derrida it uses
logic in short sequences and draws limited conclusions; but unlike
Derrida, when a "case can be made" for both of two logical interpre-

tations of a given passage, say, it can count on the charism of the Spirit).

The first examination we undertake will be twofold: it will indicate how the magisterium has worked to deconstruct logocentric theories of Trinity, and it will show how *dédoublement* can lead to a less entitative and, indeed, more orthodox *prise* of the Trinity. Throughout I shall cite the *Enchiridion symbolorum definitionum et declarationum de rebus fidei et morum*,[20] the well-known compendium of official Church declarations.[21] The problem which attracted theologians at the start was that implied in Philippians 2: 5–7: "In your minds you must be the same as Christ Jesus: His state was divine, yet he did not cling to his equality with God but emptied himself to assume the condition of a slave, and became as men are. . . ." If Jesus "did not cling to his equality with God," but "became as men are," what was His relation to God, the Father of all? He tells us "The Father and I are one" (John 10: 30), but also "the Father is greater than I" (John 14:28).[22]

Neo-Platonism played an important role in the two rational 'systems' which, broadly speaking, tried to 'solve' the contradiction. One broad systemic movement can be called 'subordinationism'.[23] Though the various schools of thought identified with this movement took care to refine themselves sufficiently so that no blatant clash with scripture occurred, the basic model remained this: the Father is the Cause (the 'Signified') and the Son is the Effect or representation (the 'Signifier').[24] Since effect is ontologically subsequent to cause (recall Derrida's treatment of logocentric hierarchy, the movement from inner to outer and from top to bottom), the Son is subordinate to the divine Father and is Himself, therefore, not divine ("The Father and I are one" can just mean, for example, that the Son is intimate with the Father). Neo-Platonism, with its very overt commitments to pluralistic unity (the 'many' hierarchically related to each other, yet orchestrated into the 'one') and to theories of Factor and Logos[25] (Image), accommodated some kinds of subordinationism. While Arianism, which became in time the main threat to orthodoxy, was Aristotelian in sympathy rather than Neo-Platonic (Arius apparently denied Christ's divinity because the Aristotelian notion of unity excludes emanationism—the Son cannot "reflect" the Father and still be divine),[26] the fact remains that Arius was very rationalist and, thus, very logocentric in an Aristotelian sort of way.[27] What is more, the model latent in his thought seems causal with a vengeance: if Aristotelian unity cannot accommodate plurality, the Son as the separate effect of the Divine Cause surely cannot share the same divine nature with the Cause.

It was the Council of Nicaea (325 A.D.) which issued a series of magisterial declarations that effectively deconstruct the subordinationist model. The Father is not the *cause* of the Son, since the Father is neither ontological nor temporal cause. The Council declares Father and Son are *co-equal*[28] and *con-substantial*,[29] so that the

Father is not the ontological cause (see also DZ 13, 39, 70, 254). And the Council declares the Father and Son are *co-eternal,* so that the Father is not the temporal cause (see also DZ 39, 68). Thus, with two deft strokes the magisterium vitiates the causal model, and it does so on the grounds which even the heretics profess—the inerrancy of scripture (since there are scriptural texts which announce the co-equality, co-eternality, and co-substantiality). And all this is very analogous to Derridean procedure which deconstructs speculative systems by way of the implicit assumptions of these very systems. The Council goes on to declare: "As for those who say, 'There was a time when he [the Son] did not exist'; and, 'Before he was begotten, he did not exist'; and, 'He was made from nothing, or from another hypostasis or essence,' alleging that the Son of God is mutable or subject to change—such persons the Catholic and apostolic Church condemns."[30] Nonetheless, the Council also insists the Son is "the only-begotten born of the Father, that is, of the substance of the Father"[31] (see also DZ 276, 462), so that Father *generates* (but does not *cause,* does not *create*) the Son. And the Eleventh Council of Toledo (675 A.D.) glosses the above formula by asserting that "the Father, indescribable substance indeed, begot the Son of his own substance in an indescribable way."[32] The workings of the Trinity, in other words, are supra-rational (Derrida's 'beyond thought' with a difference[33]), or what is technically called *mysterium,* a mystery. The Church, however, through a process similar to *sous rature* (as we shall see) provides a diascript of *generatio,* and of the other trinitarian operations.[34]

A second speculative system advanced in order to solve the contradiction between scriptural texts asserting the oneness of Father and Son, and texts asserting the priority of the Father over the Son, can be called *modalism.*[35] Here the latent model is even more facilely Neo-Platonic than is the subordinationist format: the Father is again the 'Signified', but the Son as 'Signifier' is so perfect an Image of the Father that the Son is just a modal *aspect* of the Father (this formulation is weighted in favor of unity, not otherness: "The Father is greater than I" can just mean that an image, *sub specie imaginis,* is inferior). Sabellius, for example, argued that the distinction between Father and Son is that between God and manifestation, and not a distinction in God Himself.[36] Against modalism, which persevered as a heterodox current for many centuries,[37] the magisterium ranged several official pronouncements. Thematically, these latter can be reduced to two: (1) the distinction between the Father and the Son is *real,* not virtual (Council of Rome,[38] Council of Florence[39]; see also DZ 278, 280); and (2) the Father and the Son are each defined by their *relationis oppositio* (Council of Florence, DZ 703).[40] Only this second is perhaps not clear *in facie,* and needs some explanation. The Church had long since affirmed that God is one Divine Nature "in" three Persons (the modern, psychological definition of "person" does not apply, of course: "Person" is the venerable translation from the Greek *prosopon,* or better, *hypostasis,* the Latin *subsistens,*[41] and implies a "really distinct" *way* in which the One God "subsists"[42] (a very Latinate verb perhaps conveyed in more common parlance by the verb "works," or even "acts").

The contribution of the Council of Florence was to affirm that "everything is one" in God, "except where an opposition of relationship [the *relationis oppositio*] exists,"[43] so that each of the three Persons *as* a Person is constituted ("defined," "established," "built," if you will) *only* by how that Person relates to the other Persons. The Church has clarified *relationis oppositio* no further, but most theologians have taken the term in the Thomist sense, so that it refers very strictly to opposite relations (daughter and mother, for example) and not to disparate relations (daughter and "dining out," say).[44] Thus most theologians have defined the Father in terms of paternity, the Son in terms of filiation, and the Holy Spirit in terms of "passive spiration"[45] (as we shall see, the magisterium affirms that the Holy Spirit "proceeds" from the Father and the Son [or from the Father through the Son] as from "one principle" [DZ 460, 691, 704] in one single spiration [DZ 691]).[46] In any case, my point here is that the *relationis oppositio* clause in the Council's decree precludes modalism. It was decreed that a Person is a Person only by virtue of an opposition of relationship to the other Persons. The Son is the Son by virtue of His difference from the Father (for it follows from the formula that whatever is not in opposition of relationship belongs to the Divine Unity rather than to one Person[47]). But modalism declares the Son is just an aspect of the Father, and the notion of aspect rides on sameness, not difference. The Son as Person subsists as Son precisely in so far as He differs from the Father (and opposition of relationship is the only difference the decree permits). The Son as Aspect of the Father is an aspect precisely in so far as He displays (that is, transmits the likeness of) the Father. Even if one chooses to regard "Father" on the one hand and "Son as Aspect of the Father" on the other, as the two terms in a relation of opposition, it is not the functioning *difference,* namely the specifically "aspect" trait of the Son, which is important in terms of the Son's activity. According to the modalist format, that the aspect trait transmits the Father is what is important. And such a formulation distorts the scriptural message, which is that the Son's difference from the Father, the Son as specifically Filial, is what is important in terms of the Son's activity (this is not at all to say His role in the "giving" of the Father is not very important, but rather that insofar as He is "like the Father" we can no longer properly speak of the Son but instead of the Divine Unity). The Councils of Ephesus (431 A.D.) and Chalcedon (451 A.D.) did much to sort out the problems implied even by our initial scriptural quotations—"His state was divine, yet he did not cling to his equality with God," "The Father and I are one," and "the Father is greater than I." These two councils distinguished what are properly christological questions (the relation of Christ to the Trinity) from trinitarian questions (the relation of the Persons to each other and to the Divine Unity). The Council of Ephesus, augmented by Chalcedon, issued benchmark decisions in Christology. The Councils declared that in Christ there are two natures, the human and the divine[48] (so in His human nature the Son was contingent but in His divine nature he obviously was not), but that in Christ there is only one Divine Person (so Christ is truly God).

We have seen how the magisterium—because of its fidelity to the 'way things really are' (and for the Christian, the 'way things really are' is revealed, though "through a glass darkly," by Christ's word)—has foiled various logocentric rationales which 'explain' the Trinity. But 'what' remains, then, shining through the glass? What "manner" of Trinity is implied? If divine revelation concerning the Trinity preempts entitative, closed 'models', what approach can better serve? For the Church, as we said at the very beginning, is not at all opposed to our 'thinking about' these matters! (Rather, it is just that logocentric theories, one after another, have always come up against a "stumbling block"; they have always, along the way, perforce violated a *donnée* of Revelation.) What the Church says about one scriptural truth, the "indwelling of the Holy Spirit,"[49] really expresses her attitude towards all scholarly meditation on the sacred mysteries:

> This mystery is enveloped in a darkness, rising out of the mental limitations of those who seek to grasp it. But We know, too, that well-directed and earnest study of this doctrine and the clash of diverse opinions and their discussion, provided love of truth and due submission to the Church be the arbiter, will open rich and bright vistas, by the light of which true progress can be made in these sacred sciences. Hence, We do not censure those who in various ways and with diverse reasonings strain every effort to understand and to clarify the mystery of this our marvelous union with Christ.[50]

My claim is that the differential mode of Derrida allows us "true progress" in apprehending the manner of the Trinity. The first zone of inquiry where differentialism comes to our aid is that of the Tri-Personal dynamic itself, the relations of the Three Persons to each other. Actually, I have already sketched, *grosso modo,* the differential scenario.[51] The Father and the Son, through the perpetual 'doubling back' of the Son in knowledge and love, release the third "subsistence"—the Holy Spirit who "proceeds[52] from the Father and the Son" (DZ 39) in infinite dispersal.[53] Clearly, an appreciation of the 'issuing forth'[54] from the Father and the 'doubling back' of the Son as *one* bilateral action is crucial here, because the Father and the Son can only be perpetually and mutually (and totally[55]) abrogating[56] each other—according to the Derridean mode—*if* they are, each of them, functioning *in the same way* towards each other. For it is this functioning in the same way, *invicem et totaliter,* which releases the third force, the 'origin as totally effect and the effect as totally cause'.[57] The third force, then, is the Holy Spirit. And we must specify, furthermore—lest we be misunderstood to be proposing heresy—that the action which we are describing, the action which has mutual 'origin' and mutual 'effect', is *not* the *generatio.* For, as the magisterium has so often declared, the Father *alone* generates, or "begets" (and is *not* "begotten" in turn), and the Son is *only* generated, or "begotten" (and does *not* "beget" the Father in turn). So we are not talking about that donation of His "own substance" (DZ 432) which the Father makes to the Son, but rather of some action which is *bilateral* and mutually *total.* What can this action be? I submit the one action is a 'knowing', a 'knowing' which can also be called a 'loving', and I here follow what are very clear scriptural assertions. Thus Christ proclaims the mutual knowing of Father and Son with the words, "the Father knows me and I know the Father"[58] (in the Greek of the scripture, too, the *same* verb, *gignoskein,* is repeated); and Christ proclaims the mutual love of Father and Son with the words "the Father loves me"[59] and "I love the Father"[60] (in the Greek, the same verb, *agapein,* is operative both times). A problem which at first glance seems to surely arise if one equates knowing, and/or loving, with mutual action is that the 'psychological' theory of the Trinity regards the Son as Truth and the Holy Spirit as Love (according to the dictum, *processio ad modum operati*[61]). Indeed, many theologians have understood the *relationis oppositio* (which, you recall, necessarily defines each of the Persons) precisely in terms of such a triad: Father as the Knower and the Lover, Son as the Known, and Holy Spirit as the Loved. If one accepts this formula, then clearly the Father cannot be Knower and Known, Lover and Loved; nor the Son Knower and Known, Lover and Loved.

However, the psychological theory,[62] and for that matter all other theories elaborating the 'manner' of trinitarian Persons, remain *speculative* and have not been ratified by the magisterium.[63] In other words, one need not affirm that the Son is the uniquely Known, the Holy Spirit the uniquely Loved, and so on, and for my part I reject this the 'psychological' theory. In regard to the distinct Persons, the magisterium has only insisted (with some attached provisions[64]) (1) on generation of the Son by the Father, (2) on the procession of the Holy Spirit from both Father and Son, (3) on the real distinction among Persons as always a *relationis oppositio,*[65] and (4) on the procession of the Holy Spirit "as from one principle" (for us, an extremely important clause I shall treat momentarily). A concordance of the above four seems to compel real definition of the Persons only in terms of Paternity (as definition of the Father), Filiation (as definition of the Son), and "Passive Spiration"[66] (as definition of the Holy Spirit). For each of these relationships is a *relationis oppositio* and also takes into account the other magisterial dicta immediately involved. And many recent biblical scholars have pointed out, with renewed emphasis, how very much these definitions echo scriptural revelation (and they also point out, vigorously, how the same *cannot* be said of the 'psychological' theory[67]). The result of all this for us is that the way remains clear for our thesis: we can maintain that the *relationis oppositio* clause applies to the real definition provided by the unique differential[68] relationships of Paternity, Filiation, and Passive Spiration. And we are free to move on and to next maintain that the "one principle" from which the Holy Spirit proceeds is what we have been calling the *mutual* knowing/loving of Father and Son.

What is conclusive is the magisterium's fourth declaration that the Holy Spirit proceeds from the Father and the Son as from *one principle:* "With faithful and devout profession we confess that the Holy Spirit proceeds eternally from the Father and the Son, not as from two principles, but as from one; not by two spirations but by one" (the Second Council of Lyons [1271– 1276 A.D.], and the Creed prescribed for Michael Palaeologus, DZ 460).[69] I foresee some arguing against me that the "one principle" defined by the magisterium is in actuality the "divine substance" (an identification the magisterium itself has never made) and that because the "divine substance" has been magisterially defined as only *given* by the Father and only *received* (and not given in turn to the Father) by the Son,—it must therefore be maintained that the Holy Spirit proceeds from both the Father and the Son, indeed, but *not* by way of what I have been calling a "bilateral" or "mutual" action. That is, my adversaries may maintain, the "divine substance" perpetually given as the Holy Spirit proceeds from one principle, as the magisterium declares, but this *one principle* does not function *in the same way* in Father and Son. The "one principle" is *given* by the Father to the Son, is *received* by the Son, and thus can be regarded either as proceeding "from the Father through the Son" so the Holy Spirit issues forth, *or* as proceeding "from the Father and the Son" so the Holy Spirit issues forth (indeed, both the formulae "through the Son" and "and the Son" are acceptable to the magisterium: see DZ 691). In other words, my adversary may argue that the Holy Spirit indeed proceeds as from one principle, but *not* from one and the same principle *invicem* of Father and Son.

Against these adversaries, I can range, it seems to me, very weighty passages drawn from the Fourth Lateran Council (1215 A.D.). But first I wish to point out that the actual words used by the magisterium in describing the "one principle" are: ". . . ex Patre *simul et* Filio, et *ex utroque* aeternaliter tamquam ab uno principio,"[70] i.e., "from the Father and *at once* from the Son, and *from both* eternally as from one principle." Thus the way is left open to interpret the action as 'bilateral', as 'mutual' (and Karl Rahner, for one, actually uses the translation "mutual"[71]). And the other authoritatively approved formula, "ex Patre per Filium," i.e., "from the Father through the Son," is accompanied by the equally authoritative provision: "ut per hoc significetur, Filius quoque esse secundum Graecos quidem causam, secundum Latinos vero principium subsistentiae Spiriti Sancti, sicut et Patrem,"[72] i.e., "that through this [formula] is meant that the Son, also, is according to the Greeks[73] indeed the cause, according to the Latins indeed the principle, of the subsistence of the Holy Spirit, and that the Father is too." It is to be noticed that the provision understands the *per Filium* not as a unilateral transmission of the divine substance to the Holy Spirit, so that the Father is the "cause"[74] and the Son the mediation of the "cause." Rather, the provision stipulates that the Son can be considered the "cause" or the "principle," just as the Father too is the "cause" or the "principle." Thus a theory of 'mutual' action is in no way repudiated.

As for any claim on the part of my possible adversaries that the Holy Spirit indeed proceeds from one principle, but that this one principle does *not* function *in the same way* in Father and Son, I answer the following. I answer that the phrase *not in the same way* necessarily implies the Father sends forth the Holy Spirit in one way, and the Son sends forth the Holy Spirit in another way, and such a formulation militates against the Church's insistence on "one principle." Indeed, what value remains to be conserved by the declaration of "one principle," if the Holy Spirit proceeds from Father and Son in different ways?[75] One reciprocal action of Father and Son—namely, the concept of 'mutualness', of an issuing forth from Father to Son which is *invicem, totaliter, et simul* a doubling-back of Son to Father—best accounts for the "one principle" clause. From the 'mutualness', understood in Derridean terms, the Holy Spirit can be 'released'. (M. Schmaus, in his *Essence of Christianity*, seems to pose an *invicem* format similar to mine, though not at all in Derridean terms: "In the Father's giving of himself to the Son, and the Son's to the Father, there springs into being from the mightiness of their giving, a third divine Person."[76])

There are two passages from the Fourth Lateran Council which, I believe, strengthen my case. There is great danger, the council insists, in regarding the consubstantiality (that "the very same being which is the Father is also the Son and the Holy Spirit," DZ 432) of the three Persons from a quantitative point of view. And I suggest that to say the substance of the Holy Spirit proceeds from the begetting substance of the Father and the begotten substance of the Son is to pose a format perilously close to quantification. The Fourth Council of the Lateran insists on the following: "But it cannot be said he [the Father] gave him [the Son] part of his substance, and retained part for himself, because the substance of the Father is indivisible, since it is altogether simple. Neither can one say that the Father transferred his own substance in generation to the Son, as though he gave it to the Son in such a way that he did not retain it for himself; otherwise he would cease to be a substance" (DZ 432).

The way is clear, in other words, for me to argue that the substance of the Holy Spirit proceeds from a reciprocal action of both Father and Son, viz., knowing/loving (both knowing and loving on the part of both Father and Son), and that the Holy Spirit does not proceed from the begetting substance of the Father and the begotten substance of the Son. And, what is more, my case is actually strengthened by the council's declaration, because to demand (as my adversaries would) that personal substance must proceed from personal substance is both to *quantify* divine substance and to treat it in a naively causal, indeed mechanical, way.

My case is further secured, I think, by the following statement from the same council: "And that reality [the "divine substance" which is "the three Persons taken together and each of them taken singly"] does not beget, nor is it begotten, nor does it proceed; but the Father is who begets, the Son is who is begotten, the Holy Spirit is who proceeds [Sed est Pater qui generat, et Filius qui gignitur, et Spiritus Sanctus qui procedit]; thus there are distinctions among persons and unity in nature" (DZ 432). In the face of this authoritative assertion, how can one claim that the substance of the Holy Spirit must proceed from begetting substance and begotten substance?

The second zone of inquiry where differentialism can, I think, come to our aid is that of the relation between the Persons and the Divine Unity. As we have seen, the church teaches that the "three persons are one God, not three gods; for the three persons have one subsistence, one essence, one nature, one divinity, one immensity, one eternity" (DZ 703); and the Church teaches that in God "everything is one except where an opposition of relationship exists" (ibid.). The theory of Saint Augustine, Neo-Platonic at base, has long been used by speculative theology to "account for" the above magisterial provisions. The theory is outrightly entitative, i.e., it analogizes from a Platonic model of the triune God. Throughout, the irrecusable implication is that the Persons are distinct modifications of a common substratum. Each of the modifications is a Person, and the substratum is the Divine Unity. Saint Augustine's speculation, as Rahner so well capsulizes it, starts "from the one divine *essentia,* from which the three Persons are so to speak subsequent determinations. . . ."[77] In other words, the 'oneness' of God somehow "makes," establishes, constitutes, the 'threeness'. But the Augustinian theory, as even some of its proponents grant, fails in very gross ways to accommodate the Church's authoritative guidelines. The Church has made very clear, as Rahner says, that the three Persons "are not the 'self-same', though they are 'the same'."[78] The three Persons are not the self-same, i.e., they do not 'share' or 'hold in common' the Divine Unity, simply because *qua* Persons anything they would share in common belongs to the Divine Unity *instead.* In other words, the rule of *relationis oppositio* excludes by definition the theory of substratum. And what I find so exciting for us is that Rahner, by following with great care the dicta of the Church in this matter, ends up by *deconstructing* the entitative model along very Derridean lines.[79] What is more, Rahner is led to an alternative account of the Tri-Unity, an account which implies that the Personal differences establish, or constitute, the Divine Unity (and not, as with Augustine, the other way around). Thus Rahner attacks any interpretation of the *relationis oppositio* which makes of it no more than a perfunctory device: a device contrived to meet scriptural insistence on distinction among Persons, and still weight the trinitarian formula wholly in favor of a 'founding' or 'constitutive' unity. As Rahner puts it, the *relationis oppositio* "must not be primarily regarded as a means of resolving an apparent logical contradiction in the Trinity. Its value in such a process would be very limited."[80] He proceeds to intensify the meaning of differential relation:

> Insofar as a relation is looked on as the least real of all realities, it loses value in explaining the Trinity, which is the most real of all realities. But the relation is as absolutely real as anything else that can be said of the Trinity. And apologetics for the 'immanent'[81] Trinity cannot proceed on the basis of the prejudice that a lifeless identity of an uncommunicated type is the most perfect mode of being of the absolute being, and then go on to eliminate the difficulty created by this prejudice by explaining that the distinction in God is 'only' relative.[82]

The crucial next move, which remains for us to make, I believe, is that we introduce Derridean *effacement* into the argument. The Church has stipulated all is one in God "except where an opposition of relationship prevails"; thus, theologians who truly adhere to the magisterium have defined the Persons exclusively in terms of differential relation (in itself, already so Saussurean a formulation— definition by use of difference alone!); and now we, equally true to the magisterium, will go on to claim that the differential relation is *"purely* negative reference." And we will go on to claim, and the propriety and richness of this thesis has dazzled me from the time it first crystallized, that the purely negative differences among Persons *constitute* the Divine Unity. That is to say, the dynamics of this constitution are analogous to the constitution of Derridean "trace" by way of "interval."[83] As Derrida's argument from *dédoublement* comes to the aid of the Tri-Personal problematic, his argument from *effacement*, in its own way, can beautifully serve the theology of the 'Three-in-One'. The case for "pure negative reference," that is, the case for its suitability when taken as the meaning of *relationis oppositio*, can best begin with a description of the competing case (and I understand the classic adversary to be the Augustinian posing an entitative model). The adversary interprets the magisterium to mean that the Father, for example, is Father, is Person, in so far as a *contrary* relationship exists between Him on the one hand, and the other two Persons respectively. And no doubt the adversary insists our position is unorthodox because we claim that the Father, for example, is Father, is Person, in so far as a *contradictory* relationship exists between Him and the other two Persons respectively. (And indeed, where it recognizes our move from the "contrary" to the "universal contradictory"—for this move is the shift to purely negative reference—the foregoing does accurately represent our position.)

We contend, however, that if the *relationis oppositio* clause is to be accepted seriously and thoroughly, the "contrary" must be understood as the *case* of the contradictory which needs "most mentioning," but not as a *rejection* of the "pure contradictory." The argument is clinched for us by that controlling phrase of the official definition, *"and everything is one"*[84] [in God] except where opposition prevails. That is, in the instance of the Father, for example, anything which would be 'common' to the Father, and the other two Persons, say, belongs *instead* to the Unity. We are talking in terms of Father and all else (the all else is non-Father); and we are saying the Church has already decided whatever "of Father" would be in so-called "non-Father" does not belong to Father at all, but belongs to the Unity instead! Whatever is left of so-called non-Father is truly and really in no way "like" the Father. Thus the Church has forced the issue and compelled our conclusion. But the Church seems to single out one zone of the contradictory, i.e., one zone of the non-Father, for special mention—that zone which is non-Father but by way of "contrary" relation. (For example, non-Begetter is the contradictory of Begetter, but the zone of contrariety within the contradictory is the Begotten-Begetter relation: the "Begotten" as a contrary still belongs, of course, to the class of non-Begetter.) And what the Church even says about the relation of trinitarian contrariety is that the norm of "negative reference" applies. The Father is the Father, for instance, not because of what "of the Father" is in the Son, but because of what is the "contradictory of the Father" in the Son (and the only contradictory of the Father in the Son is the contrary of the Father in the Son—because the Church has declared all else but the contraries between Father and Son would be not contradictories at all, but "likenesses" and therefore belong to the Divine Unity—and not to the Persons at all!). In other words, the Church all told has prodded us by her very criteria to "purely negative reference."

What I am saying about contrariety and contradiction, and their involvement in trinitarian doctrine, is perhaps, more easily expressed by way of symbolic logic.[85] Nonetheless, because many readers may find the notation of symbolic logic uncongenial, I now rehearse the problematic in a more concrete way: an analogy—admittedly, very inexact—will be drawn to color distribution. What the entitative model proposes is that the color ebony (the Father), say, indeed has as its contrary the color white (whether white/ivory, the Son; or white/alabaster, the Holy Spirit), but that all three colors share the admixture beige pastel, say (the substratum, or Divine Unity). The entitative theory argues, furthermore, that our contending formulation, that ebony is defined by *total* ("pure") non-equivalence to its contradictory, non-ebony, excludes the necessary presence of the beige admixture (that is, excludes the substratum of Divine Unity necessary for the establishment of the three distinct Persons). In answer, the differential theory with which we identify would contend (*if* the Church's *relationis oppositio* clause applied to color distribution—please bear with me!) that the possibility of common admixture—whether the admixture be beige pastel, green, orange, or any other color, or all other colors together—must be ruled out because by definition common admixture can be "no part" of ebony or white ("no part" of Father, Son, and Holy Spirit). Indeed, this is the same as saying that ebony is *total* non-equivalence to its contradictory, to non-ebony of any or all colors. But by definition it would so happen that the only non-ebony (the only contradictory) that could exist would be the contrary, namely white (white/ivory and white/alabaster)—since all admixture is ruled out—AND thus the norm of *pure negative reference* prevails.[86]

My next claim is that the further *déroulement* of Derridean protocol, namely, the phases characterized by erasure, and by preservation of diascript, can accommodate the Catholic notion of mystery (*mysterium*, as a technical theological term, means a true state-of-affairs which is beyond the power of human reason to apprehend, but which is known nonetheless to "be the case" because Jesus Christ so revealed it). Derrida's *déroulement* of erasure and diascript brings him, of course, to the brink of what I can only call an obscure agonizing. Catholic Christianity, on the other hand, preserves the Divine diascript with (1) the *security,* indeed the certainty, of faith,[87] and, by way of its own mystics, with (2) the *apprehension* of mystical intuition[88] (the latter has its many analogies with the differential mysticism of Nagarjuna, of course, and is in many ways already the subject of much East-West dialogue[89]). We shall address shortly the roles of faith, mystery, and logocentric theology in Catholicism, and their relations to Derrida's overall problematic. Now it suffices to indicate, briefly, the last two phases of the Derridean *déroulement* in terms of the differential Catholic 'theology' we are tracing. Differentialism deconstructs the entitative model of the Trinity, as we have seen (and does so in much the same way Derrida deconstructs entitative presence), and differentialism leads us instead towards other conclusions. *Dédoublement,* for example, leads us with what seems a relentless logic[90] to a Father and Son who are, each of them, *totally* knowers and *totally* knowns. But every step in the reasoning process which directs this conclusion can occur only because the principle of contradiction informs this very process (i.e., the principle informs the linguistic and logical syntax). To say X is totally Y is to say it cannot be partly or wholly Z. To say the Father is totally the knower is to say He cannot be partly or wholly the known as well, or else logic cannot make any distinctions at all. Likewise, in the case of the *effacement* argument, how can one maintain the possibility of negation, of *is not,* without pari passu validating the existence of presence, of *is*—and if these concepts are indeed binary, how can the notion of pure *is not* make any sense at all? It may seem all very well to insist, as Derrida often does, that by *is not* he does not mean the formal 'contradiction' of *is,* but the problem that really lays siege here is that reason itself, our very instrument, is founded on the law of contradiction in the most formal sense. Thus the differential Trinity, as a logical outline of some kind, must come "under erasure." The differential Trinity, even under erasure, does emit some truth however: the differential Trinity, from beneath its crossing-out, emits its trace, its diascript—just as Derrida's 'pure signifier' *sous rature* is palimpsest. In Catholic terms, what can the notion of differential Trinity *sous rature* mean but that reason can give us some understanding of the Blessed Trinity, but in a way so feeble and fractured that we cannot even identify the exact nature of the fracture, nor how the Truth somehow escapes and reaches us? The Church in the First Vatican Council suggests the progress of reason and how reason must balk before *mysterium:*

> It is, nevertheless, true that if human reason, with faith as its guiding light, inquires earnestly, devoutly, and circumspectly, it does reach, by God's generosity, some understanding of mysteries, and that a most profitable one. It achieves this by the similarity with truths which it knows naturally and also from the interrelationship of mysteries with one another and with the final end of man. Reason, however, never becomes capable of understanding them the way it does truths which are its own proper object. For divine mysteries of their very nature so excel the created intellect that even when they have been given in revelation and accepted by faith, that very faith still keeps them veiled in a sort of obscurity, as long as "we are exiled from the Lord" in this mortal life, "for we walk by faith and not by sight."[91]

The above citation also shows, of course, how the Christian is delivered from Derridean anxiety: the Christian knows through the experience of faith (and sometimes through mystical awareness[92]) that it is entirely *appropriate* for reason to fall short; the Christian knows that the trinitarian diascript beneath the crossing-out is God; finally, the Christian knows that his future can be a thorough frequenting of the Divine.

It is my own surmise that Derrida's treatment of prototrace, the *différance originaire,* will donate much to a new "theology" (*en guillemets!*) of the Blessed Trinity, a differential theology which can devote long studies to the Trinity as "Interval," to the Trinity as "and/or between and/or," and so on. If entitative theology—the theology of three "bonded" Persons—is deconstructed, it is so a better appreciation of trinitarian *dynamis* can prevail. Perhaps the anagogic message of Johannes Reuchlin, whose obscure cryptography was published five hundred or so years ago,[93] makes "sense" once more: as the four-lettered and hence "stable" name of God (the Tetragrammaton, יהוה, or Yahweh) is "destabilized" by a fifth letter to make the Messianic name (the name of "Jesus," i.e., Joshua, יהושע , adds the letter *shin* to the Tetragrammaton and means "Yahweh saves"), so too does Christ's trinitarian teaching subvert an entitative notion of God and announce a God of perpetual alterity. In various essays I have planned for the future, my intent shall be to show that a "theology" of Divine drift, of God as "free act . . . deployed in the divinization of the world in the Holy Spirit,"[94] can be very orthodox indeed. Notice what Rahner, while studiously faithful to the Holy See, already feels justified in claiming:

> . . . it follows that what is different from God, namely man, can attain God in the same measure in which God in himself opposes himself as different. Hence the more substantial the inner differentiation in the divine, the more substantial must be the divinization of man. . . .
>
> Hence an orthodox modalism must begin with the fundamental mystery of Christian faith, and take its stand fundamentally on the total and all-embracing self-communicability of God—where unity grows in proportion to difference.[95]

Rahner's claim, clearly, is that the differentialism which constitutes unity in Trinity must necessarily characterize, in its own way, relations between the Trinity and man.[96] It follows, I believe, that the argument we have developed from *effacement* can serve, and serve at the side of orthodoxy, such inquiries as God the "preserving Cause," God as "uncreated Grace,"[97] and so on (and specifically that 'constitution through pure negative reference', as a concept, can rescue from the problematic of pantheism, a problematic which may seem implied at first blush both by differentialism and by a Christian "Nagarjunism"). Likewise, in Derridean *déroulements* such as "errance" and "discontinuity," notions so often regarded as "fatalistic," I see future possibilities for the solution—or better, the orthodox dissolution—of such troublesome antinomies as Divine Providence and free will. It is my hope many collaborators will join me in this work.

We turn now to perhaps the most taxing problematic of all, in terms of our overall endeavor. We have claimed our purpose is to reinstate "theories of presence" while benefiting even more from the Derridean trajectory than Derrida himself does. The way, or better the wayward way, that we traced earlier led to Derrida's longed-for *exergue*, the *tathatā* realized not by Derrida but by the differential mystic. The *tathatā*, or "crosscut" as we have called it, is a mystical frequentation which allows the wise one to move at will in the "world-ensconced" (the logocentric) and the "ungathered" (the differential). But if the process of Derridean deconstruction invariably begins with a "proof" that a logocentric formula is *illogical,* why should we want to *reinstate* it at all? Why should the wise one return to "error" and "move" in it? Several 'centered' mysticisms of the Orient (that is, 'centered' on the non-logical as a kind of supreme identity) have of course asserted that the enlightened man resorts to logic when it suits him and moves in the logocentric at will, as a *convention.* That is, as long as one is "in the body," as long as one must converse with the non-enlightened, and so on, a precise command of logic is important as a *convenience.* However, our proclaimed concern is to reinstate "theories of presence" (of organic criticism in literature, for example; of logocentric formulae in speculative theology, for example) in their integrity, not as mere conveniences. Christian teaching, for one, rightly insists on the truth-bearing potential of human reason and on the truth value of dogmatic assertions expressed in terms of logical syntax (as we shall see). We wish, then, to rehabilitate the truth claim of logocentrism, but—unlike a "reactionary" reinstatement—we wish to frequent differential truth too. In sum, we intend a reinstatement of "presence" in the mode of *as,* not the mode of *as if* nor the mode of *as only.* How can we justify a real but not exclusive reinstatement? And (perhaps the most insidious threat of all) how can we prevent *tathatā*—which is described, after all, as competence to interchange logocentric and differential—from establishing itself in its own right as a kind of mystic "site," a "point of oscillation," as it were? Does not the motif of *tathatā* restore, through a kind of underground dialectic and at an Archimedean remove, the whole notion of 'center' we claim to escape?

Let us first attempt the justification of a "real but not exclusive" rehabilitation. The lead I have followed here is that of Nagarjuna himself, for—as my treatment tried to make clear at the time—I am convinced the true Nagarjunism is differential, not purely rational nor centrically mystical. Indeed, if Nagarjuna were simply a rationalist, then his demonstration that ontological causality, that entitativism (and so on) are illogical, would simply establish "theories of presence" are *false,* and there would be no justification for their reinstatement. In their stead, *śūnyatā,* demonstrated as logically true, would be the way of both truth and right behavior. If Nagarjuna were simply a centric mystic, his relentless logic would shatter "theories of presence," but just to show that all logic subverts itself—so as to facilitate the leap to the non-rational center. In this case, any return to the logocentric would indeed be just for the sake of convenience. The reader must recall, however, that the Nargarjunist version of the Buddhist "two truths"—as we established it—affirms the valid functioning and the integrity of the logocentric realm and the differential. Thus Mervyn Sprung's insistence, you will recall, that the Nagarjunist wise man "takes things in their truth. *We* may describe his way of taking things as 'as if,' but that is for our purposes, not his; the everyday for the yogi could not be 'as if' because there is nothing outside of the middle way for it to be as. . . ." (see p. 127). Without retreat into centrism, the "two truths" are somehow a wayward way: "the limits of *nirvāṇa* are the limits of *saṃsāra*," and "*samvṛti* is *paramārtha*." But Nagarjuna actually tells us precious little about *how* the wayward way avoids monism, and nothing at all about *how* the logocentric can maintain *as* rather than *as if* status if logocentrism is by nature self-contradictory. What Nagarjuna does give us, you will recall—and it is a precious communication (indeed, for us at this point a *sine qua non*)—is the assurance that the realization of the two truths is not a *reasoning* but a special sort of *prajñā*-knowing. That it is a very special sort of *prajñā*-knowing, when compared to the various cognitions typically associated with mysticism, becomes obvious on two counts. For one, Nagarjuna proceeds to enlightenment by way of *prāsaṅgika*, which (you remember) is precisely the skilled use of logic. That is, through Nagarjunist "negative dialectic" logocentrism is deconstructed, and eventually *śūnyatā* appears beneath an erased alternative (and the alternative is usually a fourth lemma). The frequenting of *tathatā*, then, is somehow laced with very methodical logic (Nagarjuna's purpose, unlike that of several Zen exercises, is never to "snap one out of logic"). On the second count, though, it is obvious that Nagarjunist *prajñā*-knowing is special because, as we said above, it is not pure reasoning. The Nagarjunist literature describes the *prajñā*-knowing as mystical and insists that asceticism and sustained good conduct are necessary for its attainment. We can already conclude, then, that Nagarjuna's knowing, his mystical realization, is neither logical nor non-logical but mysteriously off-logical.

Our next "lead" comes from Derrida himself (our Nagarjuna *manqué*), whose perhaps most unique contribution is to describe in natural terms the very *condition* which Nagarjuna frequents mystically. Derrida's great contribution is surely not the proving that certain logocentric speculations are illogical (this has been done so many times!). His great contribution, rather, is the discovery that the logical disproof of logocentrisms such as self-identity reduce finally to a disproof of the very syntax of language, the very syntax of logic, the very syntax of thought; furthermore, that such disproof invalidates the disproof itself; and furthermore, that one nonetheless *cannot* (literally *cannot*) reject the disproof *nor* reject logic. One rides in-between, as it were, and—as we saw—overhead the closing canopy and obscure fissure suggest entrapment rather than sure liberation. It is this very same condition, *natural* and anguished in Derrida, that is in Nagarjuna *mystical* and liberating. For Nagarjuna, too, in other words, there is differential activity which neither rejects the disproof of logic nor rejects logic, but in him differentialism is sure and secure. Realized, not unrealized. Redeemed, not *irredenta*.

If, on our own, we proceed now to an accounting of *why* this mysticism is off-logical, we can, I think, explain at last how a full reinstatement of the logocentric is possible. My claim, simply put, is that it is not purely logical to allow logic to deconstruct itself. From a purely logical point of view, it is absurd to embark upon a demonstration against the principle of identity, say, precisely because the efficacity of the demonstration depends on the principle of identity. If one embarks upon a logical demonstration, he is committing himself a priori to the necessary assumptions of logic. When he makes the necessary assumptions of logic themselves the content of a logical demonstration, he is committing himself a priori to the understanding that a conclusion denying the necessary assumptions can only result from a mistake in the demonstration. What I am claiming (and here Derrida would disagree) is that *as soon as* one embarks upon a "disproving" of logic, the whole project is *mixed*, is *off-logical*. Granted that the step-by-step *déroulement* of the logic is methodologically "relentless," the whole project is still impure *in radice*. To say this is not to belittle the enterprise. In fact, I would maintain it is inhuman and very ill-advised to be purely logical (or to seek to be purely logical) all the time when dealing with life's important questions. Derrida, I am convinced, is so lionized by contemporary intellectuals exactly because he has localized and identified the "quandary" to which human history has inevitably led. And differential mysticism can transmute this one and the same condition of quandary to condition of miracle. Given all the above, the reinstatement of a real logocentrism comes about in this wise. I argue that logocentric formulae are the proper and only conclusions of purely logical operations and that it thus makes sense to talk of purely logical truth in terms of modal activity: logocentric formulae can be really true "in terms of logic" as long as they correspond in these terms to reality (i.e., they should be formally "valid," and they should be "true"); the Derridean *déroulement*, from the deconstruction of logic all the way through an alternative conclusion, erasure, and diascript, is from the very start another activity—capable of real truth "in terms of differentialism, of off-logic." Of course, to practice these two truths with command and certainty, and to move with the freedom of *tathatā*, require mystical realization—the realization mustered at long last[98] by discipline, sustained goodness, and differential analysis (all working together).

Does not *tathatā*, the crosscut, function surreptitiously as a mystical center, so that we are reviving logocentrism once more? This is the last question remaining for us before we begin an affiliation of these ideas and Christian theology. The answer comes easily, as long as we recall Derrida's treatment of the 'interval' (the 'differential between', as we called it) and how it contrasts with a 'logocentric between'. The latter negotiates, in time and space, between two entities—and is thus necessarily conceived as a 'site' (though it is, of course, a site of absence, generated logocentrically as part of the dialectical exchange with 'presence'). The former, the 'differential between', is a sort of

Bishop's diagonal which slips past time and space—it constitutes as the 'difference' between two musical notes, say, constitutes. *Tathatā*, the crosscut, is a 'differential between' which enables and constitutes two activities: a logocentric activity (the "gathered") and a differential activity (the "ungathered"). As such, the crosscut is a *virtus*, an enabling power (understood differentially, of course) whereby the wise one moves at will "between" the world taken in purely logical terms and the world taken in differential terms. The crosscut, a 'differential between', itself escapes the problematic of logocentrism, then. And its thematic history can function for us as emblematic, too, of the two donors who have helped our own thesis: Derrida, after all, is the thinker whose theory can apply to the crosscut, but Nagarjuna, after all, is the mystic whose persistence attains to the frequenting of it.

Given all the above, why is it the case that Catholic Christianity,[99] perhaps very unexpectedly for some, is so well-suited for differentialism? The contributing factors are best recognized by way of analogy. Catholicism has been, historically, the defender within the Christian tradition of reason's integrity (see DZ 1622–27, 1799): her consistent rejections of "fideism" (the teaching, identified with much of conservative Protestantism, that reason cannot function as a source of religious knowledge) are well known.[100] Yet, Catholicism has rejected also the "autonomous rationalism" (see DZ 1667–74, 1703–9, 1810, 1811) of the secular rationalist (and of those elements of liberal Protestantism which, she maintains, are too secular): rationalism must, for the Catholic, defer to *mysterium* (NOT because reason cannot afford religious truth, but because reason cannot give enough of religious truth—a *mysterium* is "beyond" logocentric thought; see DZ 1795, 1796, 1816). Differential activity, then, when it is characterized—the way I have—as "off-rational," shares the adherence to ratiocination we find in Church teaching; differential activity eschews the non-rational, much as the Church eschews fideism; finally, differential activity, the way I have described it, is neither purely logical nor centrically mystical but a very special "frequenting"—a "frequenting" that in Nagarjunism becomes an affirmed "beyond logocentrism," somehow analogous to the truth-status Catholicism sees in *mysterium*.

In the context of all this, we must discuss too the role that our earlier rehabilitation of pure logocentrism plays in relation to Christian theology; on the other hand, we must discuss as well the role of Christian mysticism, especially since the Church has been intentionally reticent in its official pronouncements concerning mysticism. Let us take up mysticism first, since it will allow us an excursus on Angelus Silesius (1624–77), in my judgment one of the greatest of Catholic differential mystics. The caution with which Catholicism, in its official documents, has handled mysticism is I think well founded, and all the more so because Catholic spirituality has produced mystics so abundantly, and, I think, so beautifully. Most Catholic mystics have experienced what we have called centric mysticism,[101] and their ecstasy has been non-logical. Ecstatic experience of this kind is of a nature different from the science of theology, and, again by nature, the authenticity of a given individual's mysticism is very difficult to evaluate. The magisterium, very properly, has not wanted to identify all mysticism with extraordinary holiness,[102] nor has it wanted to relegate the great masses of faithful to some kind of secondary status among the people of God. Mysticism, centric or differential, is not necessarily the same as holiness. Indeed, repeatedly the *magisterium* has emphasized holiness is dependent on love, not on a mystical experience which has, historically, been enjoyed by very few. What is more, the virtue of faith in terms of Catholicism has been defined, in the main, as consent of the intellect and will to supernatural truths; it is understood that these truths are affirmed by the believer, under the influence of grace, because God has revealed them, and He cannot "deceive nor be deceived." In the Church's judgment, to limit faith to the ecstatic experience of the mystic would be to succumb to a gnosticism, to a dangerous elitism, if you will.[103]

What I wish to indicate is that the Church's history has been replete with differential mystics—mystics who have, in and through Christ, frequented par excellence what we have called the workings of *tathatā*. Furthermore—and here I take a quite novel approach to the purpose, or at least the role, of Angelus Silesius and his poetry[104]—what I wish to indicate is that the differential mystic sometimes does more than proclaim the differential experience: he also articulates a kind of differential theology of his own. I have already argued, of course, that both scripture and official conciliar documents have from the beginning provided *points de repère* which thwart[105] logocentric systems of interpretation, and I have argued that only now are formal theologians in a historical position to readjust their sights accordingly and produce a differential theology. But it is now my claim that differential mystics such as Angelus Silesius were already doing a kind of differential theology (I have much more evidence from many mystics[106] than what follows, but what I have space for here is already in its own way convincing, I think). In regard to mystical literature, the problem which confronted the Church in the seventeenth century (and before) was basically this: How does one cope with the truth-status of an epigram such as the following?

Gott weiss sich keinen Anfang

Du fragst, wie lange Gott gewest sei, um Bericht?
Ach, schweig: es ist so lang, er weiss es selbst nicht.

God Knoweth Not His Beginning

How long hath God been God? Be silent, ask not this!
So long, God knoweth not Himself how long it is.[107]

Taken as a theological statement and judged in logocentric terms, this verse implies heresy. God is eternal and necessarily knows Himself and His infinity 'from all eternity.' Given God's attributes, for His knowledge not to reach the infinite range of His own eternity is, in logocentric terms, impossible. But the Church, observing the devout Christian practice and the orthodox protestations of so many mystics who employed this literary manner of speech, had by this time come to the conclusion that such literature was not theological but phenomenological. That is to say, the purpose of the mystic when he uses this kind of language is not to assert logical propositons, but to describe an experience. And it is easy enough to recognize that the mystic, rapt in ecstasy, say, *experiences* God—like in the epigram above—as "so" infinite that even He is forever exploring Himself and never finding His own "end." Or, in a clearer instance, the mystic may sing that God and he are "one," so that God is the mystic and the mystic is God: in the absence of contrary evidence, the Church came to the judgment in such cases that the mystic is describing an *experience* of oneness and that he is not affirming pantheism or theosis (theosis is the heretical claim that the human soul is self-identical with God). When linked with a literary appreciation of hyperbole—and perhaps a conceptual spin-off in terms of paradox—this account of the mystic's 'style' has served well, especially for centric mysticism, since the latter is non-logical and (as Derrida himself points out) claims an affective focus well-articulated by paradox (for Derrida, paradox is the "telltale" figure of literary logocentrism, since it maintains "an apparent opposition" to be "not really so"[108]).

While agreeing with the Church, of course, that mystics as such are not adverting to a logocentric theology, I claim that mystics of the differentialist sort—besides doing a phenomenology of their experience—may be sometimes trying to establish, in their own way, a differential theology. For example, the epigram "Gott weiss sich keinen Anfang," cited earlier, may be an attempt to shatter the closed doublet of Knower and Image, the logocentric model of God which we have already deconstructed in the Derridean manner. The epigram, which happens to be in fact one of Silesius's own, could be deconstructing the model of God's knowledge which poses God as Knower ("er weiss") knowing His own infinite duration ("er weiss *es selbst*"). To set up the Divine format in these terms requires, tacitly at least, that God know Himself across infinite time: in other words, the entitative formula of self-identity, the closed doublet of knower and known, is—in God's case—extrapolated to infinity, as it were. But Silesius's epigram, of course, perhaps with an eye to the shock-effect, rejects the entitative formula with a final and defiant negative ("er weiss es selbst *nicht*"). That Silesius frequents the differentially mystic[109] is clear from his many poems of the *Ungrund* (the "Unground"), of which the following is typical:

Wie gründet sich Gott?

Gott gründt sich ohne Grund und misst sich ohne Mass;
Bist du ein Geist mit ihm, Mensch, so verstehst du das.

(I:42)

How Is God Grounded?

God is grounded without Ground and measured measurelessly;
Mankind, if you are one in Spirit with Him, then this you'll surely
see.[110]

God as *Ungrund* is not here the God of Void (i.e., God is not, in
Derridean terms, the mere dialectical variant of Presence), and many
of the Silesian's *Reimsprüche* prove it. Take, for example, the following:

Die geheimste Gelassenheit

Gelassenheit fäht Gott; Gott aber selbst zu lassen,
Ist ein' Gelassenheit, die wenig Menschen fassen.

(II:92)

The Mystical Abandonment

Abandonment ensnareth God; but the Abandonment Supreme,
Which few there be can comprehend, is to abandon even Him.[111]

To "let go of God Himself" ("Gott aber selbst zu lassen") is to let go
of 'God as Present' *and* 'God as Absent': to relinquish God is to dissolve God as a logocentric focus of any kind. God is frequented,
instead, as differential but Divine *mise-en-abyme*. The dissolving of
entitative consciousness reaches to all 'things', of course, including
the entitative 'self': "Ich bin ein selig's Ding, mag ich ein Unding
sein, . . ." (I:46)—"I am a blessed thing, may I be an un-thing"; and
this dissolving is always under the auspices of "realization": " . . .
Und weil ich es nicht *weiss,* drum hab ich es *erkiest*" (I:43)—"And
because I do not know [logocentrically] it, I therefore have realized
[mystical/differential awareness] it." The many poems of 'realization',
sometimes called the Vertigo epigrams, make it clear that Silesius's
'bracketing' of rational thought occurs only at the proper moments
and that he possesses the enabling power of the Christian *Tathatā*, (or
Christian 'crosscut'). Much like Nagarjuna, who realizes *"Saṃsāra* is
Nirvāna," Silesius realizes the Christian version of the "two truths"
that are really the *off/one way:*

Die Zeit und Ewigkeit

Du sprichst: Versetze dich aus Zeit in Ewigkeit?
Ist dann an Ewigkeit und Zeit ein Unterscheid?

(I:188)

Time and Eternity

You say—Get yourself out of time and into Eternity!
Is there then a distinction between Eternity and Time?[112]

"Zeit ist wie Ewigkeit und Ewigkeit wie Zeit" (I:47)—"Time is as
Eternity and Eternity as Time," insists the Silesian in the face of a

logic which insists on the distinction, and he proclaims the "keines Schrittes breit"—the "not a step's [i.e., stride's] breadth," or "no stride's breadth" which is the crosscut:

Wie weit der Weg in'n Himmel

Christ, schätze dir die Reis' in'n Himmel nicht so weit:
Der ganze Weg hinein ist keines Schrittes breit.

(V:67)

How Broad [or Far] the Way to Heaven[113]

Christ reckons for you that the journey to heaven
   is not so broad [or far]:
The entire way from here is no stride's breadth.[114]

The movement from the logocentric mundane to the differential and back again is purely attitudinal, and its facility is expressed so appropriately by the figure of litotes (a rhetorical trope which is very 'Derridean', in that it defines by *effacement,* absolute negative reference).

The aphorisms above, besides their descriptive role (as testimonies to differential realization and the crosscut), are often theological too—but perhaps the differential theology of Silesius is more visible in an aphorism of the following kind:

Die Gottheit gründet kein Geschöpf

Wie tief die Gottheit sei, kann kein Geschöpf ergründen;
In ihren Abgrund muss auch Christi Seel' verschwunden.

(V:339)

No Creature Fathoms the Godhead

How deep the Godhead is, no creature can fathom;
In its Abyss [*Abgrund* etymologically isn't non-Ground but off/ground] the soul of Christ must also
vanish [literally, "be lost," i.e., disappear from sight].[115]

Though Silesius is subject to the influence of an earlier German theology which was often heretical when it distinguished between "Godhead" and "God," in Silesius the "Godhead" is easily taken as the Divine Unity, and "God" taken as God the Father—both very orthodox notions, surely. In any case, the above epigram concerns only the relation between Christ (and remember that Christ's divine and human "operations," though "two," are "harmoniously united," DZ 264) and the Divine Unity. Logocentric theology demands (all the more so in the seventeenth century) that Christ fathom the Divine Unity to its infinite depth (the *mysterium,* for the logocentric theologian, insists on the "paradox"). Inasmuch as Silesius shows Christ not *fathoming* (not reaching the "other infinite end," as it were), the poet breaks the closed dyad conventionally used to explain the relation between Christ and the Divine Unity.[116] Christ just "keeps on going" in the Divine *mise-en-abyme* which is Himself and the Divine Unity.

   Derrida, you will recall, followed his deconstructive phases with
sparse accounts—in part logical, in part descriptive—of what the
constituting interval, differance, the diascript, may be like. Silesius
does much the same—in the following aphorism he dispatches the
logocentric between of "and/or," and in the aphorism I cite below it he
evokes the *differential between* of "and/or between and/or." First, the
attack on the logocentric middle:

Die Mittelwand muss weg

Weg mit dem Mittelweg; soll ich mein Licht anschauen,
So muss man keine Wand vor mein Gesichte bauen.

(II:43)

The Dividing-Wall [*Mittelwand*, "Wall in the Middle"] Must Be Done Away With

Away with the middle course; if I am to look upon my light,
No one should build a wall in front of my face.

Then, presented so appropriately as the 'working' of the Trinity itself, the differential between:

Der Punkt, die Linie und Fläche

Gott Vater ist der Punkt; aus ihm fliesst Gott der Sohn,
Die Linie; Gott der Geist ist beider Fläch und Kron.

(IV:62)

Point, Line, and Planes

God the Father is the Point; from Him flows God the Son,
The Line; God the Spirit is the Plane [the "Flat," the "Base,"
a horizontal plane] and the Crest ["crown," or the "end of a line"
of a triangle] of both.

   Until the last clause, the geometric analogy of this second epigram
implies a conventional theology (the Son flows from the Father).
Then, suddenly, we are given the Holy Spirit defined as "Crest" and
"Plane," two geometric terms which in relation to the analogy do not
"make sense." If the Father and Son are point and issuing line respectively, no spatial *enclosure* is possible. And if the Holy Spirit is the
crest (possibly the "crest" at the top of an inclined line, the Son; and
also the "crest" found at the cornered point, the Father), how can
the Holy Spirit also be directly opposite, as the "base" of both? The
Holy Spirit, after all, is not here defined as the third side of a
triangle, but as a horizontal and a crest at the same time; the definition, in other words, is oppositional. And this, despite the prior
presence on the site of only a point and issuing line, not two lines
(i.e., not two sides of a triangle). There can be then no closed
triangle, no *entity*. Instead of placement as a third side of a Divine
Triangle (as in conventional diagrams of the seventeenth century),
the Holy Spirit is a triangle's crest and base, but *not a third side*. The
logocentric third side (the conventional Holy Spirit, in other words)
which is supposed to connect crest and flat *is missing*. If the crest and
flat are oppositional, the gap, the *interval* "between" them, leaves the

doubly would-be triangle *open*. The Holy Spirit, for Silesius, is liberating energy, is *dissémination*. Can it even be the case that Silesius's "Beschluss," the last (but open-ended) poem in *Cherubinischer Wandersmann*, is in some inspired or at least (fortuitously) emblematic sense, a Derridean poem?

Beschluss

Freund, es ist auch genug. Im Fall du mehr willst lesen,
So geh und werde selbst die Schrift und selbst das Wesen.

(VI:263)

Conclusion

Friend, it is enough now. If you wish to read more,
Go and yourself become the writing and its condition.[117]

Having examined the roles of differential mysticism, we now turn once again to the Church's attitude towards ratiocination. There are three zones of inquiry involved: (1) at the microscopic level, logic, as we have seen, pervades the syntax of thought and language themselves; (2) at the theological level, logic informs the logocentric system identified thus far with speculative theology; and (3) at the doctrinal level (i.e., the *presentation* of "truths" that *must* be believed), logic structures both the scriptural and traditional revelation itself, and the magisterial decrees which formally proclaim these doctrines. Apropos the first, the Church has not officially addressed the situation, since formal Western philosophy has only recently broached it. Since, however, the Church has officially pronounced that logic can provide truth (DZ 1649–51), surely it must be assumed that the syntax of ordinary day-to-day thinking and of language, insofar as they are logically structured, can provide truth (i.e., they can offer awareness of real "goings on," awareness of how matters really "work"). Apropos the second, which concerns the theological level and by necessary retroactive implication the microscopic level which "founds" it, the key is quite certainly the concept of "limited availability to logic." That is to say, God is logically knowable by man, but this logical knowing is inadequate—and inadequacy here always means that God cannot be *completely* targeted by logocentrism, He cannot be "comprehended" in the sense of circumscribed, "grasped all the way around" by logic, even when logic is operating upon divinely revealed truths. As the very orthodox theological encyclopedia, *Sacramentum Mundi*, puts it, "God is held to be knowable but incomprehensible ['unsurroundable'] while man is understood as a being created in order to know and love God, who finds therefore his true self in being blessed by God and giving himself to God."[118] And Vatican Council II itself opens the door to differential "theology" as well as logocentric theology when it officially declares: "For the deposit of faith or revealed truths are one matter; the manner in which they are formulated without violence to their meaning and significance is another."[119] The admonition that no violence be done to the messages of Divine Revelation warns us that *all theology* (whether logocentric or differential, then) must be faithful to scripture and Divine Tradition. We have attempted to show that differential theology follows with great scrupulosity the signals of Revelation, and on this very basis deconstructs the logocentric speculation identified with logocentric theology. And we have also tried to show that deconstruction—in the case of differential theology, a deconstruction compelled by the signals of Revelation—is a *mixed process*, a process not purely logical (since pure logic cannot permit itself to 'self-deconstruct'). Thus we maintain that the interpreting of logocentric theology, as a purely logical mode of treating Revelation (especially when facilitated by Divine grace), retains its truth status. And as true, this status is worthy, of course, of the utmost respect and its conclusions worthy of assiduous study. Since one of our overall purposes, also, is to reinstate literary theory and practice which is logocentric, perhaps it is important to assert here the following two points: (1) Derridean literary criticism, as differential, is *mixed process*[120]; and (2) logocentric literary theory and criticism, so often founded on organicism of one kind or another, is in our specialized terms 'purely logical'[121] and thus perfectly proper according to its own mode of truth (the splendid work of Cleanth Brooks, and the best of the other American New Critics, are good cases in point).

If we are to adhere always to the "deposit of faith," to Revelation, another question quite naturally arises. Though many of the signals from scripture and tradition, and from the magisterium which proclaims and defines the Revelation, lead to differentialism, logocentrism obviously pervades much of the Revelation. Scripture, for example, in much of its imagery, its thematology, and its linguistic structure is logocentric. And scripture, for the believer, is after all God's message, even if mediated through the culturally-bound minds of human authors. Needless to say, decrees of the magisterium, too, are structured in many ways according to the norms of logocentrism. And for the believer, when these decrees concern dogma and are intended as binding definitions, they are necessarily faithful to Revelation, and thus true. The proper understanding of this problematic, I think, is afforded by the following passage from Vatican Council I: "Reason, however, never becomes capable of understanding them [the mysteries presented by God in scripture and tradition, and proclaimed by the magisterium] the way it does truths which are its own proper object. For divine mysteries of their very nature so excel the created intellect that *even when they have been given in revelation* and accepted by faith, that very faith still keeps them veiled in a sort of obscurity . . . ."[122] Some of the total Revelation, in other words, is communicated as logocentric and is apprehended and proclaimed logocentrically, but there remains in the Revelation itself, a Divine Surplus. We must take great care, surely, to preserve and love the logocentric communication, as the Church insists: "Therefore, let there be growth and all possible progress in understanding, knowledge, and wisdom whether in single individuals or in the whole body, in each man as well as in the entire Church, according to the stage of their development; but only within proper limits, that is, in the same doctrine, in the same meaning, and in the same purport."[123] But still God's Revelation cannot be circumscribed by any one mode of formulation, including the logocentric. The Vatican Council II declares the following about the Revelation which has been "handed down from the Apostles":

> This tradition which comes from the Apostles develops in the Church with the help of the Holy Spirit. For there is growth in the understanding of the realities and the words which have been handed down. . . . For, as the centuries succeed one another, the Church constantly moves forward towards the fullness of divine truth until the words of God reach their complete fulfillment in her. . . . Through the same tradition the full canon [content] of the sacred books becomes known to the Church, and the sacred writings themselves are more profoundly understood and unceasingly made active in her; and thus God, who spoke of old, uninterruptedly converses with the Bride of His beloved Son [the Bride is the Church]; and the Holy Spirit, through whom the living voice of the gospel resounds in the Church, and through her, in the world, leads unto all truth those who believe and makes the word of Christ dwell abundantly in them (v. Col. 3:16).[124]

By thus approving of authentic developmentalism, the Church leaves the way (or off/way!) open for differential theology.

Having discussed the relation of both mysticism and logocentric formulation to the differential, we can now address the issue of gnosticism— for it is possible, at first blush, to regard the Christian crosscut,[125] with its beautiful liberation from Derridean anguish, as the unique preserve of an elite. At a time when this kind of anguish is becoming widespread, at least among intellectuals, it is difficult indeed to envision the Church restricting liberation from the 'quandary' to a few full-fledged differential mystics. And indeed, throughout the history of the Church, gnosticism in its various forms has been condemned precisely because of its exclusivity. In terms of Christianity, I argue that the liberating security of the crosscut, though perhaps in a more inchoate 'working' than in the Christian differential mystic, is accessible to all Christian believers who need it, and that it is accessible through the virtue of faith. (In terms of Nagarjunism, it is surely accessible as *tathatā* to those who do not sense themselves called to Christian differentialism; and no doubt similar charisms are 'at work' in other individuals and communities.[126])

The problematic of the virtue of faith, briefly put, is this: the Church has refused to identify faith with an extraordinary perceptible experience,[127] in part because the latter is so difficult to authenticate, and so easily confounded with natural emotion; yet she has also refused, as indeed is to be expected, the identification of faith with a natural reasoning process, since it is clear from scripture that faith is a supernatural gift of God. Largely in reaction to an excessive emotionalism which characterized some non-authentic spiritualities in past Church history, the formula that became established identified faith as the assent to Christ's Revelation made by reason, and made by reason *because* Christ "cannot deceive nor be deceived." Though initiated by God and accomplished through His grace, the actual working of grace in and through the reason was understood to be in most cases imperceptible; indeed, the believer knows God is at work in that act of faith, but the believer need not experience this working in an extraordinary way. Vatican Council II, while of course reaffirming the above 'intellectualist' definition of faith, added to it. The addition was probably motivated by a sense, on the part of the Council Fathers, that contemporary man is "ready for" (and can have a sounder appreciation of) a *realization* which is neither emotional nor exclusively logocentric. Thus, after calling "The obedience of faith" an obedience "by which man entrusts his whole self[128] freely to God" (and "self" necessarily includes more than the logical faculty), Vatican Council II declares:

> If this faith is to be shown, the grace of God and the interior help of the Holy Spirit must precede and assist, moving the heart and turning it to God, opening the eyes of the mind, and giving 'joy and ease to everyone in assenting to the truth and believing it.' To bring about an ever deeper understanding of revelation, the same Holy Spirit constantly brings faith to completion by His gifts [and most of the "seven gifts of the Holy Spirit," a very specialized enumeration in Catholic theology, are not *logical* realizations].[129]

The virtue (*virtus*, or "enabling power") of faith is not, then, only an intellectual assent, but rather a special mode of realization[130] which can include the differential (the off/rational).[131]

As already constated, the venerable history of Nagarjunism offers the richness of *tathatā* for those so summoned, and there are as well other analogous contexts—some perhaps localized in scope, so they are esthetic, theological, or mundane. Each of these, and each in its own way, constitutes a liberating poise at what is for the anguished Derridean the "fissure" in the "canopy," but is for the differentialist what Karl Rahner calls the summons of the "Whither."[132] We must follow Discipline—"Look at September! / Look at October! / The yellow leaves, falling, falling, / To fill both mountain and river."[133] If I may indulge a pun fabricated in the paucity of my own very meager stores:

Be WAYWARD,—

A Ward of the Off/Way,

And there'll be no limbus to your nimbus!

Or, if I may indulge an anagogic allusion, drawn from an elegant Storehouse endlessly more copious than my own:

". . . and the broken pulley falls into the well."[134]

O Divine *mise-en-abyme*!

Und doch ist Einer, welcher dieses Fallen
unendlich sanft in seinen Händen hält.
—Rainer Maria Rilke

Whorlèd wave, whelkèd wave,— and drift.
—Gerard Manley Hopkins

Appendix

Deconstructive *Démarches*

Everything and Nothing:
A Demonstration of the Third Lemma

The first of the two essays here collected as an Appendix has as its purpose the demonstration of an alternative third lemma "way of proceeding." A third lemma position, you will recall from part 3, asserts that "*X* is both *Y* and non-*Y*." The classic third lemma position is a Heideggerian pluralism, which is founded—in our terms—on a Taoist *plenum* of sorts. This "way of proceeding" we treated at length in part 2. Here in the Appendix, as the first essay, I provide an alternative kind of Taoism, perhaps best understood as a Taoist void of some kind. The influence of Heidegger—this time from his studies of negation—is still noticeable, and so is the influence of centric Ch'an/Zen Buddhism. I hope the reader will recognize that the crossing-out ventured at the end as a possibility is a Heideggerian *sous rature,* and not at all Derridean. In short, the *regressio ad infinitum* reveals a mystical center. This essay was originally presented at an American Philosophical Association meeting in Washington, D.C., and addressed essays by Morris Weitz and M.H. Abrams, who represented, respectively, analytic esthetics and "humanistic pluralism."[1]

In his paper "M.H. Abrams' philosophy of Critical Theories," Professor Weitz says that the pratfall which is "essentialist" definition does not occur in his own work and that it does not even happen in the essay of Professor Abrams, who (despite his faults) is "guilty of no essential definition of critical theory" (W76).[2] I think, however, that essential definition, overt or implied, occurs in both Weitz and Abrams, though it is much more pronounced in the case of Weitz. My own treatment maps out what I consider the merits and demerits of the case advanced by each party. Concomitantly with this task, I plan to show how each of the two disputants, when measured by his own protestations, falls into self-contradiction. Actually, their latest encounter has been somewhat star-crossed, since Abrams often assumes that Weitz opposes all theory, and Weitz intends only to attack essentialist theory.[3] As I critique their debate, I shall indicate my own sympathies with the meta-theory of Abrams (for whom I have such great esteem), and cross-reference my own part 2 where the Heideggerian tradition lends support to "pluralistic interpretation." I shall also offer a personal response to the most salient charges, one that can be regarded as equally applicable to Abrams's work and to the Heideggerian mode.

First among Weitz's *démarches,* and cleverest, is a kind of misrepresentation. In accordance with his own "elucidations" of descriptive, interpretative, and evaluative activity, Weitz is committed to the proposition that only description can legitimately utter true/false assertions. Interpretation and evaluation can only involve degrees of plausibility. (As for poetics, his fourth mode, its essentialist assertions are by nature false.) The upshot of all this is that Weitz can only declare Abrams's many propositions false if he reduces their status, and the status of their relevant discussions, to the level of description. (He exonerates Abrams of essentialism, so he cannot deny Abrams's proposals on the grounds that they are essentialist.) For example, Weitz says that Abrams mis-describes Aristotle, that Abrams mis-describes how meta-theory often operates, and that these two mis-descriptions are not just implausible but wrong.

Weitz employs the same legerdemain to defend his own positions. When Abrams utters the charge that Weitz is a definitionist and at times a closet-essentialist, Weitz can cover his tracks by saying he is just performing "Adequate description" (see, for example, W62, where Weitz denies his treatment of criticism is "definition"; and see W75, where he defends the doctrine of literary autonomy against the charge of essentialism; consult also, W70, where he "turns the tables" and calls Abrams's interpretation of critical theory a description, so he is then free to label it "false"). It behooves us, therefore, to submit Weitz's notion(s) of description to a closer scrutiny. Let us observe at the outset that for Weitz description is not at all the same as "working definition," which he eschews (W62, 66); I assume the disavowal occurs because a working definition, though understood by both Weitz and Abrams as distinct from essential definition, nevertheless operates on the level of plausibility rather than true/false assertion. Weitz implies at least three definitions[4] of description as such, though he speaks, of course, as if he uses the word homogeneously. One is that description takes as its object the "verifiable" (that is, data which is available to the scientific method; see Weitz, *Hamlet,* pp. 237, 238, et passim).[5] Weitz's example is the descriptive statement, "Horatio asks, 'What, has this thing appeared again tonight?'" (W72), wherein the critic just quotes a passage from Shakespeare's *Hamlet.* Abrams accepts this and only this definition of descriptive activity, since only this kind of description accommodates what is usually called 'empirical verification'. A second clandestine definition is exemplified by attributes such as the following: Hamlet is "shy, retiring," and "fearful, too pure" (WH231). Abrams rightly points out that attributions of this type are interpretative (A31); they are not the *données* Weitz makes them out to be. Weitz himself asseverates that interpretations (which he identifies with "explanations") "are not factual, yielding true or false answers as the descriptive issues do, but explanatory, to which more or less adequate answers can be given" (WH252).

I respectfully submit that attributions to the Hamlet character such as "shy" or "fearful" match Weitz's own definition of interpretation, and not description. Surely these attributes and others like them have been debated by reputable scholars over a long span of years, and surely the history of the controversy has provided no consensus of opinion (though even if it had, "conclusion by consensus" cannot, according to Weitz's own tenets, transmute into fact[6]). But Abrams has already made this very valid point. My further claim is that Weitz's assertion about Aristotle, namely, that Aristotle's use of definition functions to prove and demonstrate definitive criteria, is OF THE SAME ORDER as Weitz's remarks about "shy" and "fearful" Hamlet. Weitz's thesis concerning Aristotle is interpretative, but masquerades as descriptive so it can contradict and therefore prove false the thesis of Abrams, namely, that Aristotle's use of essential definition is instrumental, and functions to illuminate dramatic texts rather than prove criteria.

Weitz's third notion of descriptive activity is "a generalization without universalization" (W62). He uses as his example the first sentence of the book he authored on *Hamlet*, "Criticism is a form of studied discourse about works of art." Weitz takes up the example because Abrams had cited it as a proof of Weitz's unwitting use of "working definition." Weitz claims instead that the statement is "description, generalization without universalization." I wish to point out, however, that this kind of description deviates from the previous two kinds. First, it is a generalization, and as such does not just apply to a *donnée* that appears before the critic and/or reader (whereas the Hamlet character is normally taken to so appear, and Aristotle's text is likewise taken to so appear). And this difference is obviously not expunged by the claim the generalization is not universal. Second, even if the generalization is not universal, it is intended to apply to critical texts which Weitz in fact has not encountered (otherwise his statement would not be a generalization), and on this score seems to attribute to such a set of texts qualities-in-common, an attribution which seems to me non-Wittgensteinian (though I do not know Weitz's personal stand on this matter). In any case, Weitz's third crypto-definition of description equates the latter with generalization, and generalization, because it includes reference to members-not-at-hand, is not empirically verifiable. Thus his third kind of description is not really descriptive, but interpretative.

At one point Weitz argues that if his statement, "Criticism is a form of studied discourse . . . ," constitutes a working definition, then so too does Abrams's statement, "Weitz's first sentence is 'Criticism is a form of studied discourse . . . ,' " constitute a working definition. Since Weitz's statement, "Criticism is a form . . . ," is patently not the definition of "Weitz's first sentence," Abrams is wrong in identifying the verb "is" exclusively with the defining process. But, in Abrams's defense, I answer that Abrams is making no such exclusive identification. That Weitz shows Abrams's statement is not definition in no way proves that Weitz's statement is not definition. Indeed, Abrams's argument does not rest on a naive univocal reading of the verb "is," but on the logical form of Weitz's statement. Abrams's sentence, "Weitz's first sentence is 'Criticism is a form . . . ,' " is, in terms of Abrams's own definition, obviously empirically verifiable (one need just look at Weitz's text) and therefore obviously descriptive. Weitz's first sentence, "Criticism is a form . . . ," is not empirically verifiable, and thus is non-descriptive. In Abrams's terms, it is rather a working definition.

Weitz winds down his argument by saying that Abrams himself finishes his own essay with a general statement about criticism and that Abrams calls his own statement description ("One way to describe criticism and related modes of inquiry is to say they are a language-game" [A54]). I answer that Abrams is obviously putting the word "describe" to a very broad use here and that he definitely means the postulation of a working definition (especially because this has been the burden of his argument, and because he does not claim his definition is empirically verifiable). In the same closing paragraph of his essay, after all, Abrams also authors the following clause: " . . . those aspects of the human predicament in which valid knowledge and understanding are *essential* . . ." (the emphasis is mine). Even Weitz would not press the claim Abrams means here that "valid knowledge and understanding" are sufficient and necessary conditions for "aspects of the human predicament"!

"Criteria" and "presuppositions" are two terms Weitz employs with considerable frequency, and their relation to what he calls description is most interesting. Abrams argues, of course, that Weitz espouses an essentialist theory of art, namely, the autonomous nature of the art work. Weitz delivers his riposte—that the "principle of organic unity" can be used by the critic apart from the "metaphysics of organic unity" (W69); that presuppositions are necessary for practical criticism but do not compel commitment to essentialist theories (W73); that presuppositions can function as non-definitive conditions or criteria for criticism (W75); and that criticism stands behind essentialist theories but can be excised from them (W66). The presupposition of literature's autonomy and the criterion of organic unity can be accepted as "commonplaces," as "undeniable" (W75). But I ask—why, pray tell? Weitz disavows essentialism, so they cannot be undeniable because necessary and sufficient. They are not the strange offspring of non-essentialist theory, because the latter cannot advance certainties. They are not products of interpretative or evaluative activity, or they would just be "plausible," not "undeniable." Finally, they are not descriptive, because they are not verifiable (indeed, prestigious modern European approaches repudiate notions of literary autonomy: could they do this in the face of "fact," the "undeniable," the "verifiable"?). Weitz's claim that the presupposition and criterion in question (autonomy and organic unity respectively) are undeniable commits the very same fallacies as do his second and third definitions of description. Like the case of the "shy" Hamlet, organic unity is impossible to verify even in a text-at-hand. Like the case of the "generalizing description," organic unity cannot be verified in texts-not-at-hand. And the same destructive paradigm applies to "autonomy." In this whole matter, I think Weitz has so positioned himself that he must be wrong himself in order to demonstrate Abrams wrong.

If we now refocus, so we examine the status of Weitz's "four logical models of critical discourse" as a whole, an even more vexatious problematic comes into sight. Abrams has charged that Weitz's four modes, which Weitz says are distinct and irreducible, do not reflect praxis: description mixes with interpretation, and evaluation miscegenates with them both. In short, it is very difficult to find a specimen of critical discourse which manifests these modes in an identifiable way. Yet Wittgenstein, who so inspires Weitz and the Anglo-American analytic movement, calls for logical models attuned to use, to the phenomena provided by "look-and-see." Weitz admits his four logical categories are not readily distinguishable in the practical order, though he adds that "these difficulties, however, reflect on the application of the criteria of my categories, not on the criteria themselves" (W72). But in fact do not the difficulties reflect on the criteria themselves? If the four logical categories and their criteria do not reflect the actuality of textual use, they cannot be description. Where do they come from, then? In terms of Weitz's elucidation of interpretative activity, neither can the four categories derive from interpretation. For if they are the result of interpretation, Weitz could not say Abrams's contradictory statement (that the modes can be reducible to each other) is false. Thus, in terms of his own understanding of the modes, Weitz should feel driven to concede that his four modes are DEFINITIONS. And what is more, they are essentialist definitions.

The four modes are essentialist for two reasons. First, Weitz consistently treats their formulae as sufficient and necessary criteria for what they claim to define.[7] Second, the four modes are essential because Weitz rejects Abrams's counterproposition (that the modes can be mutually reducible). If Weitz's propositions apropos irreducibility were insufficient and unnecessary, he could not make bold to declare Abrams's opposing position false. As for the mode which Weitz at tributes to Abrams, the mode of "evaluative interpretation,"[8] I am sure that Abrams's justification is that such a mode does a more adequate job of reflecting what happens in critical texts. Weitz avers that since "evaluative interpretation" is also a mode, it "distorts" the fluidity of practical discourse just as surely as Weitz's own modes do. I answer that Weitz is here performing a false analogy (that is, he assumes entities alike in one way are necessarily alike in another way). The analogy would work if Abrams were indeed claiming that Weitz's modes fail because they are modes. However, Abrams is claiming that Weitz's modes are factitious because they are not modeled on praxis. And here Abrams's mode is unlike those of Weitz, because the former does reflect praxis.

In another of his argumentative sequences, Abrams shows that "criticism presupposes theory." This issue involves the relation of theory and practice, of course, as the other sequences have. But so strategic a formulation here forces a kind of crisis. Weitz utters his *Je t'accuse:* practice and its criteria are misjudged by Abrams, in that they need not presuppose theory. Weitz reasons that one can accept Plato's doctrine of a priori knowledge without accepting his doctrines of reminiscence and preexistence of the soul (that is, these doctrines are "integral," but a person can nevertheless accept one without the other). Why then can't one accept particular criteria without accepting the theory which has, perhaps, historically founded the theory? I respond that Weitz is again pretending to display a logical simulacrum, but it is not really similar to its *donné* (in other words, Weitz is not doing what he thinks he is doing)! Weitz examines the relation of one theory to other theories. Abrams's position here is that you cannot have practice without theory; Abrams is not saying you cannot have theory without theory! The substance of the whole discussion takes fearsome turns, however. If, as Abrams says, criticism and practice presuppose theory, and if theories (each of them implied by genuine criteria and practice) contradict each other, what does one do? It is crucial to observe that Abrams—at least overtly—at no point "takes a stand" on contradiction. The most he declares is the following, that "The aims, fields, and rules of various critical language-games are sufficiently similar, however, so that some of their assertions are conflicting rather than alternative; but to determine which assertions these are, and how to decide the conflict between them, is a difficult exercise in the comparative grammar of language games" (A26).

In this context, nevertheless, Weitz senses a vulnerability. In what seems to be an unjustified maneuver, he converts Abrams's "stand" on alternative theories and practices into a "stand" on contradictory theories and practices. Throughout Abrams's essay, a constant claim is that alternative approaches can be simultaneously valid. Weitz takes Abrams to say that contradictory approaches are, by necessity, simultaneously valid. Thus misrepresented, Abrams becomes easy prey. Weitz declares that Abrams is ensnared in self-contradiction: Abrams professes that contradictory theses are both "true," and then pronounces Weitz's theses (which contradict those of Abrams) false! (Permit me a parenthetical *aparté:* of course, even if Abrams really argued contradictory theses are both necessarily valid, and if he were caught in self-contradiction, judged by the premise attributed to him self-contradiction could not make any difference to him anyway, could it?) But Abrams does not say that contradictory theses are both true! And in all instances where he disagrees with Weitz, he contradicts Weitz! To find Abrams in open self-contradiction, Weitz must show Abrams labeling false a thesis of Weitz that is an alternative to, not a contradiction of, his own.

So much for a comparison of Abrams's professed position on disagreement, and the actual form of his general arguments against Weitz. But what about the form of Abrams's arguments against Weitz specifically in so far as they reveal assumptions—possibly independent of formal "stands"—about the nature of disagreement? Here I find that in the dispute over Weitz's four modes of criticism, and in the dispute over Aristotle's use of definitions, Abrams assumes contradictory claims need not be both true (and indeed, in these disputes, Abrams says Weitz is wrong). But in the dispute over the autonomous nature of the literary work, the waters are muddied. Abrams believes the claim a literary work is autonomous has the status of "theory."[9] And it is clear he sees this theory to be in contradiction to other theories (and he affirms the latter theories). Yet he designates the theory of autonomy valid (A47). Thus I conclude Abrams believes contradictory theories can be, but need not be, simultaneously valid. I find much of this very interesting, and very supportive of my own attitude towards contradiction.[10] And it is to be noted that none of Abrams's above premises (overt or latent) concerning disagreement are inconsistent with each other.

I suggest that Professor Abrams is inconsistent, though, when he approaches the issue of "essentialism." Needless to say, despite the fervor of my polemic I have enormous respect for both Professor Weitz and Professor Abrams, and I treasure what I have learned from them over the years. In any case, it is on the topic of essentialism that I think Weitz best displays the analytic acumen for which he is so renowned. Abrams has maintained his version of Aristotle's use of definition is true, and Weitz's version false. Weitz then adds, "If it [Weitz's reading] is sterile, it is not wrong; it is only different from other, fertile readings. If it is incorrect, what objective textual evidence would decide that it is?" (W65). In other words, Weitz points out that Abrams's true/false assertion here does not "square" with interpretation as Abrams understands it, nor with description as Abrams understands it (that is, description as empirically verifiable). (Of course, Weitz's charge functions as a kind of Dantean *contrapasso*—it comes back to haunt him—since, as we have already seen, his own readings are not verifiable either.) I said, however, that I think Abrams falls into essentialism (a position he, like Weitz, consciously rejects). My rationale is simply put. Given his premises, only one recourse remains for Abrams, if he indeed wishes to justify his rejection of Weitz's reading (of Aristotle). Abrams must declare his own reading an essentialist definition, that is, a statement which is a sufficient and necessary account of the overall use to which Aristotle puts definitions in the *Poetics*. If Abrams's account were insufficient and unnecessary, he could not declare Weitz's account false. Actually, Abrams's reading is an INTERPRETATION, but he has precluded the possibility of so naming it.

In his section entitled "Does Metacriticism Presuppose Theory?" Abrams reasons that Weitz's anti-theory is itself a theory (and I think Abrams's charge is correct). Weitz parries by saying that if this be the case, anti-ontology is an ontology, anti-essentialism is an essentialism, and so on—a situation, he says, which is patently absurd (W74, 75). But I suggest that Weitz's logical model is here too gross and needs refinement. One way I justify for myself Abrams's claim is the following. Let us first examine the statement, "Anti-love is a love." I do not consider this utterance true, because "disposition to serve the beloved" is an ESSENTIAL quality of love, but NOT an ESSENTIAL quality of "anti-love." However, in the statement "Anti-theory is a theory," the ESSENTIAL components of "theory" are found also in "anti-theory." I can exemplify by saying that theory has "presuppositions" as an essential component, and anti-theory has presuppositions as an essential component. In fact, I personally go a crucial step further, and say that the presuppositions themselves are essentialist, so "essentialist presuppositions are an essential component . . ." (but more of this later). And if time and space permitted, I think I could similarly list other essential components shared-in-common by theory and anti-theory.

In any case, the formula I advance reads as follows: "If anti-X has the same essential qualities as X, anti-X is actually X." The irony that so impresses me is that Abrams and Weitz use this very formula regularly if subliminally against each other! How they wield that double-edge sword! For example, Weitz says the following of Abrams:

> In rejecting my account of the nature and role of theory in aesthetics, philosophy of the arts, and criticism, Abrams must also reject the notion that the concept of art is open, in order to claim instead that it and its subconcepts are all governed by definitive sets of criteria and are therefore amenable to the essentialist definitions he vainly tries to convert into working ones. (W78)

In other words, Abrams's non-essentialist position has the essential components of the essentialist position, and therefore is actually essentialist! And Abrams, in a much more overt way, uses the same formula against Weitz! An adjunct to this situation offers still another irony: the formula "works," you will note, only if the qualities common to anti-X and X are essential (sufficient and necessary). So even in this way Abrams and Weitz "structurally" commit themselves to essentialism!

The part of Abrams's essay that I find most relevant, and indeed, most poignant, is that entitled "Certainty, Rationality, and Critical Knowledge." Professor Abrams, humanist and *polyhistor,* calls almost plaintively for a return to the "human." Professor Weitz has singled out as his *termini a quibus* the assumptions of science and logic, two disciplines mired even more than most in the "Cartesian split,"[11] and so ill-adapted to truly human "thinking," to what Heidegger calls "originative thinking." Recall that Heideggerian hermeneutics takes as its origin the pre-objective ONENESS of interpreter and phenomenon (be the latter a literary text, or in the case of meta-critical activity, critical practice). And Heideggerian hermeneutics sees in interpretation a reading that is faithful to this oneness. To rephrase it, the interpreter "experiences" the phenomenon—he proceeds in understanding (*Verstand*); the interpreter then "interprets"—that is, he "articulates" or "phenomenologically describes" the oneness constituting *Verstand* (the oneness of interpreter and phenomenon), so as to achieve interpretation (*Auslegung*); finally, the interpreter (if he chooses) "makes a case" for his interpretation, or makes logical assertion (*Aussage*).[12] This very treatment I now render, in other words, operates on the level of *Aussage*. I recognize how my critique is "at a remove" from the zone where the most important and most human activities are "going on." To engage in logical demonstration is human too, of course, and an often necessary adjunct to other kinds of awareness. But *Aussage* is authentic only in so far as it reflects *Auslegung*.

If I may return to Professor Abrams's assessment, Abrams says Weitz is unfaithful to the "forms of life" (ultimately to what Heidegger calls *Verstand*). I do not think Weitz ever answers this contravention, other than to say Abrams likewise "distorts" (but recall my earlier treatment of Weitz's "four modes," where we found Abrams is truer to critical praxis). There is also, of course, Weitz's remark about "traditional ontology," which, "though it satisfies a deep human need and purpose, that of metaphysical solace," functions nevertheless "as no language-game at all but only as a language-idling, on holiday" (W60). Certainly Wittgenstein and Heidegger too reject "traditional ontology," though for different reasons. What disturbs me, rather, is Weitz's patronizing tone in reference to human need. Man's need for "metaphysical solace" is THERE in his very being, and is consequently a "form of life." For a Heideggerian, authentic philosophy (that is, "meditation on Being") and art provide "metaphysical solace,"[13] and do so legitimately, by interpreting (primarily) and sometimes asserting (secondarily) the nature of humankind. In this context, I find it significant that Weitz (faced with the widespread controversy over what Wittgenstein really MEANS) exclaims almost petulantly, " . . . the philosophical writings of Wittgenstein have now attained the dubious logical status of works of art" (W60)! Heidegger, of course, would regard such a characterization of his work as a great compliment.

Analytical philosophy reduces language to logical grammar, and then evaluates this grammar in terms of internal relations (that is, if the *signifiants* relate to each other logically, the statement in question is valid)—whence Weitz's remark that ontology "considered in its various drops of grammar," (W60) can be shown to be language-idling. With Weitz, Heidegger too accepts logic as an important factor operative in *Aussage*, but his point here is that logic can "go wrong" if it is not steadily pegged to *Auslegung* (thus the danger in relating *signifiants* in an internal forum as if they were independent of reality: this is real "language-idling"!). When reality and logic clash, the Heideggerian says, "revise your laws of logic; do not give up belief in the real (or belief in the knowability of the real)!" An even more important point is that logical grammar does not satisfy enough of "human need." What is art FOR, if not to satisfy human need? Such a question, by the way, is a metacritical one, is it not? And what are criticism and metacriticism FOR, if they do not indicate the positive relation between art and human need? When criticism and metacriticism abrogate their responsibility, their use of language is, par excellence, "language on holiday."

I now return to a consideration of essentialism. In order to facilitate discussion, I continue to accept the definition of essence identified with the "Analytic" tradition (among others). So I shall understand essential definition to mean the setting forth of criteria sufficient and necessary for the identification of all members of a set. Let it be said at the beginning that Weitz and even Abrams practice essentialism because it is impossible to do otherwise, as long as one is operating within the first three lemmas. A Heideggerian would claim the "instinct" revealed by such a practice is actually a very sound one: man's nature is, and man's philosophy ought to be, oriented towards discovery of what is the same in two entities, three entities, and ultimately all entities (that is, man should meditate more on the Ground which is Being, and not just on differences among beings). In order to appreciate "what is the same," one must hold in abeyance the object-object dichotomy (one entity as different from another) and even the subject-object dichotomy ("myself" as one sector, and the "outside" as another). As a means of achieving this new *modus entis,* one must recognize that all "meaning" really involves "forestructure,"[14] or a "way of experiencing" that is biologically and culturally influenced (so each person's forestructures are somewhat different from those of other people, and somewhat alike).

Let us keep in mind that in Heideggerian hermeneutics, forestructure engages an "apsect" (an "As-which") which is "other," so that "meaning" becomes the implication (enfolding) of fore-structure and aspect. The enfolding is the oneness manifest as *Auslegung*. Meaning is not "in the subject" or "in the object," though on the level of *Aussage* one (to a greater or lesser degree) "talks about" meaning as if it were thus compartmentalized. Even when talking in terms of subjects and predicates, however, one is not being "objective," since one's fore-structure contributes to the meaning involved. (When I first read Abrams's essay, I was so pleased with the way much of Abrams adequates to a Heideggerian account of "meaning": especially, see Abrams, pp. 33, 34.) Fore-structure includes presuppositions, and, in my opinion, Heideggerian fore-structure necessarily includes definitions that are "essentialist" (and in some cases valid: essentialism does not preclude validity[15]).

Regarding the debate over essentialism, let us "bring the crisis to a head," as it were. You may assert, "One need not use 'sufficient and necessary' definition to do practice and theory." I answer, "You are wrong,—prove the truth of your assertion!" If you wish to model your position on "forms of life," you look to the phenomena—in this case, a representative array of theory and practice. You declare, "An objective description of the phenomenon reveals that sufficient and necessary definition is not used by all theorists and practitioners." I answer, "There is no such thing as objective description [cf. Heidegger's *Sein und Zeit*, 7th ed., pp. 156–60]. Premises in your fore-structure engage the phenomenon, and a meaning occurs. You are treating the premises as sufficient and necessary. Otherwise you would have to grant that my counterproposition can be also true." An anti-essentialist statement, posed within the mode of the three lemmas, therefore necessarily implies an essentialist statement.

I shall wind down my paper with some remarks on contradiction. It is clear Professor Weitz does not believe contradictory assertions can be both true. My own presentation, in part 2, claims contradictory assertions (and these are or imply essentialist assertions) can be simultaneously true. But I essentially define "meaning" and several other classes of phenomena in this very critique of the Abrams-Weitz debate. And more to the point, I contradict Weitz, and in my own earlier book contradict E. D. Hirsch (who says literary meaning is exclusively the "author's meaning"[16]). Is not my stand "ensnared" in self-contradiction? Again I answer by "pushing the whole question to its limits." I say that contradictory propositions can be simultaneously true. You say they cannot. For those who have taken in my own part 2, I think it will be clear that what I am about to say now unfolds deliberately, coldly, logically, from the propositions to which I have committed myself there. (I choose to be consistent with what I have said elsewhere, and to be logical to the End of the three lemmas.)

In terms of Heideggerian hermeneutics, you have two options. The first option is to accept or reject an assertion, in this case my assertion that contradictory propositions can be both true. (Notice that contradictories CAN be true; that is, they NEED NOT be—see my part 2). You, in other words, may judge that my proposition does, or does not, ultimately reflect Being (that is, reality, or "the way things really are").[17] The second option is that the two contradictory propositions can both be true. In short, it may be the case that contradictory statements can be both true AND contradictory statements cannot be both true. (Does not this entail *regressio ad infinitum*? Does it help us to recall that, literally rendered from the Latin, this phrase means "A going back to the infinite"? And isn't this "infinite" the mystical center of Heideggerian thought?) If these contradictories are both true, the propositions involved seem to cancel themselves, to put themselves "under erasure." Heidegger surely regards "logic which self-erases" as the most fecund "hermeneutical circle" of all.[18] Heidegger yields to what medieval theologians called the *mysterium*. But what practice should one follow in doing theory and practice, then? The practice that says contradictories cannot be true? The practice that says they can? Both practices? Neither practice? Within the third lemma, the choice is yours. Is this my purpose here? To liberate the reader, . . . responsibly?[19] To hurry all of us along the way? The matter is put appositely by Seng Ts'an, third Ch'an patriarch in China: "At the least thought of IS and IS NOT, there is chaos and the Mind is lost . . . In its essence the Great Way is all-embracing."[20]

Next to Nothing:
A Demonstration Just Short
of the Fourth Lemma

The fourth lemma, "X is neither Y nor non-Y," can translate into literary theory as follows: the literary work is not a question of logocentrism and non-logocentrism. This version of a fourth lemma position can be affiliated to "deconstructionist literary criticism," in that the latter regards the literary work as off-rational (off-logocentric, in other words), a state of affairs to be distinguished, as we know, from the dialectic of logocentrism and non-logocentrism. J. Hillis Miller, perhaps the foremost spokesman for the "new Yale School," avows the practice of deconstructionist criticism, and identifies in principle with what we are calling the fourth lemma position.[21] I maintain, however, that many of his programmatic assertions, and some of his practice, reveal him to be a logocentrist—though his logocentrism, a kind of Taoism (in our terms), is very "deep-structured." Miller organizes his criticism as constructive (the positing of a monologic reading) and deconstructive (the subversion of this reading), and my argument is that even this organization, as dialectical (as, in short, a deep pattern of construction and deconstruction), qualifies—according to Derridean thought—as a kind of logocentrism. For Derrida, after all, all "framed" thought, all formulae (even formal ones) which "leave no surplus," are *ipso facto* logocentric. And, since it is a closed pattern structured as a formal opposition, the logocentrism in question is a Taoist third lemma positioning. As such, I frankly do not find the pattern all that different from the formal contraries which characterized the American New Criticism.[22] (Even the aporia cultivated by J. Hillis Miller seems to reduce to the formal paradoxes of Cleanth Brooks: formal and thematic aporia, after all, is for Derrida a symptom of logocentric closure. Likewise, what is intended in Derrida to be textual self-deconstruction by way of *emblem* often lapses, in Miller, into *allegory*, and allegory requires a "correspondence theory" of truth, and thus a logocentric epistemology.[23]) Nonetheless, and this I also wish to emphasize, many other of Miller's deconstructionist techniques are genuinely differential in effect. Given the success of these individual techniques, the result is a literary criticism which maneuvers "just short" of the fourth lemma.

This essay of mine was originally delivered as an invited paper,[24] and I include it in the Appendix because of two reasons: (1) a practical demonstration of deconstructionist techniques (many of them associated with J. Hillis Miller) is provided—students will, I hope, find this section very serviceable; and (2) the logocentric lapses of Miller are indicated with some thoroughness (they deserve mention because an authentic Derridean literary criticism has yet, in my opinion, to be generated). I wish to make clear, however, that for better or for worse, the *application* to *Hamlet*[25] which follows is entirely my own, though the techniques are not.

If we are taking stock of present deconstructive practice, surface aporia (despite my private objections) should appear formally as the first of the *procédés*. And so I treat it first. That sound cases can be established for the existence of contradictories in *Hamlet* has long been held, of course. There is, for one, the theme of fiction and reality, supported by elaborate image motifs: the paints and varnishes that reveal and conceal; the robing and disrobing which masquerade and expose; even the elaborate verbal trickery which plays with words like "show," "act," "presume," and "play." At one and the same time, Hamlet's world—even to himself—seems real and seems illusory. And there are so many other simultaneous contradictories. Is the ghost (if there is a real ghost) "a spirit of health or goblin damned" (I.iv.40), the father's true soul or a devil in disguise? Equally good cases can be made for both interpretations. Likewise, Hamlet is an anti-heroic egomaniac, and Hamlet is a hero of the finest moral sensibility. Ophelia is an immoral seductress, and Ophelia is a sweet and holy maiden. The point to be remembered here, however, is that Miller does not see contradictions of this kind as a mirror held up to life's wholesome polarities. Rather, it is asserted without proof, contradictories engage in mutual vitiation—a vitiation which sends chills down the spine.

But aporia splits apart not only themes, and not only images, but individual words themselves. The play *Hamlet,* as everyone knows, is profuse in its puns. A deconstructor would claim that when Hamlet says of Ophelia, "Conception is a blessing, but as your daughter may conceive, friend, look to it" (II.ii.185), the word "Conception" splits in two. Since "Conception" means "to conceive of flesh" (become pregnant) and "to conceive of thought" (ratiocinate, perhaps to the point of madness), the pun becomes a symbol of Ophelia's (and everyone's) shattered self-identity. Other kinds of verbal aporia depend on either textual variation or diachronic changes in meaning. One early version of the play (Q_2) prints the words "sallied flesh" (I.ii.129) and "sallied" in subsequent editions is modernized to "sullied." Another early version of *Hamlet* (F_1) prints "solid flesh," which in context can reverse the meaning of "sullied flesh." Arguments for the "validity" of each of the two contradicting words seem equally strong. The adjective which modifies "flesh" is thus sundered in two, or better yet, perpetually nullifies itself—since there are really two adjectives forever canceling each other out.

Diachronic change in meaning achieves much the same effect. That is, the word "doubt" in Hamlet's line, "I doubt some foul play" (I.iii.256), meant "suspect" (or "think probably true") to its seventeenth-century audience but can mean just the opposite ("think probably false") in the twentieth century. The deconstructionists— and here they are like the Heideggerian phenomenologists they so deplore—believe that the meaning of words need not be those of the historical author and/or his culture, but can freely relate to modern lexics as well. Accordingly, both of the contradicting meanings are valid, and the word sign "doubt" becomes dialogous.

The next *procédé* I call emblematics, and is a revival of the reading associated with *Midrash.* The deconstructionist can read some images as EMBLEMS of dialogy. Emblematic reading, though in an original form, has been revived by the Yale School. Recall too that in the sixteenth and seventeenth centuries an emblem was an image (usually an engraving or woodcut) symbolizing a concept or motto; the connection between image and concept would be effected by a short gloss or commentary. The Yale School frequently expropriates an image from a literary work, and in most unorthodox fashion, converts it into an emblem for a Derridean concept. The rampart or guard platform of act I (scenes i and iv) zigzags through the primeval dark and mist. The whole scene can easily become emblematic of Derrida's "universe," and—for a deconstructionist— necessarily of *Hamlet's* world as well. Manned by sentinels and later by Hamlet and his friends, the rampart dissects (cuts in two) a world of darkness. When the ghost appears to Hamlet, the ghost summons the prince "to a more removed ground" (I.iv.61) and possibly to a "flood" or abysmal "cliff" (loc. cit., 69, 70). The motif of solid ground (I.i.14), removal, and shifting ground (I.v.156) is a subtle but persistently recurrent one. When associated emblematically with the "strange eruption" (I.i.69) metaphor of the first rampart scene, the whole scenario allegorizes the 'rupture' (break, rip) of which Derrida and Paul de Man so often speak (needless to say, I could instead read fragmentation and sundering as glimmers of *śūnyatā*). The rampart sunders the world in two, and this first 'rip' sends fissure after fissure down the whole 'ground' of Being. The metaphysics of Being—all concepts of Being and Origin and all societies founded on them (the case in point, of course, is the Kingdom of Denmark itself and the unity provided by an integral ruler) are imagistically fragmented. "Something is rotten in the state of Denmark" (I.iv.90); and, for Derrida and Miller, in the so-called 'world' and 'human condition'.

The third deconstructive inquiry seeks the dissolution of those links which build the communicational chain, at least as traditionally understood. The technique avoids the problems of aporia. Authorial intention breaks with language, language dissolves its relation to referent, and audience is isolated from authorial intention and from language as well; and all of these excommunications are reciprocal—so the sequence of dissolution moves in the other direction too, from audience back through reference and language, and so on. First let us focus on the link between authorial intention and language. Here the history of Shakespearian redaction, of the many versions of *Hamlet* and the heated debates over valid and invalid texts, provides a deconstructionist goldmine. There are, after all, three early versions of *Hamlet*—the First Quarto (Q_1), the Second Quarto (Q_2), and the First Folio (F_1). Shakespearian scholars, even if they be fairly well agreed that William Shakespeare was the real author of the plays, still do not know if any of the three oldest versions are faithful to the manuscript as Shakespeare originally wrote it. The problem is complicated further because the three versions differ significantly from each other. All of these considerations so combine as to justify the questions: Who is the author of the *Hamlet* text we have before us, and are reading? What was his authorial intention? Such interrogation surely weakens the liaison between intention and the language. What is more, in the earliest editions there have been apparent mistakes (deviations from the text the printer was copying) in printing, most of them seemingly unintended by the printer. So parts of the *Hamlet* text we have are purely gratuitous—they have no author other than "chance." In so far as it applies, this realization seems to sever the link between authorial intent and text.

And a final redactional problem also has deconstructive implications. The standard *Hamlet* text used around the world today is a collation of the Second Quarto and the First Folio, and also includes some words and phrases which are either from other versions or from the emending and conjecturing hands of Shakespearian scholars (hundreds of them). So we are compelled to conclude, as it were, that the standard *Hamlet* text, since it is a collation, is not and cannot be Shakespeare's *Hamlet* at all. And doubly not his *Hamlet* because the text abounds in emendations certainly not his. Again, authorial intent, the deconstructionist says, has been effectively severed from the text's language.

Next, within the third inquiry, we can focus on the narrative and imagery of the play itself. Do they propagandize the scission of intent and language? Look at act V, scene ii, when Osric's language is systematically stripped from Osric's own intention, and is appropriated in effect by Hamlet himself—so that Osric does not say what he himself means but what Hamlet means (lines 90-105). And look at how the letter sent to England by Claudius and intended by Claudius to engineer Hamlet's death, escapes such an intention—and indeed accomplishes quite the opposite, the murder of Claudius's own emissaries. If we regard the poisoned sword and poisoned drink of the play's last scene as bearers of intention (and thus as symbols of language), we note that they too escape Claudius's intention, and kill those whom Claudius least wants killed, Laertes and the Queen. Indeed, the plot of poisoned sword and drink even becomes an allegory for how ALL LITERARY TEXTS work. Sword and drink issue from the hand of Claudius, escape his control, and trigger a series of events which result in Claudius's own death. And in like manner, literary text issues from its author, escapes, and then turns back to devour him. Hence the secret meaning of a strong Shakespearian motif, lines such as "Hoist with his own petard" (III.iv.208), and "The foul practice / Hath turned itself on me" (V.ii.818, 819).

We have questioned the problematic nature of any alliance between purpose and language, and can now turn to the alleged internal dynamic of language itself. Following Ferdinand de Saussure, many linguists regard language as a coupling of the "signifier" (that which represents, such as the typical phonic form "the cat" in English and "le chat" in French) and the "signified" (the concept of "sense" which is represented by the signifier; the sense "feline mammal" in our example, correlates to the signifier "the cat" or "le chat").

But, true to form, the deconstructors try to attenuate or even slash apart this coupling of signifier and signified. After the death of Polonius and departure of Hamlet, when Ophelia strews flowers—"There's fennel for you, and columbines. There's rue for you, . . . There's a daisy. I would give you some violets, . . ." (Iv.v.179–183)—each of them functions as a "signifier" different from the others (on this all scholars are agreed), but what is the matching "signified" for each of these "signifiers"? There has been heated controversy for centuries, but the upshot is that no one really knows. We have a case here of signifiers without operative signifieds, a situation deconstructionists call the phenomenon of the "free-floating signifier." It should be clear, then, that surveyed from this vantage point, the letter to England, the poisoned sword, and the poisoned drink, are free-floating in a derived sense. That is, their signifieds change from "Death for Hamlet alone" to "Death for others instead or as well." And in the case of the sword and drink, the change of signifieds is purely arbitrary, an act of chance.

Then there is the case of Osric again, who in act V, scene ii (106–12) speaks so flamboyantly that his language-as-signifier outruns its signifieds. Hamlet parodies this surplus of signifiers over available signifieds in his own speech, lines 113–21. For this "surplus phenomenon" deconstructors often reserve the term "supplémentation." The relation of signifier-signified debilitates in still another way. When Polonius warns Ophelia of what he considers Hamlet's deceptive use of language, Polonius says: ". . . Ophelia, / Do not believe his vows [words, after all], for they are brokers [procurers, pimps], / Not of that dye which their investments [garments] show, . . ." (I.iii.126–28). That is, just as garments show forth false color (dye), Hamlet's words (signifiers) proclaim false signifieds (the signifieds do not match his real purpose).

The second meretricious link in the communicational chain, say the deconstructionists, is between language and referent (referent is the entity-in-the-world to which the "signified" or "sense" of the signifier correlates). Much has been said by critics already about the chaotic beginning of *Hamlet's* act I. The personages on the rampart, blinded by the darkness, cannot find each other; there is a confused sequence of "Who's there?" and "Bernardo?" and "What, is Horatio there?" and so on. In short, names are flung out like a fisherman's net, but cannot catch their referents. The chaotic beginning sets a latent theme of the whole play: not only is self-identity cast in doubt, but words as such cannot identify the world and other people. Are we naming the ghost properly when we name him the king, Hamlet's father? The ghost may or may not be the father, so our name meets no sure referent. Speaking of the ghost, Marcellus asks, "Is it not like the King?" (I.i.48). Horatio answers enigmatically, "As thou art to thyself." The name chosen for the ghost is as uncertain as the name (or identity) we ascribe to ourselves!

When language does not doubt correlation to referent, it may camouflage correlation to referent. Such is the purport of Claudius's lines, "The harlot's cheek, beautied with plast'ring art, / Is not more ugly to the thing that helps it / Than is my deed to my most painted word" (III.i.50–54). In other cases, language itself (like the signifier we saw earlier) "free-floats," and settles on various referents. When Horatio names himself "poor servant," Hamlet answers, "I'll change [exchange] that name with you" (I.ii.163). The play *Hamlet* even provides a bold emblem for grammar's failure to shoot referential target, failure to hit bull's eye. In the famous confrontation scene between Hamlet and his mother, he hears a voice behind the arras (tapestry), interprets it as the voice of Claudius, and accidentally kills Polonius instead (by blindly thrusting his sword through the tapestry). The voice or language misdirects Hamlet, so he finds the wrong referent. The tapestry can even be taken as an emblem for Derridean *différance* itself,—in that the tapestry, like the operation of *différance*, fatally off-tracks transitive action from its target.

The communicational chain has a third problematic link, the alleged bond between intention and language on the one hand, and audience on the other. After her father's death, the "poor Ophelia / Divided from herself and her fair judgment" (IV.v.135)—and on this score already a fine symbol of humankind as dialogous identity—utters only erratic speech. The "Gentleman" accompanying her must declare "Her speech is nothing, / Yet the unshaped use of it doth move / The hearers to collection; they yawn at it, / And botch the words up to fit to their own thoughts" (IV.v.7–10). In short, there is no communication from Ophelia, nor is there even communication from any language bracketed off from Ophelia. The audience projects its own meaning on nonsensical language. The deconstructor regards this situation as just a more obvious example of what is, in attenuated fashion, universally the case.

If Ophelia's language bears no message, the language released by Claudius to his subjects bears a false message. Thus the ghost may aver, "So the whole ear of Denmark / Is by a forged process [false account] of my death rankly abused" (I.v.36–38). Audience abandoned and audience deceived is superseded only by audience negated, and the play *Hamlet* offers an emblem of such annihilation in the "foul fratricide" itself. That Hamlet's father is poisoned through the ear, the organ of perception, is not coincidental. It is Claudius's poison, emblematically the bearer of evil tidings, that nullifies the very perceiver.

The deconstructionist's fourth deconstructive inquiry is perhaps the most ingenious, and resorts to a revival of an old discipline, rhetoric. Deconstruction puts the old discipline to uses identified with Midrashic method,[26] however, so be forewarned! We can begin with what are textual ellipses of a sort. In act III, scene iv, *circa* line 140 (at the beginning of Hamlet's long response), the Folio version includes the word "Ecstasy?"—whereas the First and Second Quarto versions omit the word. Thirty lines later, all three early versions omit a word (in context, necessarily a verb) which the grammar and sense of the sentence seem to demand: "For use almost can change the stamp of nature, / And either . . . the devil, or throw him out with wonderous potency." In this case the editors "supply" the verb, and usually choose "curb" or "master." The deconstructionist fastens on omissions, and their history, because they become apposite emblems for Derrida's notion of *différance*. Recall that the vocalized A of *différAnce* disappears (since it is "heard" as an E), and this disappearance comes to represent the unnamable and unknowable "differance" which enables man to "make" any and all "definitions" he makes. Mindful of the two cases of ellipsis described above, the literary deconstructionist can aver that in the first case the word "Ecstasy?" of the Folio is not named in the Quartos, and that this absence represents unnamable, unknowable "differance." And the literary deconstructionist can aver that in the second case the "supplied" word "curb" or "master" (or whatever) disappears in the original three versions, and that this lacuna also epitomizes unnamable, unknowable "differance."

An alternative turn but same end result comes from deconstructionist use of another rhetorical trope, catachresis. Catachresis is the forced employ of a word to represent a sense which the word does not mean—either popularly or in terms of a formal lexic. Recall that the "mad" Ophelia's hearers cannot understand her nonsense speech. In attempting to describe the hearer's response to her "prattle," the text says "they yawn at it" (IV.v.9). Shakespearian scholars seem agreed that the word "yawn" does not "fit." The usage is catachrestic, and the deconstructor glosses this trope by saying catachresis too is emblematic. Since Elizabethan English does not supply an appropriate word for what "Shakespeare" wishes to name, he presses into service an unsuitable word (and, what is more, mutilates the word thereby). The catachrestic function becomes emblematic, says the deconstructor, because it tries to name the unnamable but fails. Sublatently, all language likewise fails, but with greater subterfuge.

The old rhetoric sometimes incorporated the graphics of print, and in their own study the deconstructionists do too. A good example is the phonic interchangeability between the grapheme U of the Second Quarto and grapheme V of the Folio. The words "heaven" (I.v.122) of the Folio and "heauen" of the Quarto are pronounced the same but the latter word bears the old Roman grapheme for the V sound. What do the deconstructionists make of this sort of data? They interpret the grapheme V as "masculine wedge," and grapheme U as "femine hollow" or "cervical trough." No matter what graphic form the editor of modern *Hamlet* texts settles upon, and uses to fill the otherwise empty space in line 122, the word chosen is still sundered in two by its two imperious antecedents, "heauen" and "heaven," each pulling the editor's graphic form in a different direction. And because doubly cleft, the word becomes doubly emblematic. It is graphically sundered, and it epitomizes sexual dichotomy as well; and all this in turn represents the dialogy of all things.

Our treatment of the fourth route of deconstructive inquiry can end with metaphor, perhaps the most pervasive of rhetorical tropes. When Hamlet sets up the dramatic play to be acted out before the King and Queen, he calls it *"The Mousetrap"* (III.ii.243). Why so?—he asks. And, in response to his own question, he answers— "Tropically." His answer is, of course, a pun. "Tropically" means "figuratively," or "by way of a trope," metaphor in this case. The play is like a mousetrap because it will trap the king. But the text also puns off the word "tropically" in and of itself, since the word suggests "trap," "trapically," "by way of trap." The deconstructor would revel in the maxim just waiting to be extracted: A trope is a trap. In "La mythologie blanche," recall, Derrida argues that clichés are at bottom philosophical propositions, but philosophical propositions showing their true colors, as it were. That is, philosophical propositions—and for that matter, all verbal statements—are metaphors (though metaphors under erasure).

In short, the metaphor's unexpressed AS (or the simile's expressed AS) leads away from what a thing really is. We cannot name an entity, so we substitute another entity for it (which, he says, is in turn displaced by another metaphoric substitute, and another, and another, ad infinitum). So tropes (in this case, specifically metaphor) are traps in that they deceive us into thinking we better know an entity on their account.

We have plotted four deconstructive itineraries—we have tracked the traces of aporia, emblematics, communicational breakdown, and rhetorical demolition. We conclude our survey of new Yale School criticism with its fifth inquiry, an inquiry into the allegorical function of literary texts.[27] The four other kinds of inquiry tried to find that texts demonstrate or "show" Derridean concepts, and that this "showing" is entirely separate from collusion on the text's part. The texts, simply by being texts, necessarily behave in Derridean ways. The fifth inquiry expects that literature actively proclaims Derridean principles under the conspiratorial form of allegory. (Indeed, sometimes the text is interpreted as if it bypasses even allegory: "To be, or not to be: that is the question" [III.i.56] would be treated as an outright declaration of *aporia* in the technical Derridean sense; and "The time is out of joint" [I.v.188] would become a "policy statement" on the temporal deferral of *différance*.)

Let us see how very ingeniously the allegorical scheme can work. To begin, we can resume our description of the ghost, since even in the first inquiry indications of allegorical interpretation crept in (as they did, too, in all of the "emblematic readings"). The ghost walks a dark universe, a universe cleft down the middle by the rampart. Recall that in the medieval and renaissance periods the King represented stability, hierarchy, the "great chain of being" as Arthur Lovejoy has popularized the term. Hence Rosencrantz expresses what was the contemporary world-view when he says:

> The cess [death] of majesty
> Does not alone, but like a gulf [Abyss] doth draw
> What's near to it; or it is a massy wheel [the circle,
> symbol of perfection, Origin] . . .
> To whose huge spokes ten thousand lesser things
> Are mortised and adjoined, which when it falls,

Each small annexment, petty consequence,
Attends the boist'rous ruin.

(III.iii.15–22)

For the deconstructor, the King can also represent Origin, Logos,
Center, Being, in the metaphysical sense. But the King has died, and
a ghost walks the night. Whether the ghost is indeed the King, or a
counterfeit, is a naggingly persistent theme in *Hamlet.* The deconstructor can translate all this to mean that the metaphysical principle
of Origin, Being, etc., has died. Some remnants of belief linger, but
they are riddled with doubt. The ghost may be a counterfeit, and in
any case, he is just a ghost. Indeed, pursuit of the ghost—continued
search for Origin—seems to lead to the bottomless Abyss. Thus
Horatio protests to Hamlet, "What if it tempt you toward the flood,
my lord, / Or to the dreadful summit of the cliff / That beetle's o'er
his base into the sea, / And there assume some other horrible form
. . . ?" (I.iv. 69–72). For the deconstructor, this is recondite allegory
for what he calls "mise-en-abyme": the infinite regression of a picture within a picture within a picture; and the plunge down through
successive "bottoms" which ogrify and collapse, each in turn, so that
one plummets downward forever and ever and ever. In other words,
when one pursues a metaphysics of Origin, each attempt to reinte-
grate Being, to reestablish a Ground, must inevitably result in yet
another collapse. And the collapse of Origin means the collapse of
all dependent holistic systems. I have argued of course that
"mise-en-abyme" need not be collapse into terror, but the "free fall"
into *śūnyatā.*

In the essay "Differance," Derrida describes as follows the A which
is written but not heard:

> It is put forward by a silent mark, by a tacit monument, or, one
> might even say, by a pyramid—keeping in mind not only the capital
> form of the printed letter but also that passage from Hegel's
> *Encyclopaedia* where he compares the body of the sign to an Egyptian
> pyramid. The A of differance, therefore, is not heard; it remains
> silent, secret, and discreet, like a tomb.
>
> It is a tomb that (provided one knows how to decipher the
> legend) is not far from signaling the death of the king.[28]

Derrida is being *précieux,* of course, in the mischievous French manner. Graphically, a capital A looks like a pyramid; and the A of *différance* is unheard just as the royal sepulchre deep inside an Egyptian
pyramid is silent and secret. Derrida cites Hegel for the motif identifying sign and pyramid: if for Hegel the body of the sign is an
Egyptian pyramid, then the body of the sign houses a tomb—a tomb
enclosing hollowness and the dead. In other words, *différance* hollows
out all signs.

How would or could a deconstructionist find and interpret such
macabre imagery in *Hamlet?* It is clear that opportunities abound,

but I single out an allegorical reading of one phrase. Like Derrida's passage quoted above, my interpretation is emblematic, and specifically graphic—that is, it depends on the physical appearance of lettering. When Horatio reports to Hamlet that the dead king's ghost has appeared, Horatio says—" 'A was a goodly king" (I.ii.186). " 'A" is seventeenth-century English for "He," but it is the graphic appearance of the letter A which is the unfailing "clue" for the deconstructionist! Hamlet's father the king, as emblem of Logos, had been "goodly"—that is, he had been a sign for security and social order. But the "goodly king" had been, in reality, the pyramidal A—all along, at the center of the pyramid lay the empty tomb. And if the king later died and returned to walk the earth, he returned—in Hamlet's words—only to make "night hideous" and "to shake our disposition / With thoughts beyond the reaches of our souls" (I.iv.54–56). That is, the beckoning of the king was metaphysical seduction; it was the call to illusion.

As the caller at a folk dance says, let's go around one last time! In act III, scene ii, Hamlet applies to his father, perhaps ironically, the "epitaph" of the hobbyhorse (the hobbyhorse was the outfit, an imitation horse, worn by performers in the Elizabethan morris dance). The "epitaph," as Hamlet calls it, reads: "For O, for O, the hobbyhorse is forgot" (line 139). Ah, the deconstructive possibilities here! The capital letter O—the Circle!—emblem of perfection, of Origin, of Logos. For the sake of O, for the sake of Logos, "the hobbyhorse is forgot." The hobbyhorse is imitation,—it represents the counterfeit. Counterfeit, reciprocal subversion, dialogy—for the Derridean deconstructionist such is the 'real'! For the sake of vain belief, humankind forgets that 'reality' is the hobbyhorse. Belief in the O is indeed "epitaph." And epitaph is inscription on the tomb of the dead.

We now broach the second aporia in J. Hillis Miller's work, one which operates at a deep formal level, and about which he seems unaware. Hillis Miller's claim, for example, is that dialogy forever subverts itself, forever metamorphoses: each dialogical event is complete change from the previous dialogical event. Each deconstruction is followed by a new kind of reconstitution which is in turn deconstruction in a new way, so there is no reiteration as such (for reiteration suggests cycle, and cycle implies Origin). But why then must Miller conclude one of his most important review-essays (on M. H. Abrams's *Natural Supernaturalism*, in *Diacritics*, Winter, 1972) with the following paragraph?

> This alternative scheme [dialogy], with its various aspects of motifs, has always been present as a shadow or reversed mirror image [of monology] within the Western tradition . . . [Abrams's] failure to recognize its pervasive presence in texts both traditional and modern is perhaps the chief limitation of *Natural Supernaturalism*.[29]

So dialogy and monology (an opposition!) have a "pervasive presence"? The lapse into "pervasive presence," and the telltale image of
the "mirror," clearly indicate *formal* "reiteration." To recombine dialogy and monology in such wise is in our terms a Taoist, and therefore logocentric formulation.

Or again, what about J. Hillis Miller's treatment of aporia in the
reading of text (see Miller's review-essay of Joseph Riddel's *The In-
verted Bell,* in *Diacritics,* Summer, 1975)? Miller's thesis here is that
deconstructive reading subverts the referentiality of a text's language, but that to make its point, the deconstructive reading must
still be referential (it refers to the text's language). Hence we have
aporia! And a further aporia arises because "The act of reading un-
dermines its own status as 'act,' since it is unable to efface wholly the
referentiality of the text in question and also unable to return in
peace to a naive mimetic interpretation."[30] Thus, and here is—in my
view—Miller's capitulation, "Each such reading moves through the
figurative complexities of a given text and reaches, in the particular
way the given text allows it, the 'same' moment of an aporia." And, to
clinch my case, Miller adds, "The repetition with different texts of
this act or non-act of deconstruction leads to a gradual clarification,
as the reading comes back again and again, with different texts, to
the 'same' impasse." The "pervasive presence" of dialogy, the " 'same'
moment of an aporia," the coming back again and again "with different texts, to the 'same' impasse," can indicate only one conclusion:
that J. Hillis Miller is within the Tao. Who is to gainsay, however,
that he dwells there quite handsomely?

Notes

Part 1

1. Jacques Derrida, *Of Grammatology* [OG], trans. G. C. Spivak (Baltimore: Johns Hopkins, 1976), pp. 10, 11. Original edition *De la Grammatologie* [DG] (Paris: Minuit, 1967). In my part 1, reference is also made to the following books by Derrida (and titles are represented, for economy's sake, by the abbreviations here bracketed). Translation and introduction to Edmund Husserl, *L'Origine de la géométrie* [IOG] (Paris: Presses Universitaires de France, 1st ed. 1962; 2nd ed. 1974); English trans. *Edmund Husserl's* Origin of Geometry: *An Introduction* [OGI], tr. John P. Leavey (New York: Nicolas Hays, 1977). *La Voix et le phénomène* [VP] (Paris: Presses Universitaires de France, 1st ed. 1967; 2nd ed. 1972); English trans. *Speech and Phenomena* [SP] tr. D. B. Allison (Evanston: Northwestern, 1973). *L'Ecriture et la différence* [ED] (Paris: Seuil, 1967); English trans. *Writing and Difference* [WD], tr. Alan Bass (Chicago: University of Chicago, 1978). *La Dissémination* [DISS] (Paris: Seuil, 1972). *Marges de la philosophie* [MP] (Paris: Minuit, 1972). *Positions* [PO] (Paris: Minuit, 1972). *Glas* [GL] (Paris: Galilée, 1974). *Eperons: Les Styles de Nietzsche* [EP] (Venice: Corbo e Fiore, 1976).

2. More weight is to be given to the word *factor* here than to *originating* (factor: doer, maker), since in what are historically the more recent versions of the signified-signifier combination, the signified does not "originate" the signifier. Yet this does not injure Derrida's thesis, as we shall see, since he is about to claim that signifieds of all kinds are—if one follows the logic consistently—signifiers too (and only).

3. Though Derrida seems to regard as "proto-Derridean" those past thinkers (such as Nietzsche and Freud) he considers particularly astute. That is, the very logic of these thinkers, in his estimation, forced them to discover the defects of logocentrism. Some of these thinkers "dissimulated," i.e., cosmetically covered over the defect; others, in various proportions, were more forthright.

4. In relation to non-transcendentals, the whole supreme Identity becomes a transcendental signified, though within the Identity there stand a signifier, and a signified. And so on down the line, in the case of all identities, as we shall see.

5. The Holy Spirit, for Derrida, would just be the reified movement of the Father begetting the Son and the Son reflecting the Father. That Derrida's estimate of trinitarian theology is simplistic and very inadequate I shall demonstrate in part 4.

6. Breath, for Derrida, is necessarily pneumatological, not grammatological. Thus, he affiliates breath to natural writing, or voice. See OG, p. 17.

189

7. OG, p. 43.

8. OG, p. 7, 244–46.

9. OG, pp. 45–47, et passim.

10. For example, see OG, pp. 67, 68.

11. OG, p. 49.

12. WD, p. 6.

13. We shall consider, momentarily, his justification for doing this.

14. Derrida retains the general Saussurean terms of *signified* and *signifier* when describing the theory of personal self-identity. For the sake of clarity, while retaining the Saussurean terms for identity in general, I shall reserve the terms *nominans-nomen* for personal self-identity.

15. American philosophers surely recognize, for example, C. A. Campbell's *On Selfhood and Godhead* (London: George Allen and Unwin, 1957), where they should consult in particular "Lecture V"; Risieri Frondizi's *The Nature of the Self: A Functional Interpretation* (New Haven: Yale University Press, 1953), where they will find, especially in part I, pp. 126, 127, and in all of part II, a Gestaltist version of self which openly accommodates self-consciousness; and H. J. Paton's *In Defence of Reason* (London: Hutchinson's University Library, 1951), in which self-reflexivity operates according to a kind of Kantian format.

16. Or, better phrased, the "appearance" of identity.

17. Both use similar arguments; see, for example, Gilbert Ryle's attack on "inside and outside" in his *Concept of Mind.*

18. See Newton Garver's introduction in SP, though Garver, in my opinion, strains to "soften" Derrida in order to render him respectable to the Analysts. The same can be said, I think, of the otherwise excellent work of Richard Rorty in this intercontinental dialogue.

19. Because it starts with the "outside" influence of graphs on phones.

20. See the quotations from Saussure provided by Derrida in OG, pp. 35, 36, 45.

21. Derrida is not discussing, of course, whether or what things are in themselves, but what they are to our "knowing."

22. See OG, p. 44; and for the various parts of the Derridean argument from arbitrariness, work through OG, pp. 30–73. The form of Derridean argument is itself almost always discontinuous, but can be "pieced together." The discontinuous style is emblematic, for Derrida, of *différance,* i.e., "the way matters really go on."

23. Derrida's attack on Saussure's case rests on what he judges to be Saussure's *inconsistency.* Thus a nominalist controversy (whether the nature of a "class" is different from its "sum total" of particulars, and so on) is not really involved, though it seems to me a broader treatment of the issues could easily shift the discussion to such grounds.

24. OG, p. 44.

25. OG, p. 36.

26. We can just as well call this argument *le débordement,* another term Derrida frequently applies to it. Let me make clear that in order to better effect

the communication of Derrida's ideas, a principle task of my part 1 (and a task I think possible, because of my own reasons as advanced in part 4), I have chosen to fix and keep constant my appellations for Derrida's arguments, and Derrida's several key concepts (I even capitalize these terms on occasion, when in the context communication is better served by capitalization). Derrida himself, as he explains in many places, does not "fix" nomenclature, since he fears such fixation will tempt the reader to 'center' Derridean motifs in a logocentric way. In point of fact Derrida's arguments—despite the transmutation of labels—remain the same throughout his work. Indeed, he uses the same several arguments again and again. (That he cannot escape doing so is part of the human quandary, as he sees it, and as he argues elsewhere.) Thus Derrida's refusal to fix nomenclature is really a pedagogical device, an acting out of one of his most important claims. I have no objections at all to his resort to such a device. However, my role at this point as communicator (and again, because of the reasons I advance in my part 4, I affirm the possibility of faithful communication) is to rescue many readers of Derrida from total confusion. (Many, for example, wrongly consider Derrida an absurdist.) In terms of communication, I am convinced my use of constant nomenclature accomplishes more gain than loss, especially if the reader is nonetheless warned (as I do, repeatedly) that in Derrida's estimation, logocentrism has a nasty way of camouflaging itself.

27. DG, p. 55.

28. See the quotations from Saussure provided by Derrida, OG, pp. 41, 42.

29. OG, p. 41.

30. OG, p. 42.

31. OG, p. 23, and note 13, OG, pp. 324, 325.

32. OG, p. 37; see also SP, pp. 61–66.

33. In itself, a very weak argument, as are the circumambient ones, since the most they show are bivalency: a given content can sometimes function as signified and sometimes as signifier. Derrida will have to show that the theory of signifier and signified, when worked out to its logical conclusion, leaves us with an impossible result: all contents are everywhere and always all and only signifiers ('pure signifiers'); or contrariwise, all and only signifieds. We shall soon go on to discuss how Derrida handles this demand.

34. See Robert Magliola, "Jorge Luis Borges and the Loss of Being: Structuralist Themes in *Dr. Brodie's Report,*" *Studies in Short Fiction,* 15 (1978), pp. 25–31.

35. Of course Derrida must go on, later, to deconstruct the empirical notion of "imprint" as well, since environmental determinism, no less than idealism, preserves the general format of signifier and signified. How Derrida is to do this is foreshadowed in OG, pp. 63–65.

36. The phrases of the Spivak translation (OG, p. 7) I have corrected I here underline in the original French (DG, p. 16) for the reader's reference: " 'Signifiant du signifiant' décrit au contraire le mouvement du langage: dans son origine, certes, mais on pressent déjà qu'une origine dont la structure *s'épelle ainsi*—signifiant de signifiant—*s'emporte et s'efface elle-même* dans sa propre production. . . . La secondarité qu'on croyait pouvoir réserver à l'écriture affecte tout signifié en général, l'affecte toujours déjà, c'est-à-dire

d'entrée de jeu. Il n'est pas de signifié qui échappe, *éventuellement pour y tomber, au jeu des renvois signifiants* qui constitue le langage."

37. David Steindl-Rast provided the example for me. See my *Phenomenology and Literature* (Lafayette, Ind.: Purdue University Press, 1977), pp. 71, 72.

38. OG, p. 7.

39. OG, p. 12.

40. Compare SP, p. 156.

41. Compare Jacques Derrida, "White Mythology: Metaphor in the Text of Philosophy," tr. F.C.T. Moore, *New Literary History*, 6, No. 1 (Autumn, 1974), pp. 32, 33, 36–41, 48, 49; original French version, "La Mythologie blanche (la métaphore dans le texte philosophique)," *Poétique,* No. 5 (1971), 1–52; reprinted in MP.

42. When speaking of word-to-word lexis, remember that in the case of the so-called "polysemous signifier," what is happening, technically, is that each idea-sound combination in the "signifying" word is a different "signifier."

43. Here and there in his work, Derrida introduces arguments involving other "causes" of this collapse. Phenomena such as "random mutation" in language, and the "immotivation" which so often subverts "intention," are cases in point: these phenomena subvert the traditional signified, "idea" as such.

44. They coexist only by virtue of their relationship, now deconstructed.

45. As long as one understands that dissemination is really inexpressible in terms of the concepts of signified and signifier, and even inexpressible in terms of the concept 'pure signifier,' since the latter term is still dependent, after all, on these concepts. So more properly stated, dissemination in terms of the "fanning out" or literally "seeding out" of pure signifiers is perhaps the best approximation in theoretical terms of what dissemination really is.

46. The "begetting" or generation of the Son by the Father, in the context of trinitarian theology, is treated at some length in my part 4.

47. The problem of free will even emerges in Format One. From where comes the *élan* enabling the originating factor to "move"? Is infinite regression involved? This question shall become critical in Nagarjuna's discussion of "self-cause," in my part 3.

48. I would use here the more popular term "co-causal," but the latter carries some connotations I wish to avoid.

49. OG, p. 324 (note 9). Derrida is explaining this situation in the context of Nietzsche, but clearly he holds it to be the case always.

50. OG, p. 7.

51. For the implications of this, see ahead, pp. 42–45.

52. See Joseph G. Brennan, *A Handbook of Logic* (New York: Harper and Bros., 1957; 2nd ed.), p. 144. And recall we are talking about contradictories in the strict sense; we are not talking about contraries (opposites).

53. For a good example of Derrida's persistent refusal to use *reductio ad absurdum,* what we have called the "dialectic," see WD, p. 77.

54. Again, for the reasons indicated in foregoing note 26, I fix nomenclature that Derrida allows to free-float.

55. The English translation of "Différance" appears in SP, 129–60; the French text is collected in MP, pp. 1–29.

56. Ferdinand de Saussure, *Course in General Linguistics,* Engl. trans. Wade Baskin (New York: Philosophical Library, 1959), pp. 117–18, 120, as cited in SP, p. 140.

57. SP, p. 140.

58. As we are about to see in more detail, when Derrida says differences *are not,* he does not mean this verbal form as simple negation of identity.

59. The word "present" can refer to "the present time" and to "those who are spatially present."

60. SP, p. 64.

61. SP, p. 65.

62. SP, p. 143.

63. SP, p. 134.

64. SP, pp. 134, 135.

65. See the quotation from Saussure above.

66. See OG, p. 71.

67. Perhaps an adversary may argue that not to know something except by what it *is not* is not the same as to establish that the thing (as thing) isn't there at all! But Derrida could answer, surely, that it is the *theory* of presence which is being deconstructed here. That is to say, negative reference vitiates any formula which posits "like quality" or "common ground" as an explanation of identity.

68. Derrida, in "White Mythology" and many other essays, affiliates ocular imagery with logocentrism. My own thesis will present means to reinstate logocentric tropes.

69. J. L. Austin, *Philosophical Papers,* p. 88, as cited in *The Encyclopedia of Philosophy,* P. Edwards, ed. in chief (New York: Macmillan, 1967), p. 124.

70. Ludwig Wittgenstein, "Lectures on Aesthetics," in *Philosophy of Art and Aesthetics from Plato to Wittgenstein,* eds. F. Tillman and S. Cahn (New York: Harper and Row, 1969), p. 517.

71. For Derrida's own attitude towards "repeating" another thinker, see the "Translator's Preface" by Gayatri Chakravorty Spivak in OG, pp. lxxxvi, lxxxvii.

72. We can say, in terms of formal logic, that the distributed middle is annihilated.

73. It is important to keep in mind that Derrida, when he measures metaphysical theory against "reality," understands by "reality" (or by "the way things really are") the "world-as-it-appears" to human kind. Derrida remains in this regard as in so many others a very continental philosopher.

74. See note 73. One might add that Derrida, though he might not care to admit it, can only judge the relative merit (when compared with other more conventional formulations) of the 'pure signifier' on the basis of "other-than-logical" experience. For the notion of 'pure signifier' in its wider logical setting is illogical, and thus comes under erasure. But it pleases me that Derrida must resort, even if *sub rosa,* to an admission that the "world-as-it-

appears" can be appropriately judged according to "other-than-logical" ways of knowing.

75. Technically, experience from which elements impertinent to genuine knowing have not yet been bracketed out.

76. See SP, p. 142.

77. Ibid.

78. Ibid.

79. If the above terms were all synonymous, Derrida would regard this as too great a temptation to hypostasis (though even he must capitulate somewhat before some constancy in meaning; thus I feel justified, when provisions are attached, to use the word Derridean *else*). If, on the other hand, the use of the above terms were not dependent on their respective "contexts," then Derrida would be abandoning the else, or *fil conducteur* under erasure, or "trace," that he is trying to preserve, and he would be handing his thinking over to complete randomness.

80. See pp. 39–41.

81. WD, p. 67; ED, p. 103.

82. Derrida, appropriating imagery associated with Mallarmé, often describes "trace" as diaphanous (this adjective functions as a poetic rejection of 'thingness').

83. We can easily play with the Latin root here: "direction" from the past participle of *dirigere*, from *dis-regere*, which can mean, etymologically, both to "rule straight" and to "rule apart," depending on the lexic value of *dis-* one chooses. So "directional" really suggests "off-rule."

84. WD, p. 78.

85. Note, for example, the following observation from "White Mythology": "The difficulties which we have just indicated become worse when we turn to 'archaic' tropes which have given to 'founding' concepts (*theoria, eidos, logos,* etc.) the character of a 'natural' language. Even the signs (words or concepts) which make up this proposition, starting with *trope* and *arché*, have their metaphorical charge. Concept is a metaphor, foundation is a metaphor, theory is a metaphor; and there is no meta-metaphor for them" (p. 23).

86. Even mathematical signs, in that they are created by language-bound, and therefore "metaphor"-bound, beings, are victims of metaphoricity, no matter how much their creators may try to strip them of humanity (i.e., metaphoricity).

87. Derrida, "White Mythology," p. 13.

88. For another and indeed different transformation of trace and sexual imagery, see Derrida's treatment of Freud, WD, pp. 196–231.

89. DISS, p. 294. Translations from *La Dissémination* are mine.

90. DISS, p. 293.

91. Through much of his work, Derrida's employ of sexual imagery, whether he wishes to accede or not, functions as a kind of Derridean permutation of religious (and specifically mystical) love poetry—and in both the religious and Derridean uses, there is a *dépassement* of, and not an exemplification of, Freudian theory.

92. See p. 24.

93. The translation by David Allison is a good one, and I deviate from it only when careful exegesis has required greater literality.

94. I.e., the present element.

95. The phrase "of marks," from "de marques," is omitted in the SP translation.

96. SP, pp. 142, 143; original text in MP, pp. 13, 14.

97. See pp. 21–26.

98. See p. 49.

99. Though clearly not in the sense of Husserlian transcendentalism nor late-phase Heideggerian mysticism.

100. See, pp. 26, 27.

101. Again, remember Derrida is talking about the "real" as what is accessible to man in experience.

102. Evocation, at least since Mallarmé, suggests a beckoning to an absent which, while remaining absent, somehow leaves a hint for the one who beckons.

103. See pp. 28, 34.

104. See p. 24.

105. This assembling or constituting, as we shall see, is not entitative. The word *assembler* itself presents some etymological opportunity. The modern French *assembler* comes from the Latin *ad-simul,* "to 'one and the same time,' " but is mediated through the Old French *asembler,,* which can mean "to assemble" [entitative implication] but also "to appear (toward), simulate (toward), feign (toward)" [non-entitative implication].

106. See p. 22.

107. Nor are the *a* and *ä* vouchsafed by some Platonic *A* and *Ä.*

108. *Altérité* is a favorite word of Derrida, and can be understood in terms of absolute negative reference: nothing is "carried over" from moment to moment, so there is no entitative continuity as such.

109. It is helpful in this regard to review Derrida's warnings, SP, pp. 134, 139, and WD, p. 71.

110. DISS, p. 240.

111. *Déborder* can mean both "to overwhelm" and "to get clear (of)," "sheer (off)."

112. See p. 14.

113. The language used to describe the slip, of course, has not successfully escaped (and Derrida will grant this).

114. That is, Voidism would argue that the apparent "constitution" is just an illusion.

115. And necessarily *all* theory.

116. SP, pp. 107–28; MP, pp. 187–207.

117. The adjective *in-forme* is a pun here, since the *in-* is privative, but via the Latin root can mean the opposite, viz., "form in," "form within."

118. SP, pp. 127, 128; MP, p. 206.

119. SP, p. 128.

120. Ibid.

121. That Derrida applies the same notion of "purpose under erasure" to both general history and individual choice is clear from his "Freud and the Scene of Writing" (WD, pp. 196–231, and especially pp. 200–205), where the notion is explained in terms of individual choice. The overall concept, then, seems to be that individual "choices," undertaken through crossed-out free will, inevitably move an epoch toward the opening, so there is *errance* of the whole epoch.

122. DISS, p. 207.

123. See p. 22.

124. See SP, pp. 129.

125. SP, p. 137.

126. See SP, p. 135.

127. See SP, p. 153.

128. For my own attitude, see note 26.

129. See SP, p. 135.

130. SP, p. 134.

131. SP, p. 135.

132. See pp. 27, 28.

133. For Derrida's "rejection" of conceptions such as experience, empiricism, and metaphysics, see WD, p. 152; SP, p. 104; OG, p. 74.

134. OG, p. 65.

135. OG, p. 4. The underline is mine.

136. OG, p. 92. The underline is mine.

137. They are under erasure, of course, because *lived experience* and *appearance* are also cut in two by differance, "the unheard difference between the appearing and the appearance" (OG, p. 65), in Derrida's own words. But such a crossing-out does not gainsay that in a quasi-unthinkable way (this will be part of Derrida's quandary) movement is "going on" and being appreciated.

138. See pp. 27, 28, 35.

139. See pp. 6, 35.

140. See p. 28.

141. OG, p. 93.

142. SP, pp. 102, 103.

143. OG, p. 93.

144. OG, p. 87.

145. SP, p. 132.

146. SP, p. 103.

147. In French, *clôture,* much like the English "closure," suggests both (1) that which is closed already, and (2) that which is coming to a close. Derrida

seems ambivalent about the historical status of our "present" epoch, and "doubly" so because differance obviates linear time.

148. From the Latin *intimare,* "to announce," "to hint."

149. OG, p. 6.

150. For Husserl's logocentric infinity, as Derrida interprets it, see SP, pp. 52, 53, 101, 102.

151. Computer languages are just a displacement, in that they are encoded according to logocentric formulae, which are authored by logocentric minds.

152. Derrida's claim that differance is "neither a word nor a concept" (SP, p. 135) is of course impossible, and he knows it.

153. Some ingenious examples: Derrida's differential reading of "gallery" and "corridor" (SP, p. 104), and of "pit" and "pyramid" (MP, pp. 79–127).

154. Pleonasm, catachresis, anacoluthon, are some favorites. There is, of course, the studied nonchalance of the puns—"aigle"-"Hegel" (GL, p. 7), and the like; and the Mallarméist toying with homophony and off-homophony (see DISS, pp. 294, 295, 304, for particularly adroit examples).

155. See p. 40.

156. See pp. 18, 19.

157. OG, p. 14.

158. SP, p. 137. This section is a carefully orchestrated onslaught on causality.

159. OG, p. 14.

160. Ibid.

161. Resonation, for Derrida, is exemplary (and a kind of reenactment of differance) because it renounces the "silence" of the "mystical (and ineffable) moment."

162. SP, p. 104.

163. See, for example, SP, p. 159.

164. OG, p. 14.

165. OG, p. 93.

166. OG, p. 14; French text, DG, p. 25.

167. OG, p. 93.

168. SP, p. 130.

169. Indeed, one of the chief arguments of Fritjof Capra's *The Tao of Physics* (New York: Bantam ed., Bantam, 1977), is precisely that the breakthroughs of modern physics are statements in another modal language of Eastern mystical thought: for example, astronomical scenarios for the history of the universe are paralleled with Hindu cyclic systems; laws of expansion and contraction, paralleled with Taoism; collapse of chronological time with Zen *satori.*

170. See OG, p. 61.

171. SP, p. 130.

172. See p. 39.

173. To track the pathway is to "reflect on the circularity" by repeating "this

circle in its own historical possibility," so there occurs an "elliptical change of site": see SP, p. 128.

174. SP, p. 159.

175. WD, p. 71.

176. OG, p. 74.

177. OG, p. 5.

178. OG, p. 92.

179. Here Derrida resembles Michel Foucault.

180. Not for the orthodox Marxist variety, however. Derrida has frequently assailed the triumphalist logocentrism of Marx. What is more, the tone which prevails in Derrida is, if anything, a caring meditation on the Tradition. Deconstruction, after all, is a kind of respectful meditation; it is not destruction.

181. I, of course, do not agree with Derrida. My own concern in parts 3 and 4 is to reinstate the viability of traditional literary theory and criticism, and to do so precisely *by way of* the differential detour. It is worth pointing out here, however, that novelists—English and North and South American as well as French and German—anticipated much of Derrida. Philosophers beginning the study of Derrida would do well to read contemporary theory of the post-structuralist novel. Though material on this subject is fast accumulating, I still recommend, at least as "starters," two of the early studies, now become classic: Robert Scholes, *The Fabulators* (New York: Oxford University Press, 1967); and Jean Ricardou, *Problèmes du nouveau roman* (Paris: Seuil, 1967).

182. OG, p. 5.

183. The term *exergue* involves elaborate word-play, of course, and space does not permit us the luxury of a more thorough treatment. As the inscription at the beginning of a book, *exergue* alludes to the Derridean version of history, which regards "writing," i.e., alterity, as prior to the era of the book, i.e., prior to the era when metaphysics comes up with the fiction of an "origin." Nor is there yet a new inscription, an *exergue* for a future third era, an era of differentialism. As the inscription on a coin, the proximity of the *exergue* to the inscribed date can imply—for a future *exergue*—an apocalyptic urgency.

184. In "White Mythology," the *exergue* is the transaction between metaphor ("originary" Derridean writing, in this case) and appellatory language (logocentric writing). When the *exergue* on the coin is worn away by "use," mankind forgets the Derridean implications of metaphor (i.e., that theory of metaphor, rightly studied, gives the lie to logocentrism, and points up Derridean writing).

Notes

Part 2

1. Heidegger, in *On the Way to Language* (Engl. trans. Harper and Row, 1971) and elsewhere, acknowledges, indeed celebrates, the proximity of his thought and the centric mysticism identified with much of Taoism and Buddhism. And the most persistent likeness between Heidegger and these latter is the teaching of the "unity of opposites." His *The Question of Being* (bilingual edition, College and University Presses, 1958) is replete with passages like the following: "Only because the question, 'What is metaphysics?' thinks from the beginning of the climbing above, the transcendence, the *Being* of being, can it think of the negative of being, of *that* nothingness which just as originally is identical with Being" (p. 101).

2. Heidegger's *Identity and Difference,* a late work, has not been sufficiently appreciated as the stimulus for much of Derrida's thinking. Derrida, of course, as pointed out in my part 1, deconstructs the Heideggerian unity of opposites—i.e., he finds in it a fatal failure to "match up" the oppositional halves. For Derrida, in short, there is no Taoist "belonging together." In part 3, ahead, we shall study Nagarjunist Buddhism, which dissents from centric mysticism and concurs with Derridean differentialism.

3. Nagarjunist "prajñapti" (see my part 3) is any formula of self-identity which, when deconstructed, leads to *différance.* Heideggerian thought is an important "prajñapti" for Derrida. Contemporary theorists such as William Spanos and Joseph Riddel have worked out excellent interpretations of Heidegger which represent his enterprise as a deconstructionist one. Their theories are well-taken, indeed, but must be understood as a creative and selective off/reading of Heidegger (much as Derrida generates a "Derridean Heidegger"), and quite apart from Heidegger's intention—which clearly (especially in his later years) was to reveal a centric mysticism.

4. Flannery O'Connor, "The River," in *A Good Man Is Hard to Find* (New York: Doubleday, Image series, 1970). Throughout, I bracket page references.

5. In recent American critical debate, the above issues (or most of them) have been skillfully treated by Monroe Beardsley, Denis Dutton, Joseph Margolis, E. D. Hirsch, and others, and many of these have disagreed radically with each other. I shall be reconstituting the problematic in phenomenological and, specifically, Heideggerian terms.

6. Martin Heidegger, *Being and Time,* trans. John Macquarrie and Edward Robinson (New York: Harper and Row, 1962). Page references are to this English translation, and enclosed parenthetically within my text. The

English translation is from the seventh German edition, *Sein und Zeit* (Tübingen: Neomarius Verlag); the first German edition appeared in 1927.

7. *Phenomenology and Literature* (West Lafayette, Ind.: Purdue University Press, 1977).

8. On the other hand, in his "Plausibility and Aesthetic Interpretation," *Canadian Journal of Philosophy*, Vol. VII, No. 2 (1977), 327–40, Denis Dutton argues that interpretation of aesthetic phenomena should operate in terms of a special kind of plausibility, rather than "truth" understood in terms of scientific verifiability.

9. In *Phenomenology and Literature*, I demonstrate that Heidegger's critical practice, and even some parts of his theoretical work, seem to imply a heuristic absolutism rather than pluralism. But in regard to theory of multiple interpretation, I think his usefulness depends on another current in his thought, and it is this second and stronger current that I here examine in detail.

10. *Being and Time*, pp. 188–95.

11. A definition of "aspect," and various insights into its functioning, will appear in several places in my presentation.

12. For definitions of "mutual implication," see *Phenomenology and Literature*, pp. 14, 61, 69, 70, 72, 76, et passim. "Implication" here bears the significance of "enfoldment," the signification of its Latin etymological root.

13. By verbal sign, we mean (and in my opinion a Heideggerian can concur) what Roman Ingarden calls a "word sound" or "typical phonic form," plus the significations (lexic values) available to this form by way of a culture's *langue*. Typical phonic form is to be distinguished, of course, from written or phonic material, such as quality of voice or shape of print, which can be individually new and different with each implementation. Thus, to use an example cited by Husserl, the word sound *Hund* transcends any individual articulation of it, and the primary German significations available to this word sound are "a dog" and "a truck used in mining." See Roman Ingarden, *The Literary Work of Art*, trans. George G. Grabowicz (Evanston, Ill.: Northwestern, 1973), pp. 34–56, for a discussion of word sound.

14. For Heidegger, the word "phenomenology" means "that which shows itself in itself." Phenomenological description delineates what shows forth concretely, *in* experience.

15. Indications of what Heidegger means by the elusive term "Being" are forthcoming in a moment. Derrida, of course, finds in this apotheosis of centric mysticism an inviting target for deconstruction.

16. The phrases "the one and the same" and *vis primitiva activa* (this latter term adapted from Leibnitz) are applied to Being by Heidegger himself. See Heidegger, "Hölderlin and the Essence of Poetry," in his *Existence and Being*, trans. and intro. by Werner Brock (Chicago: Regnery, 4th prnt., 1965), p. 278; and Heidegger, "What are Poets For?" in his *Poetry, Language, Thought*, trans. and intro. Albert Hofstadter (New York and London: Harper and Row, 1971), p. 100.

17. Heideggerian origin, while logocentric, is not a monist formulation: the origin is for man always a "belonging together" which is concealment/disclosure, a "reserved proximity."

18. For Derrida's lengthy deconstruction of Heidegger, see the long essay "Ousia et grammè," in *Marges*, pp. 31–78; and the shorter but powerful treatments in *Of Grammatology*, pp. 19–24, and *Speech and Phenomena* (from the essay "Differance"), pp. 153–60.

19. The term *Deutung* is adapted from Husserl.

20. For a comparison of "correspondence theory," which "matches," and "commemorative truth," which "brings forth," see *Phenomenology and Literature*, pp. 65, 66.

21. In order to avoid what may seem to be the jargonistic timbre of the actual Heideggerian terms, all of which feature the prepositional "as," I offer the alternate terms provided within the parentheses. Hereinafter, where possible I will substitute the alternate terminology. But it is important to recognize that Heidegger features the prepositional "as" for the sake of precision and emphasis: we shall see that the interpretative question takes the text *as* something; the textual aspect, for its part, is taken *as* something; and the interpretation proper is textual aspect *as* something. Heidegger, like Derrida after him, invents new terms because conventional terminology reflects a world-view he repudiates. Moreover, Heideggerian terms are no more "jargonistic" than the phraseology of American "New Criticism," for example, or even so-called Analytic philosophy—just less familiar to an Anglo-American audience.

22. As we shall see, for Heidegger if a relevant aspect is lacking, the interpretation is invalid.

23. I do not use Husserlian nomenclature, *noema* instead of "As-which" or "textual aspect," because Husserl's *noema* (at least in his later philosophy) may "be distinguished from the real object" (see Aron Gurwitsch, the great Husserlian specialist, in "On the Intentionality of Consciousness," *Phenomenology,* ed. J. Kockelmans [Garden City, N.Y.: Doubleday, 1967], p. 128). Heidegger's As-which, on the other hand, is a facet of the real object, the text. Nor is my surrogate term for the Heideggerian As-which, namely, "textual aspect," to be confounded with Husserlian "aspect"; the latter is usually adjudicated unreal (see R. Ingarden, *The Literary Work of Art,* sections 40 and 42, where Ingarden speaks as a faithful Husserlian). As for Husserlian *noesis,* it is unlike Heideggerian "As-question," since Husserl's *noesis* bestows meaning (see *Phenomenology and Literature,* pp. 98–101) and Heidegger's As-question does not.

24. Heidegger's As-structure reminds one of Husserl's old maxim, intentionality is at one and the same time the grasp and the grip which grasps it.

25. Take care not to confuse the terms "fore-structure" and "As-structure."

26. Perhaps not enough Heideggerian phenomenologists have realized that Husserl, with his notion of *habitus,* approximates some of what Heidegger means by fore-structure. For example, Husserl says that each experience causes a *habitus,* or "new abiding property" which further determines the ego; and the ego, thus habituated, goes on to its next experience in a different (i.e., proportionately modified) way. See Husserl, *Cartesian Meditations,* trans. Dorion Cairns (The Hague: Martinus Nijhoff, 1960), pp. 66, 67, for his discussion of *habitus.* However, when dealing with formal interpretative activity, I am quite convinced that Heidegger would endorse some fore-structures that Husserl would consider "presuppositions" in the technical sense, and thus "bracket out."

27. See *Phenomenology and Literature,* pp. 97–104.

28. See ibid., pp. 146, 148, 151, 156, 157, 160, 161, et passim.

29. The term and the procedure are adopted from a long-established interpretative tradition identified with Schleiermacher and Dilthey; Heidegger, of course, has not only adopted it, but very much *adapted* it.

30. Derrida's attack on Heideggerian "authenticity" in general can be found in "Ousia et grammè," *Marges,* pp. 73, 74.

31. Derrida's deconstruction often aims at the Heideggerian distinction between "originary language" (which conceals/discloses the "belonging together") and the word-and-concept language of philosophical discourse. Derrida argues, as is to be expected, that so-called Heideggerian originary language is really disguised word-and-concept language, and thus subject to the debilities of the latter. See, for example, *Of Grammatology,* pp. 20, 21.

32. I use the term "signification" in lieu of the more common term "sense," because of what has been a knotty problem for translators. Husserl's and Ingarden's word *Sinn* has been customarily translated "sense," but Heidegger's word *Sinn* is translated "meaning," and Heideggerian "meaning" is very different from the Husserlian or Ingardenian notion of "sense." When I mean an idea and/or image operative in a culture's *langue,* I resort to the word "signification"—not to be at all confused, by the way, with E. D. Hirsch's term "significance."

33. Contrast Roman Ingarden, who speaks of the "bestowal of meaning" by the author's "sense-giving acts." See *Phenomenology and Literature,* pp. 110, 115, 116.

34. Hans-Georg Gadamer, *Truth and Method,* trans. by Garrett Barden and John Cumming from the second German edition (New York: Seabury, 1975), p. xix.

35. Gadamer, *Le Problème de la conscience historique* (Louvain and Paris: Publications universitaires de Louvain, and Editions Béatrice-Nauwelaerts, 1963), p. 75.

36. See *Phenomenology and Literature,* pp. 73–78. Notice, however, that Heidegger uses As-questions even when involving the author's "willed significations." Heidegger is by no means "objective" in his own practical literary criticism.

37. In this respect, several critics have read the by now famous ending to Derrida's essay "Differance" as a mix of poignancy and suppressed tragedy: "After this laughter and dance, after this affirmation [Nietzschean affirmation of *différance*] that is foreign to any dialectic, the question arises as to the other side of nostalgia, which I will call Heideggerian *hope.* I am not unaware that this term may be somewhat shocking. I venture it all the same, without excluding any of its implications . . ." (*Speech and Phenomena,* p. 159).

38. Consult *Phenomenology and Literature,* pp. 185, 186, for the examples I provide from Nathaniel Hawthorne's short story, "My Kinsman, Major Molineux."

39. Ibid., pp. 186, 187.

40. Cited from Heidegger's *Vom Wesen des Grundes* (1929) by Theophil Spoerri in "Style of Distance, Style of Nearness," anthologized in *Essays in Stylistic Analysis,* ed. Howard Babb (New York: Harcourt, Brace, Jovanovich, 1972), p. 78.

41. Heidegger's "Dialogue on Language" appears in *On the Way to Language,* pp. 1–54. Chang Chung-yuan's book is *Tao: A New Way of Thinking, A Translation of the Tao Tê Ching with an Introduction and Commentaries* (New York: Perennial Library, Harper and Row, 1977).

42. Heidegger, *Poetry, Language, Thought,* pp. 131, 132.

43. Heidegger, *The Question of Being,* pp. 88, 89, emphasizes the "estrangement" of Being, a motif which Derrida permutates into the "always not enough" of *goings on;* that is, for Derrida *goings on* always "fall short" of metaphysical formulae of completeness (of "closure of the circle," of "self-identity," if you will).

44. Heidegger, *Identity and Difference,* trans. and intro. by Joan Stambaugh (New York: Harper and Row, 1969—bilingual text). In many sequences of this work (see, for example, pp. 64, 65, 71), Heidegger emphasizes the "overwhelming" which characterizes Being, a motif which Derrida alters into the "always too much" of *goings on; goings on,* Derrida claims, always "overrun" the neat and closed circle which constitutes a "definition." For Heidegger, estrangement and surplus are "stellar traces" of that centric mystery which is beyond metaphysical definition. For Derrida, estrangement and surplus *are* the only *goings on* there are; estrangement and surplus are, indeed, "trace" without a star (may the off/tended rhyme not offend).

45. *Bonum diffusivum sibi:* "Goodness is diffusive of itself."

46. See *Being and Time,* pp. 193, 194.

47. Compare Derrida, "Differance," *Speech and Phenomena,* p. 160.

48. Ingarden, *The Literary Work of Art,* p. 142 (though it must be kept in mind, certainly, that the Ingardenian norms for "opalescence" are somewhat different from Heidegger's).

49. See *Phenomenology and Literature,* pp. 67, 73, et passim.

50. For the convergence of "das Gevierte" to generate human *Dasein,* and for the *"Dif-ferenz"* between *Welt* and *Seienden,* see *Phenomenology and Literature,* pp. 69–72, and its composite of quotations from Heidegger.

51. Heidegger, *Poetry, Language, Thought,* p. 40.

52. For the communal nature of *Dasein,* see Heidegger's "Remembrance of the Poet" and "Hölderlin and the Essence of Poetry" in *Existence and Being.*

53. R. H. Blyth, *Games Zen Masters Play* (New York: New American Library, 1976), p. 14.

54. *The Teachings of the Compassionate Buddha,* ed. with commentary by E. A. Burtt (New York: New American Library—Mentor series, 1955), p. 228.

55. William Barrett, to his great credit, and long before the idea seemed due, recognized the possibility of correlating Heideggerian and Oriental thought. See Barrett, *Irrational Man* (New York: Doubleday—Anchor series, 1962; original ed., Doubleday, 1958), p. 234, et passim.

56. See pp. 98–104.

57. Ch'an/Zen Buddhism climaxes its development several centuries after Nagarjuna (ca. 100–200 A.D.), and its various masters reflect sometimes differential and sometimes centric Buddhism.

58. Chang, *Tao: A New Way of Thinking,* p. 108.

59. Ibid., p. 106.

60. Heidegger, *Poetry, Language, Thought,* p. 63.

61. Chang, *Tao,* p. 150.

62. Heidegger, *Identity and Difference,* p. 27.

63. For more passages where Heidegger affirms the simultaneous validity of contradictories, see the quotations from Heidegger in Chang, *Tao,* pp. 14, 61, 108, 124, et passim.

64. René Wellek and Austin Warren, *Theory of Literature,* 3rd ed. (New York: Harcourt, Brace and World, 1956), pp. 177, 178.

65. E. D. Hirsch, *Validity in Interpretation* (New Haven and London: Yale University Press, 1967).

66. Hirsch, *The Aims of Interpretation* (Chicago and London: University of Chicago Press, 1976).

67. Take care not to confuse "signification" and Hirsch's term "significance."

68. Hirsch, *Validity in Interpretation,* p. 230.

69. *Webster's Seventh New Collegiate Dictionary* (Springfield, Mass.: G. and C. Merriam, 1963), p. 154.

70. See Heidegger, *Being and Time,* pp. 377–80; and Heidegger, *On the Way to Language,* p. 34.

71. But see my discussion of an inconsistency in Heidegger's practical criticism of literary works, *Phenomenology and Literature,* pp. 77, 78.

72. Denis Dutton, in his own way, also argues effectively that norms for "scientific truth" should not function as models for the adjudication of literary interpretations (see my note 8).

73. But see Dutton's article, pp. 331, 332, his footnote 2. Many scientists are coming to regard the "scientific method" as "plausible," not "certain."

74. Heidegger, *Being and Time,* p. 197.

75. Flannery O'Connor, *Mystery and Manners,* eds. Sally and Robert Fitzgerald (London: Faber and Faber, 1972), p. 153.

76. Ibid., p. 41.

77. See ahead specifically pp. 149–53; 159–61; also part 3, pp. 119–29.

78. See Mervyn Sprung, "Being and the Middle Way," in *The Question of Being,* ed. Mervyn Sprung (University Park: Pennsylvania State University Press, 1978): Madhyamika "is the school of the so-called Middle Way— strictly, the school of the 'middlers' or 'middle-mosters,' which derives from one Nagarjuna, of the second century A.D." (p. 129).

Notes

Part 3

1. Nagarjuna, *Mūlamadhyamakakārikās* (in English, literally rendered as *Fundamental Verses on the Middle Way;* the title the *Middle Stanzas* is often used as a shorter rendering), chapter 15, verse 7 [MK XV: 7], as cited in Th. Stcherbatsky, *The Conception of Buddhist Nirvana* (Leningrad: Academy of Sciences of the USSR, 1927), p. 49. My citations to the *Mūlamadhyamakakārikās* use in the main two English translations: Kenneth K. Inada, *Nagarjuna: A Translation of his Mūlamadhyamakakārikā with an Introductory Essay* (Tokyo: Hokuseido, 1970), hereafter represented in my text as MK __:__, IN; and Frederick J. Streng, "Fundamentals of the Middle Way," which appears as an appendix in Streng's *Emptiness* (Nashville: Abingdon Press, 1967), and is hereafter represented in my text as MK __:__, S. Both translations are very competent, and each has its advantages. Inada's version comports the virtue of literal rendering; Streng's version has the virtue of that greater comprehensibility which comes from more stylistic English prose. Occasionally I cite Th. Stcherbatsky's pioneering "Madhyamaka Sastra of Nagarjuna," a translation into English of chapters I and XXIV of the *Mūlamadhyamakakārikās*, to be found in his *The Conception of Buddhist Nirvana* (see above), and appearing in my text as MK__:__, STCH. I shall also make reference to Candrakirti's seventh-century commentary on the *Mūlamadhyamakakārikās*, the *Prasannapadā*, of which Stcherbatsky's *The Conception* translates chapters 1 and 25, and which in my text as PRAS. The reader should be aware too of Stanislaw Schayer's *Ausgewählte Kapitel aus der Prasannapadā* (Krakowie/Paris: Nakladem Polskiej Akademji Umiejetnosci / Librarie franco-polonaise, 1931), which translates into German chapters 5 and 12– 16 of the *Prasannapadā*. Inada and Stcherbatsky both supply the Sanscrit text of the *Mūlamadhyamakakārikās*, and the Sanscrit text of the *Prasannapadā* appears in Louis de la Vallée Poussin's monumental critical edition, *Mūlamadhyamakakārikās de Nāgārjuna avec la Prasannapadā Commentaire de Candrakīrti* (Saint Petersburg: Bibliotheca Buddhica, 1913).

2. Stcherbatsky, *The Conception,* p. 50.

3. Here put *en guillemets,* to indicate the guarded use of the word. Nagarjuna, who professes himself a man of "no views," is like Derrida opposed to philosophy understood as metaphysics.

4. By causality here, entitative theories of causality are meant. However, if the reader wishes to investigate Madhyamikan sources privately, let me advise him that sometimes English translators render as 'causality' or 'Buddhist causality' the Sanscrit word for 'dependent co-arising'. As we shall see, the

latter does *not* involve entitative causality. To avoid confusion, I always use the English word 'causality' to mean entitative causality.

5. The Middle Path (*madhyamā pratipad*) is a Way of the Between, a differential between in our Derridean terms, and thus I render it. To represent the Middle Path by nomenclature such as *central* 'philosophy', or some of the other common translations, takes undue risk that the western reader will misunderstand it to mean a logocentric middle.

6. For a dazzling introduction to the intellectual riches of the East, I would recommend to the beginner several volumes in the Columbia University series, Introduction to Oriental Civilizations: *Sources of Chinese Tradition,* compiled by Wm. Theodore de Bary, W.-T. Chan, and Burton Watson (New York: Columbia University Press, 1960), in two volumes; *Sources of Indian Tradition,* compiled by W. T. de Bary and others (New York: Columbia University Press, 1960); and *Sources of Japanese Tradition,* compiled by Ryusaku Tsunoda, W. T. de Bary, and Donald Keene (New York: Columbia University Press, 1964), in two volumes.

7. A perusal of the section meetings on American Philosophy Association programs, American Comparative Literature Association programs, and so on, quickly convinces anyone of this; and so too does the proliferation of professional journals specializing in East-West dialogue.

8. Remember that we are using the word 'Taoism' in our own specialized sense, though derived from a metaphysical attitude common to much (but by no means all) of historical Taoism.

9. MK XV: 10, S.

10. Again, by 'knowing', here, is meant knowing by way of logic and language. And Buddhism argues that logocentric knowing, and its dichotomies of subject and object, can be 'dissolved down', so all is 'devoidness'.

11. Nagarjuna's reinstatement of the logocentric depends on his version of the Buddhist doctrine of the two truths. See ahead, pp. 119–24.

12. For the translation of *śūnyatā* as 'devoidness', I am indebted to Mervyn Sprung. See his "Being and the Middle Way," in *The Question of Being,* ed. Mervyn Sprung (University Park: Pennsylvania University Press, 1978), pp. 132, 135.

13. That is, Nagarjuna does not posit a randomness, but wishes to preserve what I called in my part 1 the 'directional'.

14. The 'thirst' caused by the flame of ignorant desire is extinguished or slaked. Again, the doctrine of two truths shall become involved.

15. I shall soon distinguish between centric and differential Zen, but for our purposes here it is enough to observe that all forms of Buddhism defy the stereotype of 'Buddhist nihilism'.

16. *Śūnyatā* is *madhyamā pratipad,* "emptiness is the Middle Path," says Nagarjuna. See Sprung, *The Question of Being,* p. 135.

17. "Now devoidness of being [*śūnyatā*] is a guiding, conductal expression based on transaction language [*prajñapti upādāya*]," from MK XXIV: 18, Sprung translation, *The Question of Being,* p. 135. The Inada translation is equally clear, rendering *prajñapti* as "provisional name" (p. 148).

18. Derrida considers paradox the privileged trope of religious logocen-

trisms. For him, religion tries to succeed where more univocal systems, such as science or logic, necessarily fail. That is, the divergencies and discontinuities of experience elude one-on-one naming, so religion tries another sleight of hand: it mislabels what are really discontinuities by calling them 'contraries', and then it asserts these 'contraries' constitute a 'mystical unity'. For humankind's urge to reduce the 'spread' of meaning to a controllable 'plurality', see Derrida's "White Mythology," p. 49.

19. Consult *The Encyclopedia of Philosophy*, ed. Paul Edwards (New York: Macmillan, 1967), Vol. 4, pp. 1, 2.

20. See Dom Aelred Graham, *The End of Religion* (New York: Harcourt, Brace, and Jovanovich, 1971), pp. 174, 175; Richard W. Brooks, "Some Uses and Implications of Advaita Vedanta's Doctrine of Maya," in *The Problem of Two Truths in Buddhism and Vedanta*, ed. Mervyn Sprung (Dordrecht: Reidel, 1973), pp. 98–108; and J. N. Mohanty, "Some Aspects of Indian Thinking on Being," in *The Question of Being*, p. 149.

21. See *The Encyclopedia of Philosophy*, Vol. 2, pp. 87, 88, 90, 93.

22. That Confucianism is, in Derridean terms, a philosophy of presence is not to say, of course, that this presence must be static and essential. In fact, Confucianism often affirms a presence generated by indefeasible laws of change, of dynamic rhythm. See Frederick Streng's "Approaches to Authentic Existence: Christian, Confucian and Buddhist," in *Philosophy East and West* (October, 1982), and especially its representation of the Confucian scholar, Chun-i T'ang.

23. And some forms of Neo-Confucianism.

24. Chang Chung-yuan, *Tao: A New Way of Thinking* (New York: Harper and Row, 1975), p. 76.

25. Ibid., p. 74.

26. Another seductive feature of Lao Tzu's thought, though here he is matched by many myths Eastern and Western, is that a logocentric 'God' is preceded chronologically in world history by the Tao (in some other myths, Eastern and Western, 'God' is preceded by Chaos): that the alleged origin of the universe is preceded by the 'other-than-logocentric' is an ancient theme, then, comparable to Derrida's proto-trace or *différance originaire*, which precedes the "epoch of God." See *Tao: A New Way of Thinking*, p. 13, for the relevant treatment of Lao Tzu.

27. See *The Encyclopedia of Philosophy*, Vol. 2, pp. 88, 90.

28. See my part 2, pp. 71–74.

29. Consult Frederick Streng, *Emptiness*, pp. 28–81, et passim.

30. Confer ibid., p. 37, for a short but effective discussion of *pratītya samut-pāda*.

31. Th. Stcherbatsky, in his *The Central Conception of Buddhism*, 3rd ed. (Calcutta: Susil Gupta, Ltd., 1961), p. 32, and Streng, *Emptiness*, p. 36, both use this translation.

32. Again, Streng provides a concise account, *Emptiness*, p. 32.

33. Ibid., p. 37.

34. Ibid., pp. 32–34.

35. It may be absolute, however, in the sense of *ab-solvo*, "loosened from," "free from" (i.e., from logos). Thus the reader is warned that some translators call *śūnyatā*, and Nagarjuna's understanding of *śūnyatā*, 'absolute' in this second sense.

36. The logocentric nature of Yogacara emerges clearly in the discussion of "The School of Consciousness Only," in *Sources of Chinese Tradition*, Vol. 1, pp. 303–6.

37. The Buddhism which develops, chronologically, after early Buddhism calls itself Mahayana, or "Greater Vehicle" Buddhism (i.e., the Mahayana claims it can save all mankind, and that the earlier Buddhism, the Hinayana or "Lesser Vehicle," cannot offer such generous means). The earlier form of Buddhism, of course rejecting for itself the disdainful Mahayanist nomenclature, takes on the name Theravada, or "Way of the Elders." See *Sources of Chinese Tradition*, Vol. 1, p. 269. For a more detailed treatment of Chinese Buddhism, see Francis H. Cook, "Chinese Academic Schools and Doctrinal Innovations," in *Buddhism: A Modern Perspective*, ed. Charles S. Prebish (University Park and London: Pennsylvania State University Press, 1975), pp. 201–7.

38. For an expert and scholarly treatment of Kumarajiva and the Three Treatise schools, see Richard H. Robinson, *Early Madhyamika in India and China* (Madison: University of Wisconsin, 1967). Concerning the use of the Madhyamika by T'ien'Tai, see Inada, p. 143.

39. For the list of these works, see Robinson, *Early Madhyamika*, pp. 26, 27.

40. For example, compare T. R. V. Murti, *The Central Philosophy of Buddhism* (London: George Allen and Unwin Ltd., 1955), who argues that *śūnyatā* is an absolute which transcends dialectical opposites; and A. K. Warder, "Is Nagarjuna a Mahayanist?" in *The Problem of Two Truths* anthology, who argues that *śūnyatā* is no more and no less than applied empiricism. A helpful survey, in this matter of definitions pertaining to Nagarjuna's *śūnyatā*, can be found in Douglas D. Daye, "Major Schools of the Mahayana: Madhyamika," *Buddhism: A Modern Perspective*, pp. 76–96.

41. I shall cite my authorities shortly, but let me make clear now that when 'building a case' it shall be my practice, especially when dealing with matters other than *śūnyatā*, to adduce evidence from all competent Buddhologists.

42. Frederick Streng, along with R. S. Misra and B. K. Matilal (q.v., below), and Mervyn Sprung, are the representatives I employ most frequently when accounting for differential Nagarjunism.

43. Streng, *Emptiness*, p. 126.

44. Ibid., p. 129.

45. In my opinion, a somewhat misleading translation: in English it can suggest, at least to the uninitiated, Hegelian triads and perhaps a leap to a transcendental unity supporting the dialectic somehow (a suggestion Streng of course wants to avoid).

46. *Emptiness*, p. 146.

47. Ibid.

48. Ibid., p. 149.

49. This is especially the case where the words have been associated with logocentric values, be they teleological and/or ontological. The Sanscrit term

paramārtha is often rendered in English as "ultimate" or "highest," but I shall choose the translation "ungathered," as the reader will note, in an effort to allay such a misunderstanding.

50. Sprung, *Question of Being,* p. 136.

51. Ibid., p. 137.

52. R. S. Misra, head of the Department of Indian Philosophy and Religion at Banaras Hindu University, is interviewed in Dom Aelred Graham's *The End of Religion,* pp. 174, 175.

53. Ibid.

54. *Sources of Chinese Tradition,* Vol. 1, pp. 303, 304.

55. Of course there were many other schools as well.

56. And the Ch'an school outlasts both the Three Treatise and the Yogacara sects. See *The Buddhist Tradition in India, China, and Japan,* ed. William Th. de Bary (New York: Random House, 1969; Vintage bk. ed., 1972), p. 355.

57. Consult David J. Kalupahana, *Buddhist Philosophy: A Historical Analysis* (Honolulu: University Press of Hawaii, 1976), p. 172 *et circa.*

58. For a brief account of the controversy involving the nature of *prajñā* (wisdom) in Ch'an, see *Sources of Chinese Tradition,* Vol. 1, pp. 348, 349.

59. *The Buddhist Tradition,* p. 360.

60. Ninian Smart, *The Long Search* (Boston, Toronto: Little, Brown and Co., 1977): "But perhaps the great paradox about Zen is its great orthodoxy. It is Japan's substitute for Lesser Vehicle Buddhism. It is (to put it unhistorically) Japan's form of the Theravada and fulfills much the same function within the overall economy of Buddhism" (p. 275).

61. The exact nature of early Ch'an is subject to much dispute among Buddhologists, and apparently the nature of early Japanese Zen was very diversified.

62. D. T. Suzuki, *Introduction to Zen Buddhism* (New York: Philosophical Library, 1949), p. 60.

63. Suzuki, *Mysticism: Christian and Buddhist* (New York: Harper, 1957), p. 30.

64. Alan Watts's famous book, in fact, is entitled *The Supreme Identity: An Essay on Oriental Metaphysic and the Christian Religion* (New York: Random House, Vintage bk. ed., 1972), and its appreciation of mysticism, while intense and fascinating, is quite thoroughly logocentric.

65. Suzuki, *Mysticism: Christian and Buddhist,* p. 30.

66. *Chinese Buddhist Verse,* trans. Richard Robinson (London: John Murray, 1954), p. 78. Note, then, that not without reason did I quote Seng-Ts'an in my part 2 as an examplar of unity of contradictories.

67. Ibid., p. 77. It is interesting also to note that Richard Robinson, in *Early Madhyamika in India and China* (p. 57) maintains there are no paradoxes in Nagarjuna's *Middle Stanzas.* How this contrasts with the absolute paradoxicality of a Seng-Ts'an or a Suzuki!

68. Cited in Jiyu Kennett, *Selling Water by the River* (Emeryville, Cal.: Dharma Pub., 1976), pp. 178–81. I cannot resist adding here, as an aside, that the very title of Kennett's book gives us (unintentionally, of course) a Derridean resonance. Since in the Orient, a river is hardly a place to sell

water (the water is already available in the river), the title is toying with the differentialist notion of 'more than more' (and by implication, 'less than less'), a variant of Derrida's 'outside the outside' and 'inside the inside'.

69. The Ancestors are the great Ch'an/Zen Masters who came after the sequence of Buddhist Patriarchs. This commentary is induced by the famous verse of Shonawashyu, "The excellent Law of Buddha has nothing to do with either mind or body." For upon hearing this while still a young monk, Ubakikuta is enlightened. The reader will find that throughout the quoted commentaries and other texts, I have tried to supply, within brackets, further explication where it seems required.

70. Zenkei Shibayama, *A Flower Does Not Talk,* trans. Sumiko Kudo (Rutland, Vt.: Tuttle, 1970), pp. 10, 11. Shibayama provides this little Buddhist story verbatim, but does not follow it with a differential reading.

71. Cited in R. H. Blyth's *Games Zen Masters Play* (New York: New American Library, 1976), p. 88. Among western commentators on Zen, I find Blyth one of the most appreciative of differentialism. His commentaries are sometimes derogated by centric Buddhists, Japanese and western, but it is important for the uninformed reader to realize such negative critiques are often conditioned by the Oriental version of what we call 'sectarianism.'

72. See pp. 126–29.

73. Cited in R. H. Blyth, *Zen and Zen Classics,* Vol. 4 (Tokyo: Hokuseido, 1966), pp. 193, 194.

74. Case XXX, from Baso (Ma-Tsu), can be found in *Zen and Zen Classics,* Vol. 4, p. 215.

75. Case XXXIII, also from Baso, can likewise be found in *Zen and Zen Classics,* Vol. 4, p. 228.

76. "Being and the Middle Way," *Question of Being,* p. 137.

77. Despite Nagarjuna's warning, in much of later Madhyamika (as we just noted) *śūnyatā* becomes identified with centric affectivity.

78. Consult Streng, *Emptiness,* 146–50.

79. The opponent is always a holder of 'views', since 'views' are ensconced by their nature in logocentric thought.

80. See Nagarjuna's "Averting the Arguments" (*Vigrahavyā vartanī*), translated in Streng, *Emptiness,* pp. 222–27; and the commentary of Streng (Ibid.), p. 96. See also Bimal Krishna Matilal, *Epistemology, Logic, and Grammar in Indian Philosophical Analysis* (Hague and Paris: Mouton, 1971), pp. 147, 148.

81. Or, to rephrase the matter once more, when Derrida and Nagarjuna argue with adversaries, they are not arguing *for* what Nagarjuna would call a 'view'; and when they show a 'view' nonsensical by forcing it to dilemma, they are not affirming the contradictory 'view'.

82. See Inada, p. 113.

83. I shall follow the exposition of the tetralemma offered by Inada, Streng, Sprung, and Matilal, since their exposition represents that of most Orientalists, and is both most faithful to the Nagarjunist understanding of the four forms, and to the native Indian tradition's general understanding of them. For example, instead of trying to 'Westernize' the third lemma, by

reducing it in all cases to two particular propositions, Inada, Streng, and Sprung usually take it as universal: All X is both All Y and All not-Y. When taken as universal, the third lemma is paradoxical, and 'mystical' in a monist and, in Derridean terms, 'logocentric' way. Nagarjuna and Derrida go on, of course, to find the third lemma 'impossible'. All this is not to deny that 'X is both Y and not-Y' sometimes means in Buddhist writing the proposition, 'All X is partly Y and partly not-Y', which is indeed reducible to two particular propositions, 'Some X is Y' and 'Some X is not-Y'. In my future discussion, when the third lemma is meant in the non-universal way, I shall so indicate.

84. Inada translation.

85. For another Nagarjunist variant of the tetralemma, see MK XVIII: 8, IN: "Everything is suchness (*tathyam*), not suchness, both suchness and not suchness, and neither suchness nor not suchness. This is the Buddha's teaching." Derrida, while not resorting overtly to tetralemma, does use a somewhat analogous arrangement on occasion—for example: "Neither matter nor form, it is nothing that any philosopheme, that is, any dialectic, however determinate, can capture. It is an ellipsis of both meaning and form; it is neither plenary speech nor perfectly circular. More and less, neither more nor less, it is perhaps an entirely different question" (*Speech and Phenomena,* p. 128). I would like to add here too that Nagarjuna's negation is not the mystical absolutism which, in several philosophies, results from the reciprocal 'canceling out' of contradictories. In other words, Nagarjuna never uses the four-cornered logic in such wise as to evoke a logocentric *aeternus modus* (nor is Nagarjuna's *nirvāna* to be understood in this way, q.v.). In my part 2, I identified the late-phase Heidegger with a logocentric mysticism conforming to the third lemma, and in my Appendix the deconstructive *démarche* which addresses the Abrams-Weitz problematic leads towards a mystical absolutism understandable either as 'canceling out' or as *plenum.* The evolution from logocentrism to logocentric mysticism to differentialism is in my own work not to be understood amelioristically, since the intention of my part 4 is to reinstate the validity of all stages. It is interesting in the context of the present part 3, however, to recall that the kind of mystical absolutism achieved by way of four-cornered logic (a logic which according to this mysticism truly 'annihilates itself') was in our own Western tradition attacked and parodied well over a century ago by Kierkegaard. In his article, "Heidegger, Kierkegaard, and the Hermeneutic Circle: Towards a Postmodern Theory of Interpretation as Dis-closure" (in *Boundary 2,* winter, 1976), William Spanos cites the assault of Kierkegaard on the 'aesthete' who cancels out contradictories and then leaps to the *aeternus modus.* Kierkegaard satirizes the aesthete who avows: "Hang yourself, you will regret it; do not hang yourself and you will also regret that; hang yourself or do not hang yourself, you will regret both; whether you hang yourself or do not hang yourself, you will regret both. This, gentlemen, is the sum and substance of all philosophy. It is not only at certain moments that I view everything *aeterno modo* as Spinoza says, but I live constantly *aeterno modo*" (from Kierkegaard's *Either/Or,* cited by Spanos, p. 465). Nagarjuna and Derrida would join in Kierkegaard's attack on the aesthete. Lastly, in the context of my part 3, I would like to alert the reader to Bertrand Russell's discussion of statements which are self-referential and contradict themselves, e.g., [The statement in the rectangle on this page is false.] I demonstrate just such a self-referential contradictory towards the end of "Everything and Nothing,"

the first essay in this book's Appendix. Russell rejects the whole quandary, and does so by affirming a distinction between 'object language', which talks about things, and 'meta-language', which talks about object language. Beginners will find a helpful summary of Russell's thesis, and its adversaries, in J. G. Brennan, *A Handbook of Logic,* 2nd ed. (New York: Harper, 1961), pp. 167–69. As for Derrida, at least eventually in his argumentative *déroulement,* he would reject it because self-referentiality 'pretends to catch itself by the tail' (i.e., self-reflexivity is a magnification of all self-identity), and not because of the rationale Russell proposes. Matilal, within the section "Sophistry and the Semantical Paradoxes" in his *Epistemology, Logic, and Grammar,* pp. 159–62, also refutes a good many arguments favoring the self-referential contradictory, and does so for the most part in Madhyamikan terms.

86. See note 31.

87. See Douglas Daye's, "Major Schools of the Mahayana: Madhyamika," pp. 84–86, 91, 92.

88. Consult Daye, p. 91; Streng, *Emptiness,* p. 37.

89. Daye's translation, in his "Major Schools," p. 81. For a lengthy, more precise, and scholarly critique of *prajñapti* than the short and somewhat popular treatment from Sprung which I quote, see Daye, especially pp. 81–95.

90. Sprung, *Question of Being,* p. 110.

91. Ibid., p. 134.

92. *Prasaṅga* is defined by A. K. Warder in his *Indian Buddhism* (Delhi: Motilal Banarsidass, 1970) as a "necessary consequence" deducible from the opponent's position, and showing "the absurdity of that position and the self-contradiction inherent in it" (p. 378).

93. *Tattvam* is the way matters truly 'go on'.

94. *Question of Being,* p. 134.

95. Ibid., pp. 134, 135.

96. Ibid., pp. 129, 130.

97. Streng sums up the formula for *pratītya samutpāda* which had become established quite early in Buddhist literature: dependent co-arising means that the "human being has no permanent essence [*ātman*] and is only a changing conglomerate of material, mental, and psychic factors [i.e., *dharmas*]" (Streng, *Emptiness,* p. 30).

98. See my part 1 for the understanding of 'self-identity' and 'personal self-identity' operative throughout our treatment.

99. See my treatment of psychology/ontology, pp. 124–26.

100. Consult Daye, "Major Schools," pp. 89–91, for differences between Sautrantikan and Sarvastivadin Abhidharma. A helpful treatment is also found in Stcherbatsky, *Central Conception,* pp. 33–36.

101. *Emptiness,* p. 37.

102. I refer by 'entitative' to any model founded on self-identical formulae, be they implicit or explicit.

103. Streng translation.

104. *Question of Being,* p. 135.

105. Inada, p. 98. For Candrakirti's own commentary on Nagarjunist *parabhāva*, see Schayer's translation, *Ausgewählte Kapitel aus der Prasannapadā*, pp. 64–67.

106. Of course, by using the argument of 'infinite retreat', Nagarjuna and Derrida are leading the reader down the road to a more radical question: Why resort to the model of 'cause and effect' at all?

107. Here the third lemma is understood in the undistributed or non-universal sense. See note 83.

108. See Kalupahana, *Buddhist Philosophy,* pp. 105, 130.

109. Chapter 1, section 48, PRAS p. 188. Candrakirti uses at least two other arguments, suitable in different contexts from this one, which pertain to potency and act. Consult Stcherbatsky, *The Conception,* p. 126 of the "Examination of Causality" section, and p. 85 of the "Analysis" section.

110. PRAS p. 189.

111. The five *skandhas: rūpa* (material form), *vedanā* (feeling), *samjñā* (awareness), *saṃskāra* (mental confrontation), and *vijñāna* (conscious play). See Inada, p. 114.

112. Ibid., p. 54.

113. An other but comparable way of showing Nagarjuna's pure negative reference can be derived from Daye's section on causation and language in his "Major Schools," pp. 81, 82. Daye explains that "a great deal of [Buddhist] philosophical discussion revolved around the two interrelated concepts of relational or dependent co-origination (*pratītya samutpāda*) and the ontological status of certain words—in Madhyamika, 'own-being' (*svabhāva*) and language-constructs (*prajñapti*). The origins of this 'causal' concept of the twelvefold prior conditions (*nidānas*) may be found in various of the earliest texts. . . . With such statements as 'this thing being, that becomes; from the arising of this, that arises; this not becoming, that does not become,' the concept of Buddhist causality seems to imply, in some scholars' eyes, a chain of physical and mental causality. However, if one combines the concept of sequential causality with the additional and equally fundamental tenet that everything is impermanent, that everything consists of a series of unique staccato-like moments, then the problem of 'causation' does *not* become one of sufficient and necessary causal conditions [that stay the same] through succeeding public moments. The problem *does* become that of trying to distinguish the ontological criteria for distinguishing what constitutes an ontological category in one succeeding moment and its relationship, if any, with a specific 'event' in a succeeding moment." And when Nagarjuna analyzes any ontological (i.e., logocentric) category attributed to a 'moment', and its 'relationship' to an 'event' in a succeeding moment, he is—within the logocentric frame of reference—led inevitably to only one ontological conclusion, purely negative reference. "The Madhyamikas," Daye tells us, "hold that although words and the world they map seem to be stable units in a changing world, identity and time are actually born [absolutely] fresh at every moment" (p. 82). The identity and time of each moment are absolutely *not* like those of other moments. Or, to put it another way, if one combines—as Daye suggests—the concepts of 'impermanence' [pure negative reference] and 'sequential causality' [relatedness], the only conclusion is that pure negative reference is the only 'relatedness' from one moment to

the next to the next. And, as we shall see, this is a fairly good statement of what 'dependent co-arising' (regarded as a 'world-ensconced truth') is.

114. Beginners can consult Sprung, *Question of Being*, p. 130, for a good capsulized treatment of the Fourfold Truths.

115. Not to be confused with entitative causality, of course, though some translations render 'dependency' as 'dependent causality'.

116. For a discussion of Nagarjuna's dispute with Abhidharmic versions of causality, see Frederick Streng, "Reflections on the attention given to Mental Construction in the Indian Buddhist analysis of Causality," *Philosophy East and West*, 25, No. 1 (1975), pp. 74–76.

117. Here is one of the cases, in other words, where the third lemma is not addressed as if its predicates were universal; the third lemma, that is, is not here regarded as mystical in its claim.

118. See Inada, p. 132.

119. Notice that Nagarjuna rejects the possibility that existence and non-existence, and light and darkness, can "be together in one place": he is rejecting the mystic unity of opposites. Nagarjuna, as I have repeatedly stressed, does not favor centric mysticism. He is a *rationalist,* and a *differential* mystic.

120. Douglas Daye, "Major Schools," p. 84.

121. The components are "epistemic" because description is constitutive in Buddhism.

122. See Daye, "Major Schools," pp. 84–88.

123. See also MK XXIV: 18 and MK XIII: 7, 8, as examples of the highest meta-language level within the Madhyamikan system.

124. Consult, for example, Murti, *The Central Philosophy*, p. 122; and Inada, pp. 179 and 183.

125. Streng, *Emptiness*, pp. 94, 95.

126. Matilal, *Epistemology, Logic, and Grammar,* pp. 152, 157.

127. Soon we shall undertake a discussion of what I call the onto-psychological.

128. Matilal is obviously not referring to 'reality' as it is rejected by all Buddhists, i.e., the reality of entitative realism/non-realism. Matilal means reality as *yathābhūtam,* or the way matters 'go on'. The specific question he is raising here is whether, *at the conventional level,* the causal law 'goes on' (as opposed to being a 'fiction', say). In other words, does entitative causality, though subject to a radical Buddhist deconstruction so as to lead to dependent co-arising and *śūnyatā* instead, still 'go on' *at the conventional level?*

129. Nagarjuna's *Vigrahavyā vartanī (Averting the Arguments)* is a remarkably condensed work in which he shows that to refute an argument is not to implicitly affirm its contradictory. Derrida concurs with Nagarjuna on this crucial question: recall our distinction between the Derridean *déroulement* and classical *reductio ad absurdum.*

130. See Streng's translation of the *Vigrahavyā vartanī,* in *Emptiness,* p. 227.

131. Case XXVI of the *Mumonkan,* cited in R. H. Blyth, *Zen and Zen Classics,* Vol. 4, pp. 188, 189.

132. *Zen and Zen Classics,* Vol. 4, p. 190.

133. Ibid.

134. Some poetic aphorisms which seem to belong to this 'genre' of instruction of the two truths can be identified as well with instruction in Buddhist 'trace' (recall the Derridean *trace* of part 1, which, like Buddhist trace, is not logocentric but still is somehow 'directional' rather than 'random'). An aphorism like the following rejects indifference and voidism, celebrating instead the subtle distinctions of the directional: "When the snowy heron stands in the snow, the colors are not the same" (from Miura and Sasaki, *The Zen Koan* [New York: Harcourt, Brace and World, 1965], p. 105). The whites of the heron and the snow are subtly distinct, yet are somehow relational and likewise devoid: they are *trace.* And note the Oriental delicacy of this 'capping phrase': "Endlessly rise the distant mountains, / Blue heaped upon blue" (Ibid.). Grandiloquent imagery, this: range upon range of blue mountains, each distinct and each an off/color of the others, so the blues pile up and back, further and further away "endlessly"—*trace!*

The Derridean 'directional' or 'trace' also has its affiliations with the Buddhist notion of *tr̥ṣṇā* ("thirst"), and much productive work can be done, I think, in the comparison of the two. Buddhist *tr̥ṣṇā* is the 'impulse on the move' which accounts for all activity, human and non-human, physical and spiritual. While early Buddhism regarded *tr̥ṣṇā* as the craving which had to be mortified, the Mahayana came to understand it as negative only when combined with egotism and thus permutated into unbridled passion. Appropriated properly, *tr̥ṣṇā* is the ongoing force of 'compassion', and so off/ impels all 'goings on'. The intriguing possibility exists, I believe, that this reworking of thirst as 'compassion' rather than 'craving' (desire) can make for a creative reworking in the west of postmodern studies of 'desire' (such as René Girard's *Deceit, Desire, and the Novel*).

135. A forever dependent co-arising which is approximated *sous rature* by Nagarjuna's 'pure effect' or Derrida's 'pure signifier' (Matilal, in his *Epistemology*, p. 150, calls this Nagarjunist co-arising by the term 'dependence only').

136. Streng, *Emptiness*, p. 37.

137. Ibid., p. 38.

138. Ibid.

139. Streng, "The Process of Ultimate Transformation in Nagarjuna's Madhyamika," *The Eastern Buddhist* (new series), XI, No. 2 (1978), p. 19.

140. Perhaps the closest Derrida comes to an 'inkling' that this 'shift' *can be* achieved is in the following passage, where *trace*'s "irreducible excess" both *escapes* logocentrism, and, by virtue of the very excess, *restores* logocentrism as well: "The trace would not be the mixture or passage between form and the amorphous, between presence and absence, etc., but that which, in escaping this opposition, renders it possible because of its irreducible excess" (*Speech and Phenomena*, p. 128).

141. Inada, p. 143.

142. See Streng, "The Process of Ultimate Transformation," pp. 17, 30.

143. This whole stanza is from Mumon's preface to the *Mumonkan*, the "Gateless Barrier" (*Zen and Zen Classics*, 4, p. 16). Read differentially, the

stanza is an invitation to Nagarjunist off/logic. Thus this first line declares that the Great Way, *śūnyatā*, is not accessible to the logocentric 'between', i.e., the 'between' which bears the gate of pure logic.

144. The Great Way is not centric, since it disseminates by off/way of thousands of by-ways.

145. While *śūnyatā* has no gate, still it is not automatically open to all. *Śūnyatā* has the "barrier" which is the differential 'between'. The barrier is, of course, not impassable, or we would be reduced to absurdism. The differential between has the remarkable (pun: re-'markable . . . ') status of mystical off/logic (see my part 4).

146. It is very significant that the reference to the notion of an "alone" (a faithful rendering of the Chinese character here) is preserved. That is, differentialism has not dissolved goings-on into indifference: what has been deconstructed, rather, is the theory of self-identity projected in an absolute sense on the goings-on. The gist of the Chinese is that one who has attained realization is *free* no matter what the circumstance.

147. While rationalism, studiously and progressively applied, can perform deconstruction, it cannot of itself bring about realization. The poem is by Karasumaru-Mitsuhiro (1579–1638).

148. Sprung, *Question of Being,* pp. 133, 134.

149. Ibid., p. 136.

150. In my part 4, I shall discuss why the notion of *tathatā* and its analogs in other philosophical traditions is *not* a lapse back into logocentrism.

151. For a good discussion of the mystic's involvement in the quotidian, see Robert M. Gimello, "Mysticism and Meditation," in *Mysticism and Philosophical Analysis,* ed. Steven Katz (New York: Oxford University Press, 1978), pp. 170–99, and especially pp. 184, 190–94. Several excellent essays which address specifically the positive relation of action to mysticism can be found in the collection, *Contemplation and Action in World Religions,* eds. Yusuf Ibish and Ileana Marculescu (Houston/Seattle and London: Rothko Chapel, dist. by University of Washington Press, 1977, 1978).

152. During the period of the *alumbrados* in Spain and the Quietists in France, the Western Church developed sophisticated norms which do much to sort out—in the face of alleged mystical claims—hallucination (and other forms of self-deception) from the eminently healthful breakthroughs of genuine mysticism, be it centric or differential.

153. Cf. part 1, p. 53.

154. Cited in Shibayama, *A Flower Does Not Talk,* p. 3.

155. I shall use the term 'crosscut' quite extensively in part 4, because this metaphor can suggest the rapid slide to and fro—the spontaneous command, if you will—characteristic of the wiseman's shift 'between' pure devoidness and the logocentric. The image of diagonality, it seems to me, further elides the conventional metaphor of 'frontal' or *en bloc* space usually identified with centric 'breakthrough'.

156. Of course, insofar as our phraseology fails here and elsewhere to escape a logocentric rhetoric, it is because we must use—as Nagarjuna says—conventional discourse, i.e., logocentric discourse, in order to 'guide'.

157. That is, logocentric formulations, while not having absolute propriety, retain *internal* propriety as long as the operations within the logical frame are themselves 'logical'.

158. That is, the pushing of logic so it can do for us *the most it can* (while granting there is much that logic cannot do); otherwise, a turn to mysticism, even differential mysticism, takes on the appearance of a not-so-artful dodge,—"fudging," if you will.

159. Cited in Blyth, *Zen in English Literature and Oriental Classics*, p. 195.

160. Cited by Alan Watts, in his essay "Haiku," at the beginning of poetry section, *The World of Zen: An East-West Anthology*, ed. Nancy Wilson Ross (New York: Random House, 1960), p. 128.

Notes

Part 4

1. See Jacques Derrida, "Structure, Sign, and Play," in *The Structuralist Controversy*, eds. R. Macksey and E. Donato (Baltimore: Johns Hopkins, 1972—pbk. ed.), pp. 248, 249, 264, 265; "White Mythology," pp. 69, 70, 72; GL, pp. 31–33; DISS, pp. 293, 294; OGI, p. 147; SP, p. 134; OG, pp. 13, 60, 65, 71–73, 89, et passim; WD, pp. 64–78, 182, endnote 17 on p. 322, and the whole of the essay on Emmanuel Levinas,—WD, pp. 79–153 (especially pp. 150–53, and endnote 90 on p. 320). See also the references to Derrida, theism, and transcendental self-identity as cited in my part 1.

2. See Derrida, SP, pp. 142, 143, and MP, pp. 13, 14 (French text); and also the relevant parts of my part 1.

3. Of course the term "prototrace" (*archi-trace*), like the term *différance originaire*, is meant to be confounding. How can a track/trace precede that which left the track/trace behind?

4. Matt. 27:51, from *The Jerusalem Bible* (Garden City, New York: Doubleday, 1966). Biblical quotations are from this version except where otherwise noted.

5. While remaining "one" (in a way which we shall try to probe somewhat).

6. John 8:32.

7. Luke 12:49.

8. *Mysterium* is the technical term for any divine truth impossible to infer from human reason alone, and thus known to man only because God has revealed it. A *mysterium,* usually rendered by the now infelicitous translation "mystery" in English, is necessarily beyond human ken—though theorizing about a *mysterium* can reap insights that are true in proportion to human knowledge, i.e., the insights are "adequate" but not "comprehensive" (they do not "contain" or encircle God). The words *mysterium* and "mystery," like the word "mysticism," Derrida finds repugnant—a repugnance I find comically miscalculated, since the etymological root for all three words is the Greek *muein,* "to close the eyes and/or mouth," that is, to "opt out" of metaphysics, and the embedded metaphors of "vision" and "voice" which constitute logocentrism.

9. OG, p. 36; French text, DG, pp. 54, 55.

10. But "ever altering," in the technical Derridean sense.

11. Compare with what has been called Derridean tetrapolarity, as in DISS, pp. 322–407.

219

12. See part 1, pp. 9–18.

13. Some of the New Testament passages which are most informative in this regard are the following: Matt. 1:23; 3:16; 10:20; 17:5; 28:19; Luke 1:16f; 4:18; John 3:34f; 5:18, 19, 23; 6:57; 10:30, 14:1, 9, 16, 26; 15:26; 16:7, 14f; 17:10; 20:21; Heb. 1:8; Rom. 8:15; 9:5; Phil. 2:5f; Gal. 4:4–8; 1 John 5:7.

14. In this context, I mean both the Catholic and the Eastern Orthodox churches. It so happens that the Church councils most important for adjudication of trinitarian problems occurred in the centuries before the sad break between Eastern and Western Christianity.

15. The trinitarian problematic and the related questions of Christology were thrashed out both in synodal and general councils. The general Council of Nicaea (325 A.D.), for example, addressed Arianism; the Council of Rome (382) treated the ramifications of the Nicenic term and concept *homoousios;* the general Council of Ephesus (431) addressed the Nestorian heresy; and the general Council of Chalcedon (451) resolved Christological questions that grew out of the declarations promulgated at Ephesus. I shall try to indicate, shortly, how and why an intransigent logocentrism (in the Derridean sense) contributed so much to the generation of the early trinitarian heresies, and I shall try to show how the early Church councils coped with challenges of this special kind.

16. "And know that I am with you always; yes, to the end of time" (Matt. 28:20).

17. Thus Saint Paul calls the Church "the Church of the living God, which upholds the truth and keeps it safe" (1 Tim. 3:15). And in Matthew's gospel, Jesus confers authority: "You are Peter ['Rock', a word not used as a name before] and on this rock I will build my Church. And the gates of the underworld can never hold out against it. I will give you the keys of the kingdom of heaven: whatever you bind on earth shall be considered bound in heaven: whatever you loose on earth shall be considered loosed in heaven" (Matt. 16:18, 19).

18. But still, by definition, necessarily *inerrant.*

19. The Church did not consider itself obliged, however, to affirm the contradictory of what it negated. The Church, in other words, did not automatically fall into what Derrida deems the trap of dialectical thinking.

20. *Enchiridion symbolorum definitionum et declarationum de rebus fidei et morum* [*Handbook of Creeds, Definitions, and Declarations on Matters of Faith and Morals*], eds. H. Denzinger and A. Schönmetzer (Rome, Barcelona, New York, Freiburg i. Br.: Herder; 33rd edition—1965, 34th edition—1967).

21. The *Enchiridion* collects, in their original languages and in chronological order, the important magisterial documents of the last one thousand nine hundred years. To better accommodate the slow but steady increment of documents, the numbering-system whereby each entry is numerated and indexed was altered in 1963. Lest older textbooks become incomprehensible because they use the pre-1963 numeration when citing the *Enchiridion,* editions of the *Enchiridion* since 1963 have run the older numeration and the newer one in parallel, next to the documents collected. Throughout my text I shall use the older (i.e., the pre-1963) numeration, because a theological source-book (see note 23) often cited in my part 4 employs it, and because the commonly available English translation (alas, it is a much abridged version) of the *Enchiridion* represents it at least parenthetically. This English

translation, selected and translated by J. Clarkson, J. Edwards, W. Kelly, and J. Welch, bears the title *The Church Teaches: Documents of the Church in English Translation* (Saint Louis: B. Herder, 1955), and it uses both its own numerical scheme, and, in parenthetical format, the cross-reference to the *Enchiridion*'s numeration. All my references to the *Enchiridion* shall be bracketed, as [DZooo]; my references to *The Church Teaches*, when I choose to utilize it, shall be bracketed, as [CTxxx]. There are cases, however, when I shall feel justified, indeed obligated, to supply my own translation. As for official Church declarations since 1963, I have found that for our specialized purposes the rich documentation of Vatican Council II (1962–65) indeed suffices, and my citations here are to *The Documents of Vatican II*, ed. W. M. Abbot, trans. ed. Msgr. J. Gallagher (New York: America Press, 1966).

22. No doubt these Biblical passages can pertain to both trinitarian and Christological concerns. But in a way this is precisely the point. Much of early theology became really the sorting out of these entrammeled issues.

23. For a concise treatment, see Karl Rahner's "Trinity in Theology," in *Sacramentum Mundi*, ed. Karl Rahner, with Cornelius Ernst and Kevin Smith (New York: Herder and Herder, 1968), Vol. 6, p. 305. *Sacramentum Mundi* is an encyclopedia of theology (perhaps better described as an anthology of theological essays, arranged topically) written in the authentic spirit of Vatican Council II. Protestant, autocephalic Eastern, and Jewish scholars alike, as well as Catholic scholars, have acclaimed the expertise of its contributors and their articles (all signatoried, and collected in six volumes). Because of the prestige of its scholarship, and because of the orthodoxy of its views (in terms of Catholicism), I shall cite it frequently. For one of the most striking features of my argument in this part 4 is that it only "works" because there is a *magisterium:* the intransigent fidelity of the *magisterium* to the ancient "deposit of the Faith" (Scripture and Sacred Tradition) is what, amazingly, *liberates* humanity from the rigidity of logocentrism. The orthodoxy proves to be the most open, most "differential."

24. It is easy to see how at first blush Heb. 1:3 can be so interpreted: "He [the Son] is the radiant light of God's glory and the *perfect copy* of his nature, . . ." (the emphasis is mine, of course).

25. How heavy the native Jewish influence, and how heavy the Greek Platonic influence, on Johannine use of the word *Logos* is much controverted today. For early theologians, however, the historical recovery of the intention of the Johannine writer was not of much concern. God's message was in the scriptural words, independent of the human author's conscious purpose.

26. See *Sacramentum Mundi*, Vol. 1, p. 95. See also CT, pp. 123, 124.

27. Indeed, Arius's intense commitment to rationalism has often been remarked by scholars.

28. DZ 6, 54, 86 / CT 1, 2, 3.

29. Ibid.

30. DZ 54 / CT 2.

31. Ibid.

32. DZ 275 / CT 299.

33. But Christian differentialism's "beyond thought," like Nagarjuna's, is secure and masterful; anxiety, stress, doubt, are not the signs of liberation.

34. At this point I cannot resist an aside. Notice that in the strategic Derri-

dean excerpt from *Of Grammatology* quoted near the beginning of this part, the "origin" is given a kind of priority, but not the priority of "simple origin." The "origin" (the "reflected"), in other words, receives what is at least rhetorical focus: that the "origin" is "split" (so it is effect) is overtly recounted; that the image is split (so it is just cause) is just implied, though clearly the third force issues from what is one *bilateral* action. I see an analogy, indeed an uncanny analogy, between the strange priority that Derrida confers on the "reflected," and the mysterious priority of the Father who *begets* (but who is not begotten), and who yet does not *cause*.

35. See Rahner, "Trinity in Theology," p. 306.

36. See Elmar Klinger, "Modalism," in *Sacramentum Mundi*, Vol. 4, p. 90.

37. And which, along with its opposite number, subordinationism, may be resurfacing in our own age.

38. See CT, p. 125.

39. CT, p. 136 and DZ 705 / CT 313. See also, Karl Rahner, "Divine Trinity," *Sacramentum Mundi*, Vol. 6, pp. 299–301.

40. Eastern Orthodox theology, instead, regards the relations as manifestative, not constitutive. See Edmund J. Fortman, *The Triune God: A Historical Study of the Doctrine of the Trinity* (London and Philadelphia: Hutchinson/ Westminster, 1972), p. 294.

41. See Rahner, "Divine Trinity," pp. 297, 301; and Fortman, *The Triune God*, p. 295.

42. See Rahner, "Divine Trinity," p. 301; and Rahner, "Trinity in Theology," p. 308 and especially p. 307.

43. Rahner's very keen translation of DZ 703, in "Divine Trinity," p. 298.

44. See Fortman, pp. 222, 223. And see my treatment of differential unity, ahead.

45. See Fortman, pp. 294, 295, for a refined yet concise study. Be on guard, too, against reading entitative implications into the Latin terminology.

46. Rahner, "Divine Trinity," p. 297.

47. I shall explain this idea more thoroughly in a moment.

48. See CT, pp. 167, 168.

49. "The Divine Persons are said to inhabit inasmuch as they are present to intellectual creatures [i.e., "rational" creatures—human beings] in a way that transcends human comprehension, and are known and loved by them, yet in a way that is unique, purely supernatural, and in the deepest sanctuary of the soul" (DZ 2290 / CT 322). The indwelling occurs only in those who are free of serious sin, and thus is not the same as God's omnipresence. The indwelling is attributed in a special way to the Holy Spirit, by what is technically called "appropriation." Appropriation is attribution to one Person of a work done by the Divine Unity, when that work reflects what is, in God's inner life, most proper to that Person. Karl Rahner makes the point that perhaps the concept of appropriation has been overextended by theologians, for it should apply only to God's efficient causality, and not to "uncreated grace" (the latter is God's gift of *Himself*). See Karl Rahner, *The Trinity*, trans. Joseph Donceel (New York: Seabury, 1974), pp. 76, 77.

50. DZ 2290 / CT 321. The quotation is from the encyclical *Mystici Corporis*, and thus exercises what is technically called ordinary rather than extraordi-

nary magisterium. *Mystici Corporis* goes on to issue a caveat, viz., that one hypothesis which had been advanced (see CT, p. 139) is *not* the case (though neither is the contradictory affirmed—the encyclical is not using negative dialectic). All this is very much to the point for us, because it shows again the *deconstructive* function of the magisterium.

51. See pp. 134–36.

52. The Holy Spirit "proceeds" from the Father and/through the Son by way of *spiratio,* and usually the term "procession" is identified exclusively with this spirating movement. The term *generatio* is limited to the "begetting" of the Son by the Father, and is not to be confused with *spiratio.* We shall soon involve ourselves in these matters with more precision.

53. As long as we keep in mind an identification of the "economic" Trinity and "immanent" Trinity (see note 81), an anagogic reading of John 16: 5, 7, suits very well the concept of the Son's perpetual "doubling back": "I am going to the one [the Father] who sent me. . . . unless I go, the Advocate [Holy Spirit] will not come to you."

54. Necessary for my thesis, too, is to establish that the "issuing forth" of which we speak here need not be the same as the *generatio,* since I shall argue the issuing forth is one bilateral action with the doubling back, and clearly the Son does not reciprocally generate the Father (to maintain such would be heretical indeed).

55. Recall that this logocentrically impossible provision was crucial for Derridean *effacement,* i.e., absolute negative reference. See my part 1.

56. Our term for that Derridean canceling-each-other-out which does not result in void.

57. See p. 135.

58. John 10:15. Christ precedes this passage with the equally famous, "I know my own [His followers] and my own know me," which will serve to illustrate how differentialism applies to the Divine Indwelling.

59. John 10:17.

60. John 14:31.

61. See Karl Rahner's discussion, *The Trinity,* p. 118.

62. Bernard Lonergan is perhaps the most famous modern proponent of what is called the "psychological" theory, both when he is discussing the "immanent" Trinity (the relations of the Persons to each other), and the Divine "inhabitation" (the "dwelling" of the Persons in the faithful). He is opposed by his Jesuit confrere, Karl Rahner, who understands the Son and Holy Spirit in terms of the "moments" of the Father's self-donating act. Though my formulation differs also from Rahner's, I find his approach much more congenial to mine than is Lonergan's psychologism. For comparisons of Lonergan and Rahner, see Fortman, pp. 295–99, 306–8, 311, 313; and Gerard S. Sloyan, *The Three Persons In One God* (Englewood Cliffs, New Jersey: Prentice Hall, 1964), pp. 105–8. A brief summary of Rahner's disagreement with Lonergan can be found in Rahner's own *The Trinity,* pp. 119, 120.

63. See Karl Rahner, *The Trinity,* p. 73 et seq., and pp. 103–20; and Rahner, "Divine Trinity," pp. 300, 302; and his "Trinity in Theology," pp. 305, 306. See also Fortman, pp. 292, 293.

64. Such as the eternality of the generation, the consubstantiality of Father and Son, etc.: see Rahner, *The Trinity*, pp. 58–79; and the appropriate references listed topically in CT, pp. 357, 358.

65. See Fortman, p. 294; and Rahner, *The Trinity*, pp. 77, 78.

66. The relation of that which is spirated to that which spirates; here the Holy Spirit defined precisely as *that which is spirated.*

67. There is a connected argument against the psychologistic theory. Many theologians maintain that we must deduce the nature of the immanent Trinity from what Scripture tells us, and Scripture only tells us about the economic Trinity; if then, the economic Trinity the Scripture proclaims speaks only of Paternity, Filiation, and the Spirit released, these economic activities are likewise the respective immanent activities of the immanent Trinity.

68. We shall soon argue in more detail that the definitions of Father, Son, and Holy Spirit respectively are established by purely negative reference.

69. See CT, p. 134; see also DZ 704.

70. From DZ 691 (the emphases are mine); see also DZ 703, 1084.

71. Rahner, "Divine Trinity," p. 297.

72. From DZ 691.

73. The Council of Florence accepts this version of the Eastern Church, as well as the *Filioque* of the Western Church, in order to clarify the matter and speed reunification of the two Churches, which had divided one from the other in the ninth century.

74. Of course, the Greek formula is not to be understood as "efficient cause" here; see pp. 137–38.

75. In fact, the formulation of my adversaries makes unnecessary trouble: why theology's long insistence that the Active Spiration (see Rahner, *The Trinity*, pp. 77, 78; and Fortman, pp. 293, 294) is virtual, not real, if there are two ways of spirating, belonging to the Father and the Son respectively? For two spirations (a premise specifically outlawed by the Florentine definition) would permit the mode of Active Spiration, and not just that of Passive Spiration, to be real. The "challenge" that procession from "one principle" establishes that "one principle" as a fourth Person would not even arise.

76. M. Schmaus, *The Essence of Christianity* (Dublin: 1961), pp. 185, 188, 189.

77. Karl Rahner, "Trinity in Theology," p. 306.

78. Rahner, "Divine Trinity," p. 302.

79. See Karl Rahner, *Theological Investigations*, Vol. 4, trans. by K. Smyth (Baltimore: Helicon Press, 1966), pp. 77–102. And of course *The Trinity*, especially pp. 24–28, 50–57, 68–73, 103–20.

80. Rahner, "Divine Trinity," p. 301.

81. In the classical theology, study of the immanent Trinity concerns the relations of the Divine Persons to each other; the study of the economic Trinity concerns the saving relations of the Divine Persons to humankind.

82. Karl Rahner, "Divine Trinity," p. 301; see also p. 303, where Rahner argues that in the formal sequence of dogmatic theology, much can be said

for placing the *De Deo Trino* treatise before the *De Deo Uno* treatise, in order to stress the former as the "basic structural principle" for what follows. Elmar Klinger, in the excellent essay on "Modalism" in *Sacramentum Mundi*, Vol. 4, uses much the same argument as Rahner (p. 90).

83. See part 1, pp. 32–37.

84. Emphases mine.

85. Putting aside for the nonce symbolization of the Holy Spirit's relationships and their "effects" (a question I shall take up at another time and place), we can illustrate what I am saying as follows. Where BRx abbreviates "x is the Begetter" (or, "whatever is of the Begetter"), and where BNx abbreviates "x is the Begotten" (or, "whatever is of the Begotten"), we can assert—The Church affiliates to the following proposition: $(x)(\sim BRx \supset BNx)$. Keeping in mind the preceding formula, my own point is that in the case of the trinitarian Father and Son $\sim(\exists x) (BRx \equiv \sim BRx)$ leads to $\sim(\exists x) (BRx \,\&\, BNx)$.

86. That each divine Person is defined by purely negative reference may seem, at first blush, to subvert my earlier argument—that the Father and Son know/love each other in "one and the same act," the "one principle" from which the Holy Spirit proceeds. However, to understand this one act of Father and Son in terms of *sharing* is precisely to relapse into the plastic model it is my point to deconstruct. Actually, the role of pure negative reference applies just as surely in its own way to the "one act," and my thesis implied as much from the very beginning—when I insisted that the bilateral "doubling-back" operates *invicem et totaliter*. That is to say, the Father totally *abrogates, abnegates* the Father, and the Son totally *abrogates, abnegates* the Son, and amazingly, from this mutual abrogation (which undoes all possibility of common substratum) the Holy Spirit proceeds. Pure negative reference may seem, at first blush, to threaten too the official doctrine of the *circumincessio* (that each of the Divine Persons is fully *in* the others, v. DZ 704 / CT 312), but again, the problem dissolves if one realizes that the *circumincessio* is *established* by the mutual exclusivity of the three Persons.

87. That is, the virtue of faith enables intellect and will to affirm divinely revealed truths with certainty, because God can "neither deceive nor be deceived." Of course, the act of faith can only be made at God's prompting; it is God who takes the initiative, as it were. See DZ 1638, 1642, 1645, 1789. And for the role of experiential realization in faith, see ahead, pp. 161–62.

88. "Intuition" not in the current vernacular sense, but in the technical sense, i.e., immediate awareness by way of experience, of "seeing into," from the Latin *intueri*, "to look at or into."

89. For example, many effective comparisons of Buddhist and Christian differential mysticism can be found in R. H. Blyth, *Buddhist Sermons on Christian Texts* (San Francisco: Heian International Publishing, 1976). Besides the anthologies cited in part 3, comparisons of Eastern and Western mysticism in general (with some differentialism included) can be found in J. M. Déchanet, *Christian Yoga,* trans. Roland Hindmarsh (New York: Harper and Row, Perennial Library series, 1972); "Word out of Silence" special issue, ed. John-David Robinson, *Cross Currents*, Vol. XXIV, Nos. 2–3 (Summer-Fall, 1974); Dom Aelred Graham, *Zen Catholicism* (New York: Harcourt, Brace, and World, 1963); J. K. Kadowaki, *Zen and the Bible*, trans. Joan Rieck (Lon-

don: Routledge and Kegan Paul, 1980); and William Johnston, *Christian Zen* (New York: Harper and Row, 1971).

90. We must recall, of course, that "figured into" the logic are certain *givens* that the non-Catholic need not accept—authoritative conciliar decrees, for example. Also, for the pertinent discussion of "mixed-state" and "pure-state" logic, see pp. 152, 153.

91. DZ 1796 / CT 33.

92. See pp. 153–59.

93. See the treatment of Reuchlin in Gershom Scholem, *Kabbalah* (New York: New American Library, 1978), p. 198.

94. Karl Rahner, "Divine Trinity," p. 299.

95. Elmar Klinger, "Modalism," p. 90. One of the main intentions of this essay is to disenfranchise heretical modalism, which is based (as we saw) on an entitative model, by advancing a differential model (where unity is constituted by negative reference). Concerning relations between God and humankind, the argument is that the same principle applies: we are divinized by our *dif-fering* from God.

96. Rahnerian theology traces trinitarian revelation from the economic Trinity to the immanent Trinity, and then back to man again—a hermeneutical movement not evident in our short excerpt. The term "economic Trinity," recall, refers to the Trinity's "missions," or Personal issuings-forth to mankind; the term "immanent Trinity" refers to relations among the Persons, and between the Persons and the Divine Unity. I would be willing to argue that the trinitarian differentialism can be found first in the economic Trinity, and can lead to the immanent differentialism we have already discussed at some length.

97. For the intriguing modern history of the theology of uncreated grace, and the controversy over "appropriation" and "distinct missions," first see Fortman, p. 308 et seq.; then Rahner, *The Trinity*, p. 76 et seq.; and Sloyan, p. 105.

98. The crosscut is not a short cut, alas!

99. And Eastern Orthodox Christianity.

100. In my opinion, some—though by no means all—of contemporary theologians of "God-language" (i.e., theologians who identify themselves with a movement to analyze the nature of religious discourse) likewise tend towards Fideism. Differentialism's off-logic would save them from the false dilemma of pure rationalism on the one hand and non-rational "faith" on the other.

101. My intention is not, of course, to devalue centric mysticism. The procedure which reinstates logocentrism as pure process applies to centric mysticism as well, since, in Derridean terms, *all* centering is logocentric. That is, all centering is founded on the dyad of signified and signifier, and its dialectical permutations (e.g., the non-logical as the dialectical mirror of the logical dyad).

102. See Ronald Lawler, Donald Wuerl, and Thomas C. Lawler, *The Teaching of Christ* (Huntington, Indiana: OSV Press, 1976), pp. 301–13; and William Johnston, *Silent Music* (New York: Harper and Row, Perennial Library edition, 1976), pp. 67, 100–102.

103. See Lawler *et al.*, *The Teaching of Christ*, pp. 258–60, 284–87, 294–97.

104. Angelus Silesius wrote both poetry and prose. Our citations will be to the collected works, Angelus Silesius, *Sämtliche poetische Werke,* ed. Hans L. Held (Munich: Carl Hanser, 1949), 3 vols; and, except where the renderings are my own, to the translations from *Angelus Silesius: Selections from "The Cherubinic Wanderer,"* trans. and intro. J. E. Crawford Flitch (London: G. Allen and Unwin, 1932; rpt. Hyperion Press, 1978), a bilingual edition.

105. Divine Revelation has encouraged what is, in our terms, off-rational interpretation.

106. Which I hope to publish in future articles. Perhaps *équipes* of scholars can help me: if structuralists can use the "team" approach, perhaps differential theologians can too!

107. The Flitch translation (p. 160) of a verse from Angelus Silesius. The German can be found both in Flitch (p. 235) and in the *Sämtliche poetische Werke*, Vol. 3, which contains the *Cherubinischer Wandersmann* [*The Cherubinic Wanderer*]. Silesius's most famous work, the *Cherubinischer Wandersmann* is a collection of "epigrams," or "rhymed sentences," in six books (so hereafter we will cite these verses by book and verse number—CW I–VI:ooo). The above verse (CW III:180) can be more literally translated: "You ask, 'How long has God been, in fact?' / Ah, be silent: it is so long, he doesn't know it [i.e., how long] himself."

108. The paradox thus bespeaks monism. Paradox is equally logocentric, for Derrida, in its 'Taoist' formulation: paradox as a binary structure of appearance (signifier) and reality (signified).

109. This is not to deny that Silesius writes epigrams in the tradition of centric mysticism as well. He does so in part because his environment and culture are stocked with so many logocentric motifs, and in part because his mystical experience no doubt functions differentially sometimes and centrically other times (that he can so "transact" is in itself a testimony to *tathatā*, the crosscut).

110. In this rendering I have tried to keep the felicity of rhyme while preserving meaning. A more literal translation would be: "God grounds Himself without Ground, and measures Himself without measure; / You be one Spirit with Him, mankind, so you understand this."

111. Flitch trans., p. 148. A more literal translation would read: "Abandonment snares God; but to let go of God Himself, / Is an abandonment which few men secure [achieve]."

112. My literal translation. Flitch has: "From Time into Eternity / Thou tellest me to get me hence! / Between Eternity and Time / Is there then any difference?" (p. 162).

113. Silesius's title is a playful permutation of Matt. 7:13.

114. My literal rendering. Flitch translates: "Think not the journey overlong if thou wouldst fare / To Heaven: take but one short stride and thou art there" (p. 163).

115. My literal translation. Flitch has: "No creature fathometh how deep the Godhead is; / Even the soul of Christ is lost in that Abyss" (p. 106).

116. See CW I:276 for a deconstruction of logocentric "first cause," and CW III:129 for a deconstruction of the theory of entitative space.

117. The verses of Silesius are "shot through" (off/pun?) with a differentialism which awaits research. See CW II:201, for example, as a very Derridean off/formula for *pure negative reference*.

118. Vol. 6, p. 313.

119. "Pastoral Constitution on the Church in the Modern World," *The Documents of Vatican II,* pp. 268, 269.

120. When it is really Derridean, and not a lapse into clandestine logocentrism.

121. Even when dealing with the "deep logic" of affectivity, archetypes, the unconscious, and so on.

122. DZ 1796 / CT 76. Emphases mine.

123. DZ 1800 / CT 80.

124. "Dogmatic Constitution on Divine Revelation," *The Documents of Vatican II,* pp. 116, 117.

125. The crosscut, moving at will between logocentric and differential, "cuts *across*" them. The Christian's diagonal transaction is by way of the Cross, which cuts across as a "double-edged sword." The term, then, is both descriptive and reverential.

126. Research into how differentialism works in traditions other than Buddhism and Christianity is an enterprise well worth the effort.

127. Thus it repudiates the emphasis of so many right-wing Protestant sects on a sensibly experienced "baptism in the spirit."

128. Underline mine. The editor of *The Documents of Vatican II* comments in his footnote, "The Council desired to get away from a too intellectualist conception" (p. 113).

129. "Dogmatic Constitution on Divine Revelation," *The Documents of Vatican Council II,* pp. 113, 114.

130. See *Sacramentum Mundi,* Vol. 3, p. 158, for an excellent discussion.

131. Faith is not a blindness. It seems to me the Church's renewed stress on faith as "realization" suggests that it is the role of man's purely logical apprehension to defer (and thus, to accept without absolute certitude *in its own terms*) to the certitude afforded by the supra-rational (possibly including, as we have seen, the off/rational) realization.

132. Karl Rahner, *Theological Investigations,* Vol. 4, pp. 49, 50.

133. See note 167, part 3.

134. Eccles. 12:6, from *New American Bible* translation (Cleveland: Collins World, 1976). The question of Oriental influence on the Book of Ecclesiastes (Qoheleth) has been discussed by many scholars. It is interesting too that the meaning of this book's famous "vanity of vanities! All things are vanity!" has, in the venerable English rendering, long been misunderstood. The actual Hebrew word rendered here by "vanity" means "the tremor of an almost imperceptible breeze," and the Vulgate's rendering seems to frequent this meaning when it uses *vanitas* (in Latin, literally "emptiness," but perhaps emptiness as ongoing? . . . as "going on"?). The makings of a good anagogic reading, at least, are surely here.

Notes

Appendix

1. The paper by Morris Weitz now appears as chapter 3 in his book, *The Opening Mind: A Philosophical Study of Humanistic Concepts* (Chicago: University of Chicago, 1977), pp. 49–90; hereafter my references to this source shall be bracketed in my text as (Wxx). The essay of M. H. Abrams to which Weitz's chapter is a response appears as "What's the Use of Theorizing about the Arts?", in a collection entitled *In Search of Literary Theory,* ed. Morton Bloomfield (Ithaca, New York: Cornell, 1972), pp. 1–54; hereafter, Abrams's essay is bracketed as (Axx).

2. "M. H. Abrams' Philosophy of Critical Theories," now accessible as chapter 3 of *The Opening Mind,* was the earlier title used at the APA meeting while Weitz's book was still in press. Concerning the term "essentialist definition" here, remember that throughout his work Weitz's intention is to fly the Analytic banner; thus essentialism (identified by the Analysts with the "established" Greco-Roman philosophy and with Scholasticism, and their descendants) is for Weitz a specious formulation, since it affirms traits-in-common, and claims they can be "named" as a whole class.

3. For example, see Abrams, pp. 35–39.

4. Weitz, of course, would not want me to call them definitions. Would he want me to call them descriptions of description? The question is not germane right now, so I pass it over.

5. The reference is to Weitz's *Hamlet and the Philosophy of Literary Criticism* (Chicago: University of Chicago Press, 1964), hereafter cited as (WHxxx). Regarding "verifiable data," word count and the cast of characters are also cited as examples by Weitz (WH229).

6. When proceeding in the mode of a Heideggerian phenomenologist, my own position here is that there is no "fact" apart from "viewpoint(s)" as such, so even the term "empirically verifiable" is misleading. "Empirically verifiable" data are what a group of people together regard as data, and regard as "empirically verifiable" (because the group accepts the "scientific method"; in short, members of this group interpret data in the same basic way). Actually, everything is at bottom interpretative in this broad sense, that is, dependent on viewpoint(s).

7. For example, on p. 271 of his *Hamlet,* Weitz defines critical evaluation: "Critical evaluation, thus, contains what we may call an 'evaluative utterance' and reasons that are given in support of this utterance." Immediately following, "examples" are provided, and it is very evident they are considered examples because they match the sufficient and necessary conditions set forth by the definition.

8. Abrams never speaks outrightly of a "mode of evaluative interpretation,"

229

though the term (coined by Weitz for Abrams!) does, in my opinion, reflect one of Abrams's latent assumptions.

9. Weitz has Abrams say that anti-theory is a helpful speculative instrument. Abrams nowhere says this. Abrams does not equate the claim for a literary work's autonomy with anti-theory (it is Weitz who makes this equation, and it is Abrams who says such an equation is wrong).

10. See my part 2.

11. See Magliola, *Phenomenology and Literature,* pp. 3, 4, 61, 75, 76, 181; consult also the remarks on "representational truth" versus "commemorative truth," pp. 65, 66.

12. This part of my APA paper sketches, very briefly, some of what is elaborated in more detail in part 2.

13. See *Phenomenology and Literature,* pp. 62–75.

14. See pp. 64, 65, 66.

15. See my remarks on Heideggerian authenticity, pp. 67, 68, 74–82.

16. See Magliola, *Phenomenology and Literature,* "The Problem of Validity: Hirsch and Husserl" (Pt. II, ch. 1), pp. 97–106.

17. See also my treatment of "intersubjective constancies" in part 2. The reader, of course, can "bring me up short" here or anytime; that is, he can refuse to follow the lexis of my reasoning further, because he thinks I am no longer true to "the way things really are."

18. This Heideggerian *sous rature* here leads to a centered voidism, the mirror opposite of the plenum we also find in Heidegger (see my part 2).

19. This may be interpreted as "openness" with a vengeance (Weitz repeatedly calls for the avoidance of "fore-closure," does he not?).

20. *The Teachings of the Compassionate Buddha,* ed. E. A. Burtt (New York: New American Library, 1955), p. 228.

21. When speaking of the movement of trace in a text, for example, Miller says that "As groundless, the movement is, precisely, alogical" (see Miller, "On Edge: The Crossways of Contemporary Criticism," *Bulletin: The American Academy of Arts and Sciences,* XXXII [January 1979], p. 31). His avowed intent is to show that deconstruction as a way of addressing a text, and text itself as the addressee of deconstruction, are both of them neither logical nor non-logical, but alogical. They operate, in other words, according to the fourth lemma.

22. For example, even Miller's affirmation of the formula "black light" to explain Wordsworth's Lucy poems (see Miller, "On Edge," p. 30) operates— thematically and formally—as a *paradox,* and not as Derridean dissemination. Cleanth Brooks, in a witty and cogent essay, "The New Criticism" (*Sewanee Review,* Fall 1979), documents the paradoxes which (ironically) ground Miller's Wordsworthian critique. And Brooks, while demurring from Miller's choice of content for most of the paradoxes, wryly adds that he as a New Critic should be abashed to quibble over Miller's resort to the *form* of paradox, that most logocentric of all devices (see Brooks, p. 603).

23. Emblem, according to Derrida's use, is almost always an image or image-cluster which in its own right acts out, and acts out "microscopically," the indigenous dissemination which characterizes the "macroscopic" field of the text (and beyond). The term 'allegory' suggests a point-for-point corre-

spondence between an image or image-cluster in the text and an extraneous schema of some kind. Miller, it seems to me, often correlates textual elements (and correlates them without indigenous justification) to his own very rigid version of Derridean thought—a version Miller keeps extraneous to the text and then "matches up" with the text allegorically and gratuitously.

24. At Gannon University, Erie, Pennsylvania, October 17, 1978. Originally delivered for Gannon's "Shakespeare Alive" lecture series, only a few revisions have been since made in the text.

25. References will be to the New American Library *Hamlet*, ed. Edward Hubler (1963); I have also crosschecked all references against the *New Variorum* edition.

26. *Midrashim* are a group of Jewish commentaries on the Hebrew Scriptures, and their method for the most part precedes by many centuries the dates of their codification (c. 400–1200 A.D.). Midrashic method permits a sort of *regressio* of interpretations—work glossing work glossing work, and so on; and it decodes the thematic import of graphs—i.e., of the shapes of letters, the size of script, etc. Derrida finds the method very adaptable in terms of his own sort of off-rationalism.

27. The paper I delivered at Gannon University presented an inventory of techniques identified with J. Hillis Miller. As indicated in note 23, Miller's version of deconstruction includes allegorical usages (as well as others I have called "emblematic" in the genuine Derridean sense). I have here left my original treatment of Miller's allegorical usages stand, though I do not consider them Derridean. The fact is that Miller's usages are interesting in their own right.

28. Derrida, "Differance," in SP, p. 132.

29. Miller's review of Abrams, p. 13. Perhaps I should add here too a clarification. Miller's version of deconstruction is a formal dyad of monological reading and a competing monological reading which contradicts and is thus said (wrongly) to "deconstruct" it then and there. My point is that no matter how much the contents of these readings change, the *form* remains that of dyad. My reinstatement of logocentric readings, as proposed in this book's part 3 and part 4, works in another way entirely. Logocentric readings are not to be negated by "alternate" readings as such—since the alternative readings would have to be in dialectical relation to the first logocentric reading, and thus could only be (1) competing logical readings, or (2) absurdist readings. A *differential* reading, as off-logical, must have its own off-ways of proceeding—off-ways which somehow frequent the "and/or between and/or" (see part 3). These off-ways in literary criticism remain yet to be "worked out," though Derrida's experiments in *Glas* provide, I think, a good lead. The frequenting of differential literary criticism may very well demand what we have been calling in a more philosophical context the Derridean *déroulement:* demonstration that the conventional logic cannot hold; movement instead in terms of a deviant solution; placement of that solution "under erasure"; and then, frequenting of what I have been calling the *diascript*, which can be read "on the bias" from the erased solution. It is upon the "realization" of frequenting that the logocentric reading(s) can be in turn reinstated, since *tathatā* is precisely the *virtus* of doing both the logical and off-logical (and the logical and off-logical, unlike the logical and non-logical, have no formal relation to each other—they are, in short, not dialectical).

30. Miller's review of Riddel, p. 30.

. . . öst/Face

> Sir, dids't not thou sow good seed
> in thy field? from whence then hath it
> tares?
>
> —Matt. 13:27

> Deux textes, deux mains, deux regards,
> deux écoutes. Ensemble à la fois et
> séparément.
> —Jacques Derrida, *Marges*

> Just a dew drop,
>   and yet,
>   and yet . . .
>   —from Japanese verse

> yea, his heavens drop down dew.
>   —Deut. 33:28

> . . . the depths have broken out, and
> the clouds grow thick with dew.
>   —Prov. 3:20

agonia

DIAGONIA

AND the fire that breaks from thee then,
a billion / Times told lovelier, more
dangerous . . .

and blue bleak embers, ah my dear,
   Fall, gall themselves, and
   gash gold-vermillion.
                    —Gerard Manley Hopkins

"O happy fault!"

                    —Easter Vigil liturgy

"The lightning seemed to me white like a flash from a lookingglass
but Mr. Lentaigne in the afternoon noticed it rose-coloured and
lilac. I noticed two kinds of flash but I am not sure that sometimes
there were not the two together from different points of the same
cloud or starting from the same point different ways—one a straight
stroke, broad like a stroke with chalk and liquid, as if the blade of an
oar just stripped open a ribbon scar in smooth water and it caught
the light; the other narrow and wire-like, like the splitting of a rock
and danced down-along in a thousand jags. I noticed this too, that
there was a perceptible [sous rature] interval between the blaze and
the first inset of the flash and its score in the sky and that that
seemed to be first of all laid in a bright confusion and then uttered
by a tongue of brightness (what is strange) running up from the
ground to the cloud, not the other way."
                    —Gerard Manley Hopkins, from his private
                    journal, the entry for July 8, 1871
                    (*A Hopkins Reader,* ed. J. Pick, N.Y.: image
                    bks., 1966, p. 105)

! Gloria tibi Domine$_{e_{e}}$eeeeeeeeeeeeeeeeee

Index

Abhāva (non-existing), 87
Abhidharma, 92, 107
Abrams, M. H., 165–76 passim, 186
Absurdism, 27
Allegorical function, 184
Altérité, 134
American New Critics, 160, 177
Analytic School, 7
Anātma (no soul), 91
And/or *between* and/or, 32, 87
Anitya (impermanence), 91
Anti-theory, 172
Aporia, 184
Arbitraire (arbitrariness), 7, 8
Aristotle, 137
Arius, 137
As-question, 64
As-structure, 64
As-which, 64
Augustine, Saint, 144
Auslegung, 62
Aussage, 62
Austin, J. L., 25
Authenticity, Heideggerian, 67
Autonomy, literary, 168

Bary, W. T. de., 97
Being and Time, Martin Heidegger, 62–82 passim
Between, the differential, 32, 127, 158; the logocentric, 158
Bhāva (existing), 87, 109
Blyth, Reginald H., 123
Bohr, Niels, 50
Brooks, Cleanth, 160, 177, 230

Catachresis, 183
Candrakirti, 110, 120
Causality, logocentric, 107, 112, 138
Cause and effect, 109–12 et passim

Ch'an/Zen, logocentric, 96; differential, 96, 100, 104
Communicational chain, dissolution of, 179
Constancy, intersubjective, 79
Contradiction, 19, 97, 170, 171, 175
Cook, Francis H., 208
Criteria, 168
Crosscut, 128, 149, 157, 161, 216

Daye, Douglas, 118
Deconstructionist literary theory, 176–87
Dédoublement, 9, 17, 106, 107, 135, 140 et passim
"Definition, working," 166
Dérive (drift), 15, 41, 49
Derrida, Jacques, passim
Derridean 'else', 28, 37, 38
Description, according to Analytic School, 166
Dharma (the Teaching), 114
Dharmas (elements), 91, 105, 114
Dharma-language, 107
Dialectical thinking, 104
Dialogy, 178, 186
Diascript, 105, 115, 117, 118, 147
Différance (differance), 20, 22, 89, 106, 133, 182, 184, 185 et passim
Differing/deferring, 20–24, 30, 31, 36, 41, 50
Dissémination, ix, 15, 16, 32, 135
Duhkha (turmoil), 91, 113
Écriture (writing), 4, 7, 8, 30, 38
Écriture primaire, 133
Effacement (pure negative reference), 21, 24, 106, 112, 145, 147, 148, 157
Einstein, Albert, 50
Ellipsis, 182

235

Emblematics, 178
Enchiridion symbolorum definitionum et declarationum de rebus fidei et morum, 133– 63 passim
Errance, 39, 41, 49, 51
Essentialism, according to Analytic School, 165, 171, 174
Evaluation, according to Analytic School, 169
Exergue, 127

Faille (crack, fissure), 51
Form of life, 173
Fortman, Edmund J., 222, 223
Foucault, Michel, 5
Four-fold Noble Truth, 120
Freudianism, xi, 32, 135

Gass, William, 51
Generatio, 138
Girard, René, 215
Gödel, Kurt, 50
Graham, Dom Aelred, 94

Heidegger, Martin, xi, 3, 5, 10, 50– 52, 54, 57– 83 passim, 165, 173– 76 passim
Heisenberg, Werner, 50
Hekiganroku, 124
Hinduism, 90
Husserl, Edmund, 28, 48, 51, 112. See also Phenomenology, Husserlian
Hypostasis, 139

Ibish, Yusuf, 216
Identity, 6, 21, 23, 97, 107, 114 et seq., 144, 145
Identity, the Supreme, 24, 25, 133
In modo reverso, 14, 16
Inada, Kenneth K., 87– 129 passim, 205
Indice (clue), 105
Indwelling, 140
Interpretation, according to Analytic School, 169
Interval, 30, 50, 158

Jabès, Edmond, 29, 30
Jaina, 122, 123
Jeu, and off/tracking, 40, 41, 47
Johnston, S. J., William, x
Judaism, 29, 30

Kalupahana, David J., 96
Karman, 108
"Keines schrittes breit," 54, 157
Kierkegaard, Sören, 211
Klinger, Elmar, 222
Kumarila, 120

Language-idling, 174
Leitfaden, Husserlian, 51
Levinas, Emmanuel, 50
Lévi-Strauss, Claude, 5
Logic, symbolic, 146, 225
Logocentrism, 7, 94, 95, 187
Logos, 3, 41, 137, 186
Lonergan, S. J., Bernard, 223

Madhyamā pratipad (way of the between), 87, 89, 91
Madhyamika, 88, 121 et passim
Magisterium, 134, 137, 144– 47, 153, 154
Mallarmé, Stéphane, 40, 41, 47
Marculescu, Ileana, 216
Matilal, Bimal Krishna, 120, 121
Meaning, as appearance in language, 6, 19, 107
Metacriticism, 172
Metaphoricity, slide of, 31
Midrash, 178, 182
Miller, J. Hillis, 176, 177, 179, 186, 230
Mise-en-abyme, 156, 157, 163, 185
Misra, R. S., 94
Modalism, 138
Monism, 27
Mūlamādhyamakakārikās, 88, 107
Mumonkon/Wu-men-kuan, 103
Mysterium, 134, 138, 148, 153
Mysticism, differential, 126, 155; logocentric, 44, 57, 71, 73, 165, 176; unity of opposites, 74

Nagarjuna, xi, 54, 87– 129 passim, 147– 49, 153, 156
Nansen/Nan-ch'uan P'u-yuan, 103
Negative dialectic, Nagarjunist, 104
Neo-Platonism, 137
Neti, neti, 136
Nietzsche, Friedrich, 49, 52
Nirvāna (the mode of bliss), 87, 94, 117
Nominans-nomen, 5, 6, 8, 17
Nyaya, 122, 123

Off/logical, 152, 160
Onto-psychology, 124
Orders of discourse, linguistic, 118

Parabhāva, 109
Paramārtha (the ungathered), 96, 119, 151
Personal identity, 5, 6, 13, 91, 107. *See also Nominans-nomen*
Phenomenology, Husserlian, 28. *See also* Husserl, Edmund
Phenomenology, modified, 27, 42
Pluralism, 57, 78, 165
Prajñā (wisdom), 96, 125, 151
Prajñapti (language-construct), 105, 118
Prāsaṅgika, 106, 151
Prasangika, subschool of Madhyamika, 92
Pratītya samutpāda (dependent co-arising), 91, 107, 114 et passim
Presupposition, 168, 170
Processio, 139, 144
Processio ad modum operati, 141
Prosopon, 139
Psychology, 11, 128, 141. *See also* Onto-psychology
Pure effect, 111
Pure Land, 100
Pure signifieds, 16
Pure signifiers, 16, 17, 25, 111 et passim

Quandary, Derridean, 44, 47, 49, 52, 134

Rahner, S.J., Karl, x, 144–47, 162
Reductio ad absurdum, 20, 104
Regressio ad infinitum, 176
Relationis oppositio, 138, 139, 141, 142, 144, 145
Retardement, 23
Reuchlin, Johannes, 149
Ricoeur, Paul, v
Riddel, Joseph, 187
"River, The," Flannery O'Connor's story, 58–61, 64, 65, 69, 76, 79, 80
Rorty, Richard, 190
Rūpa (material form), 111
Rupture, 179
Russell, Bertrand, 211

Sabellius, 138
Sacramentum Mundi, 159
Saṃgha (the Buddhist order), 114
Saṃsāra (the mode of the quotidian), 87, 89, 119–24, 156
Saṃvṛti (the gathered), 96, 119, 151
Saussure, Ferdinand de, 4, 8, 9, 10, 13
Schmaus, M., 143
School, Three Treatise, 96
Scientific revolution, new, 50
Seng-Ts'an, 97
Shibayama, Zenkei, 210
Signifier and signified, 3–5, 7, 11, 12, 110, 135, 137, 138, 180 et passim. *See also* Pure signified, Pure signifier
Silesius, Angelus, 153–59
Skandhas (components), 91, 111
Slide, 110, 116
Sloyan, Gerard S., 223
Smart, Ninian, 97
Solace, metaphysical, 173
Sous rature (under erasure), 17, 18, 35, 106, 109, 116, 117, 147, 148
Spanos, William, 211
Spatiality/Temporality, 33–36, 42
Spiration, Passive, 141, 142
Sprung, Mervyn, 94, 150, 151 et passim
Stcherbatsky, Theodor, 87–129 passim
Streng, Frederick J., 92, 120, 125 et passim
Subordinationism, 137
Sūnyāta (devoidness), 89, 93, 113, 114, 116, 150, 179
Supplémentation, 29, 181
Suzuki, D. T., 97
Svabhāva (self-existence, 'own-nature'), 106, 107
Svatantrika, 92

Taoism, xi, 17, 90, 135, 177
Tathāgata (he who comes/goes *thus*), 99
Tathatā (thusness/suchness), 54, 126–28, 150, 154
Temporality, 24, 33, 112, 113
Tetralemma, 104, 105, 117
Theology, differential, x, 133–63 passim

Theology, logocentric, 133–63
    passim
Trace, 21, 100 et passim
Trinity, 3, 133; co-equality of per-
    sons, 137; co-eternality, 138;
    con-substantiality, 137, 143;
    differential, 135; immanent and
    economic, 223, 226; logocentric,
    135, 140
Tropes, rhetorical, deconstruc-
    tionist uses of, 182, 183
Tṛṣṇā (thirst), 215
"Two truths," x, 119–24

Ubakikuta Sonja, 98
Undecidability/decidability, 39
Ungrund, 155

Verstehen, 62
*Vigrahavyā Vartanī (Adverting the
    Arguments),* 123

Void, logocentric, 25, 28, 37, 95,
    113, 116
Vorgriff, 65
Vorhabe, 65
Vorsicht, 65

Warder, A. K., 212
Weg, Heideggerian, 51
Weitz, Morris, 165–76
Wellek, René, 75
Wittgenstein, Ludwig, 26, 169 et
    passim

Yale School, New, 176
Yathābhūtam (the 'going on'), 124
Yogacara (School of Consciousness
    Only), 96

Zen. *See* Ch'an/Zen, logocentric, if
    you can, or preferably off/see it
    (Ch'an/Zen, differential, *thus*)